Musical Beauty

Musical Beauty

Negotiating the Boundary between Subject and Object

FÉRDIA J. STONE-DAVIS

CASCADE *Books* • Eugene, Oregon

MUSICAL BEAUTY
Negotiating the Boundary between Subject and Object

Cascade Books
An Imprint of Wipf and Stock Publishers
199 W. 8th Ave., Suite 3
Eugene, OR 97401

www. wipfandstock.com

ISBN 13: 978-1-60608-557-8

Cataloging-in-Publication data:

Stone-Davis, Férdia J.

    Musical beauty : negotiating the boundary between subject and object / Férdia J.
Stone-Davis.

    xviii + 210 p. ; cm. 23 — Includes bibliographic references and index.

    ISBN 13: 978-1-60608-557-8

    1. Music — Philosophy and aesthetics. 2. Boethius, d. 524. 3. Kant, Immanuel, 1724–
1804. I. Title.

ML3845 .S78 2011

Manufactured in the U.S.A.

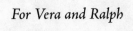

For Vera and Ralph

Contents

Acknowledgments

I WOULD LIKE TO acknowledge the financial support that has enabled this project to come to fruition, including the Arts and Humanities Research Board, the Faculty of Divinity, University of Cambridge, and The Worshipful Company of Musicians.

I would like to thank Jeremy Begbie, Denys Turner, Patrick Sherry, Patrick Masterson, Simon Waters, Andrew Bowie, Mark Elliott, and Marcus Plested for comments on the manuscript. In particular I would like to express gratitude to Jeremy Begbie and Denys Turner for their continued dialogue and encouragement.

I would also like to thank Daniel Healy for his invaluable support.

Introduction

Although of course it [the art of tone] speaks through mere sensations without concepts, and hence does not, like poetry, leave behind something for reflection, yet it moves the mind in more manifold and, though only temporarily, in deeper ways.

—Kant, *Critique of Judgment*, §53, 5:328, 205.

Indeed no path to the mind is as open for instruction as the sense of hearing. Thus, when rhythms and modes reach an intellect through the ears, they doubtless affect and reshape that mind according to their particular character.

—Boethius *De Institutione Musica* 1.1.181.

THAT MUSIC MEANS IS beyond dispute. How it does so is not. For at some level we can say what music is, namely the temporal organization of tones generated by vibrations of air.[1] We can examine how it impacts upon the human person as well as tracing its social and cultural functions. At another level, however, the musical mechanism remains elusive, resisting definite articulation. Hence the exploration of the nature of music, its "quiddity" so to speak, is found within a variety of spheres: scientific, socio-cultural, philosophical, and theological, as well as amidst the flux of music practice. This book is not situated within any one of these domains in particular but is concerned rather with something foundational to them all. It is an ontological enquiry and as such is concerned with musical quiddity in a simple sense, that is, with music *qua* music. Specifically, it is concerned with the structure by virtue of which music exists *as such*. That is, it is concerned with music *as physical*,

1. In defining music thus, I am attempting to be inclusive of different forms of music whilst maintaining a distinction between music and sound-art. The tones used in music are structural in nature: they are shaped by means of rhythm, melody, and harmony. It is this that differentiates music from sound-art. On the complexity of defining the concept of music, see Hamilton, *Aesthetics and Music*, 40–65.

specifically, music as sound and as embodied practice. For it is here that music's first-order mode of being reveals itself.

Attending to the physicality of music may seem an obvious task. It is not. Contemporary philosophical modes of discourse regarding ontology remain at some level of detachment from it. Such discussions often focus on musical "works," centering upon the conditions distinguishing one sort of "work" from another.[2] Yet more abstractly, they focus on "whether musical works are classes, types, or kinds, over whether they are universals or particulars, over whether they are created or discovered, and over whether musical works, as well as performances, consist of sounds."[3] There are exceptions to this, such as that presented by Bruce Ellis Benson who, approaching music phenomenologically, shows how the notion of "work" breaks down in music practice. Indeed the relationship between composer and performer proves far more dynamic within the activity of music-making than their categorization implies.[4] My own purpose is different. I will explore music not simply as manifest through its practice, although this will be essential to the enterprise, but will examine music's physical mode of being (ὤν), the way in which it *is* as physical.

Attending to the meaning latent within music's physicality is not unproblematic, since a priori frameworks of meaning often obscure some of its crucial elements. Given its indefinable nature, witnessed to by the variety of meanings within the different spheres outlined above, frameworks are often imported from elsewhere in order to throw a halo around musical meaning. Such frameworks include analogies with phenomena that are more readily intelligible, key elements of which are then transferred into the realm of music for exploration. One clear example is the analogy of music and language: their common ability to evoke,

2. Davies distinguishes three types of musical "work": works for live performance, works that emerge as masters from which copies are replicated (typically tapes, discs, MP3's), and works that emerge within a studio environment (employing technologies that are not normally available in live performance). Davies, "Music," 495.

3. Ibid., 496. See also Thomasson, "Ontology of Art"; Davies, "Ontology of Art"; Goodman, *Languages of Art*; Wolterstorff, *Works and Worlds of Art*; Wollheim, *Art and its Objects*; Ingarden, *Work of Music*; Levinson, *Music, Art, and Metaphysics*; Kivy, "Platonism in Music"; Scruton, *Aesthetics of Music*.

4. Benson invokes the idea of improvisation (as found within renaissance and baroque music practice) in order to subvert the idea of "work" and to better describe what occurs in practice. *Improvisation of Musical Dialogue*.

express, and represent suggests a connection between the two. Indeed, linguistic metaphors are valuable to our understanding of music. It is for this reason that they have become ingrained within our language about musical meaning: "passages in music are conceived as sentences, with individual notes or clusters of notes taken to be equivalent of words."[5] Likewise, we talk about musical ideas, musical sentences, propositions, punctuation and musical questions.[6] Some accounts of musical meaning, however, have been governed entirely by the analogy and assert that music *is* a kind of language. Thus, within Deryck Cooke's controversial book *The Language of Music*, he takes music's capacity to express and evoke emotion as his starting point. He claims that similar melodic phrases, harmonies, and rhythms found within the work of different composers within the tonal tradition are used to communicate identical emotions. On this basis he suggests that music can be considered a language, since it has idioms affording specific meanings.

Analogies are, of course, structurally advantageous since they have the capacity to preserve the integrity of the concerned parties, recognizing which connections obtain and which do not, which are helpful and which hinder. In this respect analogy has the ability to prevent reduction or totalization. In practice, however, one partner often becomes dominant, the understanding of one negatively affecting the other. This, in fact, has often been the case with the analogy of music and language, resulting especially from the frequent presumption that determinate and verifiable content underpins linguistic communication.[7] Against this criterion, to which music does not measure up, "it is erroneously concluded that music is a second-class citizen of the intellectual world."[8] This is the case with Peter Kivy's use of the analogy. In brief terms, Kivy favors the content provided through language and thus fails to acknowledge the possibility that music has content because it does not comply

---

5. Johnson, *Meaning of the Body*, 235.

6. See Johnson's treatment of the metaphor of "music as language." Ibid., 235.

7. See Leo Treitler on the relationship between music and (particular understandings that underpin) language in "Language and the Interpretation of Music," 23–56. The emphasis upon determinacy is brought out in relation to beauty by Paul Guyer. In particular, he relates the destabilization of the concept of beauty within philosophical circles to the verificationist theory of meaning and the positivist equation of scientific explanation and prediction. Guyer, *Values of Beauty*.

8. Johnson, *Meaning of the Body*, 260.

with the nature of everyday (and poetical) linguistic content.[9] Music is thus viewed simply as pleasure since it is non-propositional. At the other extreme, but on the very same basis (most notably within the Romantic understanding) music has been thought to surpass words, communicating the ineffable.[10]

The nature of musical meaning, considered through its physicality, is also often clouded by frameworks built upon aesthetic categories and principles. These provide a lens through which the arts in general are viewed. Such broad-sweep approaches tend towards a certain homogenization across their range and thereby result in distortion within accounts of individual arts. The uniqueness of the arts is not fully attended to. The specific category that will provide the focus for the task at hand is beauty. Beauty features within current aesthetic and theological discussion (standing more peripherally within the domain of philosophical aesthetics).[11] Historically, however, it has been a dominant concept, acting as a cipher for underlying presuppositions that themselves comprise broader frameworks, both philosophical and theological.

It is on this basis that the two central figures of our narrative present themselves: Anicius Manlius Severinus Boethius (c.480–c.525) and Immanuel Kant (1724–1804). Both are of immense significance within Western intellectual history, contributing to the development of accounts of the arts and advancing the theory and practice of music. An examina-

9. Kivy, "Kant and the Affektenlehre." We will return to Kivy's understanding of music in chapter six. Theodor W. Adorno states that "Music resembles language," but maintains that anyone who takes the resemblance literally "will be seriously misled." "Music and Language: A Fragment," 1–6. We will see that Kant upholds the connection between music and language. The latter dominates his conception of communication and his understanding of the fine arts. Music suffers as a result.

10. Discussing the Romantic understanding of music Carl Dahlhaus says: "If instrumental music had been a 'pleasant noise' *beneath* language to the common-sense estheticians of the eighteenth century, then the romantic metaphysics of art declared it a language *above* language. The urge to include it in the central sphere of language could not be suppressed" (*Idea of Absolute Music*, 9).

11. Until quite recently the majority of philosophical discussion has centred upon the notion of beauty: it is now marginal although not without advocates. These include Mothersill, *Beauty Restored* and Zangwill, *Metaphysics of Beauty*. See also Guyer, *Values of Beauty*, chap. 13. Within theology the attention paid to beauty has been consistent. This is due in large part to the objective ground for beauty provided by belief in God. Recent works include: Harries, *Art and the Beauty of God*; Sherry, *Spirit and Beauty*; Aran Murphy, *Christ and the Form of Beauty*; Hart, *Beauty of the Infinite*; Nichols, *Redeeming Beauty*; Viladesau, *Theological Aesthetics*.

tion of their respective accounts of beauty will allow the frameworks underpinning them to be *deciphered*. For their contrasting conceptions of
beauty are intrinsically connected to their understandings of the nature
of physicality and its capacity to offer knowledge of the world, conceptually understood. In this way, epistemological concerns surface, for it is
within the space that the concept of beauty opens up that the boundary
between the perceiving subject and the perceived object is negotiated
and, thereby, that the relationship of the self and the world is constituted. In addition, it will show how their particular understandings of
beauty mold their evaluation of music. As a result two aspects central
to music will become clear. These ultimately devalue music within both
the Boethian and Kantian schemes but are not only central to music
ontology but provide a means through which music acquires its variety
of meanings and functions. These features are the *physicality* of music
(its existence as sound) and, its corollary, *indeterminacy* (that is, the absence of propositional knowledge from music's physicality). Attention to
music itself will draw these features out.

Before sketching an outline of the path that our exploration will
take, a word is needed about the music which Boethius and Kant have in
mind for it would be wrong to presume that both thinkers are concerned
with the same type. Indeed, to talk about music in its non-specificity
would be to perform an abstraction. Hence, a glimpse at the history of
Western music reveals the difference between the types of sounded music that Boethius and Kant have in mind. There are two major developments that are relevant here. The first is a progression from the sequential
tone-pattern (exemplified in chant) to the polyphony of the sixteenth
century and the second is a movement away from "Pythagorean tuning" towards "equal temperament."[12] Hence, whereas for Boethius music
emerges horizontally from the melodic sequence of tones, using a musi-

12. The Pythagorean scale gave way to tempered versions because of the dispro-
portion inherent within its construction. Stuart Isacoff notes, "The fact is, octaves and
fifths, when created with Pythagoras' pure mathematical ratios are incommensurate:
The further they move away from a common starting point, the more the structures
built from these 'perfect' intervals diverge." Thus, in the production of a scale, a series of
octaves or fifths will never be exactly in tune with one another. Isacoff, *Temperament*,
40–42. A good summary of the shift from Pythagorean tuning to forms of temperament,
including "meantone tuning" and the "just scale," is found in Backus, *The Acoustical
Foundations of Music*, 134–60. Cf. also Rasch, "Tuning and Temperament," 193–222. A
brief historical survey of other forms of early music tuning is found in Covey-Crump,
"Pythagoras at the forge," 318–20.

cal scale that is tuned according to the octave (*diapason*), fourth (*diat-essaron*), and fifth (*diapente*), for Kant music is conceived vertically as well as horizontally, in the harmony that contextualizes a melody, using a musical scale that tunes according to the octave and therein consists of equal semi-tone intervals. Even though these changes are substantial and the types of sounded-music that Boethius and Kant have in mind are different there is enough continuity to justify their juxtaposition for the purposes of this discussion, namely the continuity that derives from music's existence as *practice*. Thus, although sounded-music is the em-bodiment of different practices that vary according to time and place, in each case there is something commonly recognizable as music, namely the temporal organization of tones.

Initially, then, we will start with Boethius for whom the world is knowable and for whom, as a result, the physical world is of value. Here, within an integrally theological framework, beauty is understood as harmony and as such is constitutive of the world: it is the principle by which the world coheres as a whole and a property of the material world. I will show how granting beauty this objectivity allows it a cosmic mean-ing or "resonance" which extends both between and beyond subjects. I will then demonstrate how the Boethian account of music illustrates his understanding of the material world and beauty. Considering beauty as the principle of harmony grants music significance in relation to both the intellectual and the material for, as physical sensation, music offers knowledge of the world. However, I shall show that ultimately Boethius stresses the intellectual to the detriment of the material, using the physi-cal experience of music as merely a stepping-stone to intellectual per-ception through form (with form finding its ideal location in God). By virtue of the satisfaction and pleasure imparted by music's physicality, Boethius' attention is re-invigorated and he is encouraged to re-focus on the world and, specifically, himself as part of the world. Ultimately, however, musical indeterminacy gives way to and is surpassed by the conceptual truths of reason.

I will then turn to Kant who displays a mistrust of sensory knowl-edge, which can never be guaranteed. The world-in-itself remains beyond human comprehension. This unknowability, and the understanding of the physical, material world as an occasion for its "appearance," leads Kant to deny beauty as, to put it simply, an objective property of the material. It causes him to assign to it a merely descriptive capacity through its reference to the harmony of the cognitive powers within the subject, the locus of aesthetic response. I will demonstrate how understanding beauty thus permits it a merely inter-subjective meaning, or "resonance," one extending between subjects but not beyond them. Thereafter I will show how Kant's account of music exemplifies his view both of the material world and of beauty as well as exploring the ambiguity of music's status within his account of the fine arts. Positively understood, the conceptually indeterminate nature of certain forms of music allies it with nature, rendering it paradigmatic of beauty. However, negatively understood, music lies on the margins of the Kantian understanding of beauty (and the fine arts) since judgments about beauty necessarily concern only a harmony of the intellectual powers. Ultimately, for Kant, the physicality of music precludes it from engaging the mind and involvement with concepts (albeit in an indeterminate way), reducing it to mere pleasure.

Finally, given this particular history of the concept of beauty and its intrinsic connection with epistemological concerns (and the implicit tendency demonstrated thereby where non-musical frameworks are imposed upon music in order to ground its significance) we will explore the physicality of music as manifested in its practice and reception. I will show how music *as sound* facilitates the suspension of the boundary between subject and object, self and world, such that each becomes open to the other. In doing so we will thereby impact upon an understanding of beauty epistemologically (but non-propositionally) understood. I will suggest that musical beauty refers to the occurrence of a pre-reflective stance towards the world wherein one focuses outwards and experiences an abundance of meaning that is not self-generated but is presented from without whilst 'resonating' within. Experienced as a sense of richness or fullness I will suggest that music can thus be said to encourage what might be called an "enchanted" mode of attention.

1

The Boethian Understanding of the World, the Role of Beauty, and the Value of Music

> It appears without doubt that music is so naturally united with us that we cannot be free from it even if we so desired. For this reason the power of the intellect ought to be summoned, so that this art, innate through nature, might also be mastered, comprehended through knowledge.
>
> —Boethius *De Institutione Musica* 1.1.187 [1]

BOETHIUS' VISION IS FUNDAMENTALLY theological: the world is an ordered whole that has its ground in God. Herein, music is the active principle of harmony. As such, it is both a means of understanding the world and of participating therein and is innate to the physical and mental existence of humankind. It is on this basis that Boethius grants the importance of music as both sound and form. However, even though the sounded nature of music is important for Boethius its formal structure is more so. Thus, one moves through and beyond contingency and indeterminacy to that which comprises its uncontingent and determinate basis. It is thus that the importance of the intellect is asserted through its capacity to comprehend the rudiments of sounded music. Underlying this simultaneous appreciation and devaluation of music *as sound* are three interconnected points within Boethius' thought: the creation of the world by God, the consequent emphasis upon the objective "form" of beauty, and the underlying contrast between that which is changeable and that which is not.

For Boethius the world is an ordered whole that offers evidence of its true nature by means of its perception. It does so because God is

---

1. Hereafter, referred to as *Fundamentals*.

its Creator, number is its foundation, and harmony is its order. Hence knowledge of the world is achieved initially through attentive observation of the world's order and thereafter through comprehension of the number that grounds it. This involves a movement away from the changeable towards the unchangeable. Thus, as the role of number comes to the fore the intellect abstracts from the sensible and the sensible becomes superfluous. In this context, beauty is synonymous with harmony, manifested by God in the form of His creation, and is a part of the fabric of the cosmos. As a result it has both ontological and epistemological value. It is both *what* we know and *how* we know.

In the light of this music is assigned a unique two-fold role. On the one hand, music is ontologically significant. Number grounds the cosmos by means of a series of ratios, and music, as the relation between numbers, comprises an essential aspect of the world itself. On the other hand, music is epistemologically important. It reveals number and thus allows humankind to achieve a fuller understanding of the world through its orientation towards the unchangeable. In this way, music stands as an active and powerful force within the cosmos, since it reveals and thereby encourages harmony. In doing so it relates diverse elements to one another, including humankind, drawing them into a coherent whole. Although it does so by means of both sound and form, the formal basis of music is valued more highly than its manifestation in sound. This is because emphasis is placed upon the unchangeable and formal basis of music which is underpinned by number.

QUADRIVIUM: THE FOUR-FOLD WAY

In order to explore the role that music plays in Boethius' thought we will first examine the system of which it is considered a part, the *quadrivium*. The *quadrivium* comprises four disciplines, arithmetic, music, geometry, and astronomy,[2] each of which occupied an important position within

---

2. Masi notes the existence of two representational traditions of the Liberal Arts, one following from the *Liber De Nuptiis Mercurii et Philologiae* of Martianus Capella and the other from Boethius. Capella's treatise was written in the fifth century and was well known throughout the Middle Ages, making a significant contribution to the study of philosophy and the arts. Therein, the allegorical figures of Liberal Arts are described in a highly pictorial manner and appear thus, geometry, arithmetic, astronomy, and music. Masi says: "The essential difference between this order of the quadrivium and the sequence demanded by Boethius depends on whether music is considered a mathematical study and is paired off with arithmetic (Boethius) or a harmonic study and paired off with astronomy (Capella)" (*Boethian Number Theory*, 13).

the classical educational system for a long time.[3] Between the years 500 and 506 Boethius wrote treatises on all four subjects,[4] a fact attested to by Cassiodorus in a letter between them.[5] However, not all have survived. All that remain are two complete books of the *Arithmetic*, five incomplete books of the *Fundamentals*, and a work on geometry, divided into two or three books (although this may not be genuine). The treatise on astronomy has been lost.

Not only did Boethius write on all four disciplines, he is said to have coined the term *quadrivium*.[6] Whether or not this is the case, the system itself was by no means new and Boethius traced it back to Pythagoras:

> Among all the men of ancient authority who, following the lead of Pythagoras, have flourished in the purer reasoning of the mind, it is clearly obvious that hardly anyone has been able to reach the highest perfection of the disciplines of philosophy unless the nobility of such wisdom was investigated by him in a certain four-part study, the *quadrivium*, which will hardly be hidden from those properly respectful of expertness. For this is the wisdom of things which are, and the perception of truth gives to these things their unchanging character.[7]

3. See White, "Boethius in the Medieval *Quadrivium*," 162–205; Bower, "Transmission of Ancient Theory," 136–67. Masi notes manuscript evidence indicating that students in schools and universities studied these disciplines in the Boethian order. *Boethian Number Theory*, 12–14.

4. Schrade, "Music in the Philosophy of Boethius," 188.

5. Cassiodorus, "Variae," i.45.4. Cf. Caldwell, "*De Institutione Arithmetica*," 137. Cassiodorus' letter from the early sixth century shows that he was at least aware that Boethius had written something on music but it does not demonstrate any knowledge of the contents of Boethius' treatise. For support of the suggestion that Cassiodorus had not read Boethius' treatise see Bower, "The Role of Boethius' *De Institutione Musica*," 161. Cassiodorus also mentions Boethius' *Arithmetic* and *Geometry* in his treatise *Institutiones*. Cassiodorus does not refer to the *Fundamentals* or the *Astronomy* here. Caldwell notes that no one has ever doubted the authenticity of the *Fundamentals* and that the lack of mention in the *Institutiones* may simply be due to its incomplete state. Caldwell, "*De Institutione Arithmetica*," 137.

6. Masi notes that the four-fold way does not derive from Nicomachus, one of his sources, but is coined by Boethius. He remarks that the earliest manuscripts consistently use the version "*quadruvium*" and that "*quadrivium*" is a later spelling. Schrade offers a contrary view, noting that Boethius seems to have introduced this term into the Latin world, probably in direct derivation from Nicomachus of Gerasa, who had spoken of "the four ways." Schrade, "Music in the Philosophy of Boethius," 189. See White, "Boethius in the Medieval Quadrivium," 162.

7. Boethius *Arithmetic* 1.1.

Vestiges of the Pythagorean reverence of number can be found in
Plato's *Republic*.[8] Specifically, it emerges in the system of education com-
mended there: arithmetic (521–526c), geometry (526–528d), astronomy
(528e–530c), and harmonics (530d–531). Importantly, mathematics is
identified as the primary discipline. There seem to be three main reasons for this. First, mathematics underpins the "quadrivial" disciplines.
Second, mathematics enables the mind to abstract from the sensible.
Third, by virtue of this capacity for abstraction, mathematics prepares
the ground for philosophy, which is primarily concerned with the realm
of the "forms."[9] These points echo within Boethius' own work, as a brief
comparison will disclose.

Mathematics as Foundation

For Plato, mathematics underpins those disciplines that later come to be
known as the quadrivium. It is for this reason that Socrates and Glaucon
choose mathematics when discussing which discipline should be com-
pulsory within the education of the *polis*. It is not sufficient to attend
merely to the sensory element of astronomy or music since, for Plato,
the sensible realm is changeable and is therefore of limited meaning.[10]
Rather, their true value lies in their mathematical core, which enables the
mind to penetrate to their real and unchanging essence. Hence, Socrates
says of "the subject of calculation" that it leads the soul "forcibly upward
and compels it to discuss the numbers themselves, never permitting
anyone to propose for discussion numbers attached to visible or tangible
bodies."[11] Thus, Glaucon draws attention to the unreliability of sense in
the case of music. For there are those who "talk about something they

8. It is important to emphasize that very little is known about Pythagoras. See
Guthrie, *A History of Greek Philosophy*, 153–68. Plato mentions Pythagoras (*Republic*
600b) and "Pythagoreans" (ibid., 530d) only once (Aristotle also only mentions them
twice in his extant writings). However, Plato treats numbers with a similar metaphysical
significance to the Pythagoreans. Guthrie, *History of Greek Philosophy*, 213–14.

9. For details on the Platonic theory of "forms," cf. Copleston, *History of Philosophy*,
163, 206; Grube, *Plato's Thought*, 1–47.

10. Plato *Republic* VI, 509d–511e. Here, the "divided line" maps modes of knowledge onto the distinction between the changeable and the unchangeable (the visible
and the intelligible). Thus, as one moves away from the visible realm towards the intelligible one proceeds from "imaging" (εἰκασία) through "belief" (πίστις) and "thought"
(διάνοια) to "understanding" (νοήσις). For further details of Plato's theory of knowledge see Copleston, *History of Philosophy*, 142–62.

11. Plato *Republic* VII, 525d.

call a 'dense interval' or quartertone—putting their ears to their instruments like someone trying to overhear what the neighbours are saying."[12] Others say that they "hear a tone in between and that *it* is the shortest interval by which they must measure."[13] There are others still who "argue that this tone sounds the same as a quarter tone."[14] In short, in each case the ears are placed before understanding.[15] Socrates is clear that such people are caught up with sense and do not use reason. They "seek out the numbers that are to be found in these audible consonances, but they do not make the ascent to problems. They don't investigate, for example, which numbers are consonant and which aren't or what the explanation is of each."[16]

The emphasis upon mathematics and reason surfaces in Boethius: the *Proemium* of the *Arithmetic* makes it clear that mathematics is "mother" to the rest.[17] Three reasons are given. First, "God the creator of the massive structure of the world considered this first discipline as the exemplar of his own thought and established all things in accord with it."[18] Second, "through numbers of an assigned order all things exhibiting the logic of their maker found concord."[19] Third, mathematics underpins the other disciplines because it precedes them. Boethius explains: "whatever things are prior in nature, it is to these underlying elements that the posterior elements can be referred." He continues, "Now if posterior

12. Ibid., VII, 531a–b.

13. Ibid.

14. Ibid. Of geometry, Glaucon states: "geometry *is* knowledge of what always is." Socrates continues: "Then it draws the soul towards truth and produces philosophic thought by directing it upwards what we now wrongly direct downwards" (ibid., VII, 527b). The emphasis upon abstraction from the sensible is present also with regard to astronomy: "Then if, by really taking part in astronomy, we're to make the naturally intelligent part of the soul useful instead of useless, let's study astronomy by means of problems, as we do geometry, and leave the things in the sky alone" (ibid., VII, 530b–c).

15. Ibid., VII, 531a–b.

16. Ibid., VII, 531b–c.

17. In his introduction to *Arithmetic*, Masi notes that the modern meaning of "arithmetic" conveys nothing of what it meant for Boethius. It was only in the Middle Ages that the term came to designate "an elementary discipline of counting and calculation." Prior to this it concerned the "theory or philosophy of number." Masi, *Boethian Number Theory*, 11.

18. Boethius *Arithmetic* 1.1.

19. Ibid.

things pass away, nothing concerning the status of the priori substance is disturbed—so *animal* comes before *man*. Now if you take away *animal*, immediately also is the nature of *man* erased. If you take away *man*, *animal* does not disappear."[20] Likewise, "those things which are posterior infer prior things in themselves, and when these prior things are stated, they do not include in them anything of the posterior, as can be seen in that same term *man*. If you say *man*, you also say *animal*, because it is the same as *man*. If you say *animal* you do not at the same time include the species of man, because *animal* is not the same as *man*."[21]

    This is translated to geometry, arithmetic, astronomy, and music. They are characterized according to their relation to number, which is prior to and therefore constitutive of them. Thus, in the case of geometry, number is implicit within its geometrical forms, such as the triangle and the quadrangle, but geometrical forms are not implicit within number. The elimination therefore of geometrical figures does not affect number but the removal of number causes geometrical figures to perish.[22] The case of music follows accordingly, since the melodic progression of sounds centers upon the intervals of an octave (*diapason*), fourth (*diatessaron*), and fifth (*diapente*). Each of these derive from antecedent numerical terms: the octave results from the ratio 2:1, the fourth is generated by the ratio 4:3, and the fifth arises from the ratio 3:2. Thus Boethius says: "the sound which is in a diapason harmony, the same sound is produced in the ratio of a number doubled."[23] Thus, music depends upon number but number is not dependent upon music. In sum, number is the foundation upon which the disciplines of the *quadrivium* are built and without which they would cease to exist.

Abstraction from the Sensible

For Plato, emphasizing mathematics as the basis of the 'quadrivium' stems from the belief that it encourages the mind to turn away from the sensible world towards the unchangeable. This movement is of utmost importance within Platonic thought, which upholds a distinction between the sensible world and the world of unchangeable "forms." The

---

20. Ibid.

21. Ibid.

22. Ibid.

23. Ibid. For a definition, see Boethius *Fundamentals* 1.16.201–19; 205.

sensible world is in constant flux and is characterized by Plato as a place of becoming. By contrast, the world of the 'forms' is unchangeable. It is a place of being and therefore of truth. It is thus crucial that one abstracts from the sensible: "If anyone attempts to learn something about sensible things, whether by gaping upward or squinting downward, I'd claim— since there's no knowledge of such things—that he never learns anything and that, even if he studies lying on his back on the ground or floating on it in the sea, his soul is looking not up but down."[24]

For Plato, it is by virtue of the capacity of mathematics to reveal the unchangeable that it is included within the education of the *polis*. Mathematics underpins music, poetry, physical training, and the crafts,[25] and studying it allows one to examine their fundamental basis. Thus, geometry, astronomy, and music are important and useful only in so far as they are related to and concern number. Their sensible aspect is not only extraneous but distracts from the unchangeable: "what we need to consider is whether the greater and more advanced part of it [the particular discipline] tends to make it easier to see the form of the good. And we say that anything has that tendency if it compels the soul to turn itself around towards the region in which lies the happiest of the things that are, the one the soul must see at any cost."[26]

In short, within Platonic thought it is the numerical aspect of the sensible that grants the "quadrivial" disciplines their importance, the unchangeable character of number facilitating abstraction. Boethius adopts the Platonic distinction between that which changes and that which does not. The *quadrivium* is "the wisdom of things which are, and the perception of truth gives to these things their unchanging character."[27] This allows one to reach the unchangeable realm: "We say those things *are* which neither grow by stretching nor diminish by crushing, nor are changed by variations, but are always in their proper force and keep themselves secure by support of their own nature."[28]

24. Plato *Republic* VII, 529b–c.
25. Ibid., VII, 522b.
26. Ibid., VII, 526d–e.
27. Boethius *Arithmetic* 1.1.
28. Ibid.

Preparation for Philosophy

The drive towards the unchangeable is manifested in the education system of the *Republic*, which is designed principally for the philosopher who is to govern the *polis* and therefore must direct his attention towards the unchangeable world of "forms."[29] The allegory of the cave depicts this: the prisoner escapes his bondage and proceeds in steps towards the light beyond the cave.[30] Only thus does he discover the true nature of things. For Plato, it is only in distinguishing being from becoming and thereby knowing the true reality of the world that the philosopher can be a 'guardian' of the people. The mathematical disciplines are formative to this end: they exercise the mind in the task of "hypotheses" and thus prepare for dialectic, which enables progression beyond to the "first principle" of all.[31] Thus, Socrates says to Glaucon:

> it would be appropriate, Glaucon, to legislate this subject for those who are going to share in the highest offices in the city and to persuade them to turn to calculation and take it up not as laymen do, but staying with it until they reach the study of the natures of the numbers by means of understanding itself, not like tradesmen and retailers for the sake of buying and selling, but for the sake of war and for ease in turning the soul around, away from becoming and towards truth and being.[32]

The idea that the *quadrivium* serves as a preparation for the study of philosophy is also present in Boethius:

> Pythagoras was the first person to call the study of wisdom "philosophy." He held that philosophy was the knowledge and study of whatever may properly and truly said "to be." Moreover, he considered these things to be those that neither increase under tension nor decrease under pressure, things not changed by any

29. For an overview of the Plato's system of education, see Grube, *Plato's Thought*, 216–58.

30. Plato *Republic* VII, 514a–517a.

31. Socrates explains: "that which reason itself grasps by the power of the dialectic. It does not consider these hypotheses as first principles but truly as hypotheses—but as stepping stones to take off from, enabling it to reach the unhypothetical first principle of everything. Having grasped this principle, it reverses itself and, keeping hold of what follows from it, comes down to a conclusion without making use of anything visible at all, but only of forms themselves, moving on from forms to forms, and ending in forms" (ibid., VI, 511b).

32. Ibid., VII, 525b–c.

chance occurrences. These things are forms, magnitudes, qualities, relations,[33] and other things which, considered in themselves, are immutable, but which, joined to material substances,
suffer radical change and are altered in many ways because of
their relationship with a changeable thing.[34]

It is for this reason that Boethius classifies the disciplines of the *quadrivium* in terms of their connection with number.[35] To explain: Boethius defines quantity as either discrete or continuous. He calls discrete quantity
multitude and stipulates its origin in unity.[36] Consequently, multitude
is concerned with the collective union of individual things such as "a
flock, a populace, a chorus."[37] In this sense, it is limited with regard to its
smallest part but unlimited in terms of its reach, potentially extending
to infinity. Of these multitudes, some are discrete in relation to themselves, such as numbers, whilst others are discrete in relation to something, "such as double, triple, and others that arise from comparison."[38]
In terms of the disciplines of the *quadrivium*, therefore, arithmetic is
linked to multitude that stands in relation to itself: "arithmetic considers

33. Bower notes in his translation that this is the first occurrence of the word *habitudo* in the *Fundamentals*, Boethius' translation of the Greek σχέσις. This term, here
translated as "relation," is used in a general sense for any relation between two numbers and is often used as an equivalent of "*ratio*" (*proportio* or λόγος). Nicomachus
frequently uses σχέσις in his *Eisagoge arithmetica*, and consequently *habitudo* often
appears in Boethius' *Arithmetic*. That *habitudo* occurs only in Books Two and Three
of *Fundamentals* is an indication of just how dependent these two books are on the
arithmetical treatise. Boethius *Fundamentals* 2.2.227–28 n. 3.

34. Ibid., 2.2.227–28. Concerning philosophy as the study of that which can truly be
said "to be," see Boethius *Arithmetic* 1.1.

35. Nicomachus, upon whose relevant treatises Boethius relied, discloses the logic of
the selection and order of subjects in his *Introduction to Arithmetic*. They are based upon
a distinction between multitudes (arithmetic and music) and magnitudes (geometry
and astronomy), of which the former were either self-sufficient (arithmetic) or referred
to something else (music), and the latter were either stationary (geometry) or mobile
(astronomy). Caldwell, "*De Institutione Arithmetica*," 137. The Nicomachan classification was not universally adopted, though it is accepted by Boethius and also adhered
to by Cassiodorus in the *Institutiones*. Caldwell notes that Isidore followed Cassiodorus
and it was from these two writers that it passed into medieval consciousness; ibid. This
is echoed by Bower, who maintains that Cassiodorus and Isidore furnished the idea of
the liberal arts, and thus of *ars musica*, for most of Europe from years 500 until 850.
"Role of Boethius' *De Institutione Musica*," 160.

36. Boethius *Fundamentals* 2.3.228.

37. Boethius *Arithmetic* 1.1.

38. Boethius *Fundamentals* 2.3.229.

that multitude which exists of itself as an integral whole."[39] Music, on
the other hand is connected to multitude that stands in relation: "the
measures of musical modulation understand that multitude which exists
in relation to some other."[40]

Continuous quantity is called magnitude.[41] In contrast to multitude, which operates in terms of discrete units and is thereby limited
by its smaller measure but infinite in virtue of the larger one, magnitudes are continuous and not separable. Examples given include "a tree"
and "a stone."[42] For this reason, beginning with a finite quantity as its
measure, magnitude is restricted with regards to its larger measure but
infinite in its capacity to divide. Thus, Boethius says, "if there is a line one
foot long, or any other length for that matter, it can be divided in half,
and this half again divided into another half, so that there will never
be any limit to dividing magnitude."[43] Of these magnitudes, Boethius
observes that some are fixed. These include "squares, triangles, or circles."
Others are movable, "such as the sphere of the universe and whatever is
turned within it at a prescribed speed."[44] In terms of the disciplines of
the *quadrivium*, therefore, geometry is allied with stable magnitude and
astronomy is connected with movable magnitude."[45]

God, Creation, and the Importance of Music

The "quadrivial" tradition that Boethius receives, shaped by the primacy
of number, is crucial to his understanding of music. In particular, it is the
intimation of a close alliance between arithmetic and music that is vital,
for arithmetic is concerned with discrete numbers and music involves
discrete numbers *in relation*. This alliance is embodied in the defini-

39. Boethius *Arithmetic* 1.1.

40. The close connection of music and mathematics is supported by mutual reference between the treatises concerning music and arithmetic and the fact that both
works depend upon the relevant works by Nicomachus. It is for this reason that Bower
suggests that Boethius' works on arithmetic and music are basically one work rather
than two: "they both treat number and are both based on related works by Nicomachus,
and many passages in the musical treatise refer to passages in the arithmetica treatise"
(Bower, "Role of Boethius' *De Institutione Musica*," 159).

41. Boethius *Fundamentals* 2.3.228.

42. Boethius *Arithmetic* 1.1.

43. Boethius *Fundamentals* 2.3.228.

44. Ibid., 2.3.228–229.

45. Boethius *Arithmetic* 1.1. The definitions of the quadrivial disciplines through
their association with number is confirmed in *Fundamentals* 2.3.229.

tions of music given within the *Arithmetic* and the *Fundamentals*. In the *Arithmetic*, Boethius observes that "harmony is the union of many things and the consensus of dissidents."[46] In the *Fundamentals*, music is defined as "quantities related to quantities" thereby incorporating all numerical proportions.[47] Structurally speaking, therefore, music is of immense importance. It not only stands alongside arithmetic as the foundation of astronomy and geometry, since without the relation of numbers there would be no magnitude (whether fixed or movable), but in virtue of this underpins Boethius' vision of a created cosmic order, even implicitly connecting directly to God (as we shall see in the *Fundamentals*).

Hence, in the *Proemium* of the *Arithmetic* Boethius cites among his reasons for placing mathematics at the foundation of the *quadrivium* the notion that number embodies God's own thought and that it assigns order throughout creation. Further on Boethius explains: "From the beginning, all things whatever which have been created may be seen by the nature of things to be formed by reason of numbers. Number was the principal exemplar in the mind of the creator. From it were derived the multiplicity of the four elements, from it were derived the changes of the seasons, from it the movement of the stars and the turning of the heavens."[48] It is clear that it is number not in isolation but in relation that constitutes creation. Creation involves the drawing together of diverse elements, and music, as the relation of number, is crucial to the achievement of this coherence.

In short, music is a fundamental aspect of the Boethian world-view. This will become more explicit in what follows. We will first examine the *Fundamentals*, for key notions of Boethius' understanding of music alighted upon here will be extrapolated in detail there, specifically those of harmony and consonance. We will then consider the *Consolation* where the active nature of these notions, configuring music's sphere of action, will be demonstrated practically through the use of music to address Boethius and assist his recovery. It is only at this point that the notion of beauty will come into focus, crystallizing Boethius' world view.

46. Boethius *Arithmetic* 2.32. "*Est armonia plurimorum adunatio et dissidentium consensio.*" Specifically, music is the power that binds all things together out of the two original and contrary "natures" of Plato's *Timaeus*, the "Same" and the "Other."

47. Boethius *Fundamentals* 2.3.229. Cf. also *Arithmetic* 1.21.

48. Boethius distinguishes two fundamental "principles" of which number consists, even and odd. These also emphasize the existence of number in relation: "These elements are disparate and contrary by a certain divine power, yet they come forth from one source and are joined into one composition and harmony" (ibid., 1.2; 2.32).

2

Inhabiting Harmony—
The World as a Series of Relations[1]

An Examination of the Fundamentals of Music

SOURCES AND MODELS, AND STRUCTURE

A S WE HAVE SEEN, the Boethian world-view largely emerges from the Platonic tradition. Indeed, it is accepted that one of Boethius' main concerns is the transmission of ancient Greek knowledge to the Latin-speaking world.[2] This is confirmed in part by Boethius' treatment of the *quadrivium*, which as we have seen arises from the Pythagorean/ Platonic schema, and his conscientious attention to the Greek sources of the *Fundamentals*, the five books of which rely heavily upon works of Nicomachus and Ptolemy.[3]

---

1. Chamberlain notes that all uses of *harmonia* in Boethius' works are not synonymous with *musica*, but that on the whole he uses them interchangeably; the music of the elements is created by *harmonia* (*Fundamentals* 1.2.188–89). "Philosophy of Music in the *Consolatio* of Boethius," 81.

2. "What stands beyond controversy is that Boethius' literary and educational programme is a faithful reflection of the assumptions and teaching practice of the contemporary Platonic schools of Athens and Alexandria" (Chadwick, *Boethius*, 20–21; cf. also Bower, "Boethius and Nicomachus," 45). Crabbe writes: "he [Boethius] had a salvage operation to perform: what might be preserved from a brilliant past for a dying civilization as the dark ages fell" ("Literary Design in *De Consolatione*," 240). Boethius characterizes his own program of study in his commentary on Aristotle's *Perihermeneias*, see Lerer, *Boethius and dialogue*, 14. For a summary of the Boethian project, see Marenbon, *Boethius*, 17–42.

3. Bower, "Boethius and Nicomachus," 1–45; cf. also Caldwell, "*De Institutione Arithmetica*."

Other precedents exist in addition to these sources, however, such as Augustine's *De Musica* and part of Martianus Capella's *De nuptiis Philogiae et Mercurii*. Of these, Augustine's *De Musica* is the Latin treatise that is closest in character to Boethius' *Fundamentals* since both treatises are concerned with what one can really *know*. This involves moving in, through, and beyond physical matter to the attainment of true knowledge, mathematical truths and, thereby, spiritual truths. However, Augustine's *De Musica* focuses on musical metre (an aspect of music not dealt with by Boethius, as we shall see) and does not deal with musical consonances.[4]

Comparison can also be made between the *Fundamentals* and the final book of Martianus Capella's *De nuptiis Philogiae et Mercurii*. Next to Boethius' work, that of Martianus provides the most complete source of musical facts from antiquity. However, as Bower notes, Martianus' thought "is seldom quantitative in any systematic way, and his approach is cursory and encyclopaedic. Compared to Boethius' thoroughly developed musical system Capella's work must be considered a superficial introduction."[5]

Given Boethius' attentiveness to his sources, opinion differs with regards to his originality. Thus, for example, Bower considers the *Fundamentals* primarily as a work of translation[6] whilst at the same time acknowledging the originality of particular contributions such as the origination of the term *quadrivium* and the division of music into "Cosmic," "Human," and "Instrumental."[7] In apparent contrast, John Caldwell maintains that the treatise "is a book by Boethius himself, however derivative in its details." He explains, although it is "dependent almost throughout on the work of existing authors, the arrangement of the materials is at least in part that of Boethius himself; he draws on the work of numerous writers, and he comments on and refutes his sources as well as translating or paraphrasing them."[8] Although Bower

4. "Although Augustine's treatise influenced metrics and musical rhythm in the later Middle Ages, it presented neither the fundamentals of musical consonances nor a rigorous mathematical system such as that of Boethius" (Bower, "Role of Boethius' *De Institutione Musica*," 159).

5. Bower, "Boethius and Nicomachus," 159–60.

6. Ibid., 157.

7. Bower, "The Role of Boethius' *De Institutione Musica*," 44.

8. Caldwell, "*De Institutione Arithmetica*," 139. Caldwell comes to this conclusion in the light of Boethius' treatise on arithmetic, which is more a work of translation. He

and Caldwell differ, it seems that they in fact articulate a similar understanding of the *Fundamentals*, namely, that it is a treatise which clarifies
the Greek understanding of music whilst drawing out its implications in
an original way. In this light, it is significant to note the contrast between
the respective purposes of Boethius and Kant. Boethius aims to transmit
the Greek tradition to the best of his ability, making it as comprehensible
as he can in the process, while at the same time having no wish to enter
into any debate as such.[9] By contrast, Kant (as we shall see) responds to
contested questions, setting forth a critique and thereby asserting his
own position.

It is likely that it is Boethius' pedagogical aim that motivates him to
clarity. This is suggested by the introduction of the *Fundamentals*, which
lucidly outlines the main issues that feature within its technical body.
Boethius says, "All the things that are to be explained more fully later, we
are now trying to explain cursorily and briefly, so that, for the present,
they might accustom the mind of the reader to what might be called
the surface of the subject; the mind will plunge into deeper knowledge
in the subsequent treatment."[10] In effect, therefore, the introduction sets
forth statements of belief that will later be rationally discerned: "All these
things I shall prove both through mathematical reasoning and aural
judgment."[11] To this end, Boethius lays down the "Cosmic" framework

---

says: "At the very least, it must be allowed that the technique of translation is freer, the
scope for insertion and (perhaps) compression greater, than in the *Arithmetic*" (ibid.,
142).

9. "Boethius' intention in his philosophical programme was, and this cannot be
overstressed, a highly technical one, that of reconciling the philosophical schemes of
Plato and Aristotle, and he himself makes no claim for it to have any greater significance
than this" (Kirkby, "Scholar and His Public," 59).

10. Boethius *Fundamentals* 1.33.223. This follows the example of Pythagoras: "Now
this has been in the manner of the Pythagoreans: when something was said by the master Pythagoras, no one thereafter dared challenge the reasoning; rather, the explanation
of the one teaching was authority for them. This continued until after the time that the
mind of the one learning – itself made stronger through more steadfast doctrine—came
to discover the rationale of these same things, even without a teacher" (ibid.).

11. Ibid. A similar statement of the importance of belief is made part way through
Book One: "Meanwhile, belief must be summoned to the present argument to make up
for modest knowledge; indeed, a firm credence in all should be summoned, since each
thing will be made clear by proper demonstration" (ibid., 1.19.205). The same methodology is found in *The Consolation of Philosophy*, as we shall see. At the beginning of
the work, Boethius affirms belief in God as the Creator of the world. By the end of the
narrative, he is able to give reasoned explanation for this belief.

that structures the antique understanding of music and sets forth key metaphysical notions that implicitly inform the technicalities of the treatise. He posits the innate nature of music, the importance of conso-nance, the threefold classification of music and, implicitly, the relation-ship between sense and reason.

Whilst it is possible that the introduction stands as an apology ex-cusing the theoretical tenor of the treatise,[12] it seems more likely that it allows Boethius to establish the existential importance of the treatise: "But to what purpose is all this? So that there can be no doubt that the order of our soul and body seems to be related somehow through those same ratios by which subsequent argument will demonstrate sets of pitches, suitable for melody, are joined together and united."[13] It is the ethical (or as it turns out to be, the existential) role of music that is of ut-most importance, as we shall see in our examination of the *Consolation of Philosophy*, and Boethius is making this clear to the reader.

Following the introduction, the second and third books are pri-marily concerned with the arithmetical aspects of intervals.[14] The fourth book discusses particular basic questions of acoustics as a preliminary to the division of the monochord with which, after a description of Greek musical notation, it is mainly concerned and the fifth book deals with "the controversies of earlier writers."[15] Given the metaphysical character

12. "This statement can be viewed as an apology for the remainder of the treatise; for the main thrust of Boethius' thought is toward knowing, grasping, and thus control-ling fundamental elements of music" (Bower, "Role of Boethius' *De Institutione Musica*," 158). Bower continues: in order for the basic elements to be securely grasped they "must be translated into discrete quantities, quantities which—unlike sound—are immutable." In turn, the quantities become the basis for a dialectical system of mathematical pro-portions. And finally, the proportions are applied to an instrument, the monochord, and only then perceived as sounds. Ibid.

13. Boethius *Fundamentals* 1.1.186.

14. The discussion of the semitone and attendant questions which forms virtually the whole of Book Three, follows naturally from the content of Book Two.

15. Caldwell, "*De Institutione Arithmetica*," 140. The last book of *De Institutione Musica* closely follows Book One of Ptolemy's *Harmonics*. Book Five is incomplete as it stands. However, we have the complete table of contents, which is compatible with a continuation to the end of the Book One of Ptolemy's *Harmonics*. The implication is that Boethius did actually complete this book. Whether or not he went on to translate the other two, or planned to do so, is another matter. Bower contends that Boethius meant to translate, or in fact did translate, all three books of the *Harmonics*. In sup-port of this he points out that those further two books of the *Harmonics* would fulfil the promise implicit in Book One of the *De Institutiones Musica*, to deal with *musica*

and foundational nature of the introduction it is upon this that we will focus our attention.

THE INTRODUCTION OF THE FUNDAMENTALS OF MUSIC

The Innate Nature of Music

The natural connection between music and humankind is crucial to Boethius' thought. In the introduction Boethius maintains first, that music is innate to humankind; second, that music is bound up with the order and harmony of the universe; and third, music therefore has the capacity to transform humankind.[16] These might be summarized as the *That*, *Why*, and *How* of music; they prepare the ground for what is to be articulated in the *Consolation of Philosophy* as the notion of likeness.

THE *THAT*, *WHY*, AND *HOW* OF MUSIC

That music is natural to and universal amongst humankind is self-evident to Boethius: the common possession of the senses through which music is perceived rendering it so. Boethius states, "Perception through all the senses is so spontaneously and naturally present in certain living creatures that an animal without them cannot be conceived."[17] It does not receive much more explicit discussion than this, but underlies the themes of the treatise. The *Why* arises from this, emerging within the inter-connection between the human capacity for music, the existence of music in the cosmos, and the attraction of humankind towards that which is harmonious. This inter-connection arises from the notion of likeness: harmony is the principle of the cosmos and it is that which is our true nature. Boethius explains by reference to ancient authority,

> What Plato rightfully said can likewise be understood: the soul
> of the universe was joined together according to musical concord

---

mundana and *musica humana*, which are not subsequently referred to in the work as it stands. Bower, "Boethius and Nicomachus," 44.

16. This all stems from the Pythagorean foundation of Boethius' treatise, which insists that the universe is comprised of numbers and their relationship and by implication maintains that although it is number per se that constitutes the cosmos, it is their relationship that is ultimately of importance.

17. Boethius *Fundamentals* 1.1.179. Cf. also 1.1.187. Bower states that the idea that music is natural to humankind becomes the foundation of the first chapter of the treatise. Bower, "Role of Boethius' *De Institutione Musica*," 158.

within us.[18] For when we hear what is properly and harmoniously united in sound in conjunction with that which is harmoniously coupled and joined together within us and are attracted to it, then we recognise that we ourselves are put together in its likeness. For likeness attracts, whereas unlikeness disgusts and repels.[19]

In brief, for Boethius, harmony is the principle according to which the world is created. It is thus that humankind has an innate capacity for music and is affected by it, being drawn to that with which it is fundamentally alike due to harmony. For this reason Boethius refers to music as the expression of the soul: "Someone who cannot sing well will nevertheless sing something to himself, not because the song that he sings affects him with particular satisfaction, but because those who express a kind of inborn sweetness from the soul—regardless of how it is expressed—find pleasure."[20]

Moreover, it is due to the sense of likeness that harmony encourages that music as sound is valued. In the first instance, it grants the sense of hearing an intrinsic ability to discern the status of a given sound apart from reason: it "very often actually finds pleasure if the modes are pleasing and ordered, whereas it is vexed if they are disordered and incoherent."[21] In the second instance, it grounds the 'ethical' nature of sounded-music: "For nothing is more characteristic of human nature than to be soothed by pleasant modes or disturbed by their opposites."[22] This is a trait universal amongst humankind and not "peculiar to people in particular endeavours or of particular ages. Indeed, music extends to every endeavour . . . no age at all is excluded from the charm of sweet song."[23] Boethius states, "A people finds pleasure in modes because of likeness to its own character, for it is not possible for gentle things to be joined with or find pleasure in rough things, nor rough things in the

18. Plato *Timaeus* 35b.

19. Boethius *Fundamentals* 1.1.180.

20. Ibid., 1.1.187.

21. Ibid., 1.1.179.

22. Ibid., 1.1.180. Later Boethius states: "a sweet tune delights even infants, while a harsh and rough one will interrupt the pleasure of listening. Certain people of every age and sex experience this: although they may differ in their actions, they are nevertheless united as one in the pleasure of music" (ibid., 1.1.186).

23. Ibid., 1.1.180.

gentle."[24] It is on this basis that Boethius supports Plato's exhortation to take great care of the musical character of the *polis:* "He [Plato] states that there is no greater ruin of morals in a republic than the gradual perversion of chaste and temperate music, for the minds of those listening at first acquiesce. Then they gradually submit, preserving no trace of honesty or justice—whether lascivious modes bring something immodest into the dispositions of the people or rougher ones implant something warlike and savage."[25] In short, music is integral to the cosmos and thus has a direct effect on humankind. It does so by virtue of harmony, which constitutes the foundation of likeness.

Having explained the basis for the effect of music, Boethius moves on to consider the *How* of music, the "radical transformations in character" that happen as a result of its impact. To do so, he extends the idea of humankind's natural attraction towards harmony and concord to the relationship between soul and body. With reference to the Pythagoreans he says, "they knew that the whole structure of our soul and body has been joined by means of musical coalescence. For just as one's physical state affects feeling, so also the pulses of the heart are increased by disturbed states of mind."[26] The body and soul mutually interact and as a result music has a direct impact upon the mind. Boethius illustrates, "This capacity of the musical discipline had become so familiar in the doctrines of ancient philosophy that the Pythagoreans, when they wanted to relieve their daily concerns in sleep, employed certain melodies so that a mild and quiet slumber would fall upon them." They likewise used other modes to purge the "stupor and confusion of sleep."[27]

24. Ibid. Bower notes that the terms *mollis* and *durus* (translated from μαλακός and σκληρός) are technical terms in ancient theory, and that at the more general level of discussion *mollis* describes music that is soft, tender, and effeminate in character, whereas *durus* describes music that is firm, austere, and masculine. Moreover, Bower notes that at a technical level, *mollis* denotes intervals, particularly semi-tones and quarter-tones, that are small and compact, whereas *durus* denotes intervals, particularly tones, that are broader and more expansive. Ibid., 1.1.181 n. 7.

25. Ibid., 1.1.180. With reference to Plato *Republic* IV, 424a–d. It is in association with this idea that Boethius talks about the corruption of music: "Music was indeed chaste and modest when it was performed on simple instruments. But since it has been squandered in various, promiscuous ways, it has lost its measure of dignity and virtue; and having almost fallen into a state of disgrace, it preserves nothing of its ancient splendour" (*Fundamentals* 1.1.181).

26. Ibid., 1.1.186.

27. Ibid.

Boethius' outline of the *That*, *Why*, and *How* of music attests to its ontological and epistemological significance: music is an integral part of the cosmos and permeates the human person as a result of its inclusion therein. Consequently, the appreciation of harmony integrates itself into the realm of knowledge. Herein, humankind comes to know the true nature of the world, and itself, by means of sounded-music and the sense of likeness that resounds therein.

Consonance and the Blending of Diversity

It is by virtue of the organization of the cosmos by means of the principle of harmony, and the ontological and epistemological import that music attains, that the notions of consonance and dissonance achieve significance. Boethius substantiates this through a consideration of sound, ratio, and movement. We will attend to each of these in turn.

SOUND

Boethius distinguishes between successive sound, which is "the distance between high and low sound" and is called interval,[28] and simultaneous sound, which results from the concurrent intermingling of distinct sounds and is called consonance.[29] An explanation of this distinction appears later in the treatise when Boethius outlines the use of the monochord (an ancient single stringed instrument with a moveable bridge) to "discover the character of the consonance of the diatessaron."[30] Of the two relevant notes he says, "if I strike them one after the other, the interval of a diatessaron will resound, but if I strike both at the same time, I come to know the consonance of the diatessaron."[31] It is interesting to

28. Ibid., 1.8.195.

29. Ibid., 4.1.302. Bower notes in his translation that these lines reveal essential elements of Boethius' modal theory: the species and the modes are interdependent (literally, the modes "exist from" the diapason species). He also points out that the word *modus* is synonymous with *tropus* and *tonus* ("mode" is a literal translation of τρόπος, *tropus* is a transliteration of the same, and *tonus* is a transliteration of another term, τόνος, which, like τρόπος is used in Greek theoretical literature to describe 'mode'); and a mode is a transposition of a whole system, not merely a segment of a system. Ibid., 4.15.341, n. 82.

30. Ibid., 4.18.348. The ratio of the diatessaron is 4:3.

31. Ibid. Bower notes in his translation: "The concept of consonance as simultaneous sounds found in this passage is wholly consistent with that found earlier in the treatise—e.g., at 1.28 and 4.1. The distinction between consonance and interval, the one struck at the same time (*simul*), the other alternately (*alterutra*), is unique to this passage" (ibid., 4.18.348 n. 92).

note that although intervals are notes in succession, and consonances are
notes simultaneously sounded, consonances provide the framework for
modes, the sounded music of ancient Greece and the early middle ages.
Boethius explains: "Tropes are systems that differ according to highness
or lowness throughout the entire sequences of pitches. A system is, as it
were, an entire collection of pitches, brought together within the framework of a consonance such as the diapason, diapason-plus diatessaron,
or the bis-diapason."[32]

Thus, with regards to the simultaneous mixture of sound, Boethius
distinguishes between consonance (*consonantia*), wherein sounds are
"pleasant and intermingled with each other,"[33] and dissonance (*disso-
nantia*), which do not "yield intermingled sound."[34] These definitions are
important, revealing the essence of the principle of harmony and the
importance of consonance as a means of understanding the notion of
likeness. Consonance draws together that which is diverse, allowing it
to coalesce. This understanding is confirmed by the contrast made between Nicomachus' and Plato's conception of consonance, and the implicit identification Boethius makes between Nicomachus' position and
his own. Plato understands consonance to be comprised of like sounds.
Boethius explains:

> A higher sound, he says, is necessarily faster. Since it has thus
> sped ahead of the low sound, it enters the ear swiftly, and, after
> encountering the innermost part of the ear, it turns around as
> though impelled with renewed motion; but now it moves more
> slowly and not as fast as when emitted by the original impulse,
> and, therefore, it is lower. When the lowered sound, now return-

32. Ibid., 4.15.341.

33. Consonance arises from "a mixture of high and low sound falling pleasantly
and uniformly on the ears" (ibid., 1.8.192. Cf. Nicomachus, *Enchiridion*, 12). Elsewhere
Boethius says that consonance is "the concord of mutually dissimilar pitches brought
together into one" (Boethius *Fundamentals* 1.3.191).

34. Ibid., 4.1.302. *Simul pulsae* is added to these definitions by Boethius or his
source. The phrase is probably a translation of the Greek ἅμα κρουσθέντες. Compare
this definition with that in 1.28.220. Here two strings are struck at the same time (see
also 1.28.220 n. 130). Dissonance is "a harsh and unpleasant percussion of two sounds
coming to the ear intermingled with each other." Boethius continues, "as long as they
are unwilling to blend together and each somehow strives to be heard unimpaired, and
since one interferes with the other, each is transmitted to the sense unpleasantly" (ibid.,
1.8.195. Cp. Nicomachus *Enchiridion* 12).

ing, first runs into the approaching low sound, it is similar, is blended with it, and, as Plato says, mixes in a consonance.[35]

This contrasts with Nicomachus' understanding, wherein consonance is the joining of *unlike* sounds: "Nicomachus does not judge this to be accurately stated, for consonance is not of similar sounds, but rather of dissimilar, each coming into one and the same concord."[36] Boethius continues, "Indeed, if a low sound is mixed with a low sound, it produces no consonance, for similitude does not produce concord of musical utterance, but dissimilitude. While concord differs in individual pitches, it is united in intermingled ones."[37]

It is the Nicomachan rather than the Platonic explanation that Boethius adopts, his definitions of consonance and dissonance involving a judgment about the relationship of diverse sounds, and their capacity to blend. Boethius writes:

> Although the sense of hearing recognises consonances, reason weighs their value. When two strings, one of which is lower, are stretched and struck at the same time, and they produce, so to speak, an intermingled and sweet sound, and the two pitches coalesce into one as if linked together, then that which is called "consonance" occurs. When, on the other hand, they are struck at the same time and each desires to go its own way, and they do not bring together a sweet sound in the ear, a single sound composed of two, then this is what is called "dissonance."[38]

Thus, in effect, consonance involves co-operation, since diverse notes in their harmony appear linked and thus produce the effect of a single sound. By contrast, within dissonance the notes appear to move in opposite directions and refuse anything but tentative association. In short, for Boethius consonance is about the blending of diverse sounds so that they emerge as one.

At this point it is worth noting by means of clarification that Boethius' understanding of consonance, as the blending of that which is diverse, does not conflict with the Platonic idea to which Boethius also subscribes, namely that the cosmos, and humankind therein, is drawn to that to which it is fundamentally alike. This is because there is a dis-

35. Boethius *Fundamentals* 1.30.221; see Plato *Timaeus* 80a–b.
36. Boethius *Fundamentals* 1.31.222.
37. Ibid.
38. Ibid., 1.28.220.

tinction between the order of the diverse parts of the cosmos, and the order within the principle of harmony which it thereby embodies. In the case of celestial order, for example, this connection is clear: the diversity of planets is rendered coherent due to the pattern which the principle of harmony manifests. However, as we shall see in the *Consolation of Philosophy*, the permeation of harmony within humankind is slightly more complex. Unlike the order apparent within the cosmos, there are factors that can cause disorder within humankind even though it bears a likeness to that which is harmonious. Thus, humankind can be attracted to that to which it is not fundamentally akin. As we shall see in our treatment of the *Consolation*, such an attraction is a matter of confused perception.

RATIO

An examination of ratio further elucidates the relationship contained within consonance. Boethius defines ratio as "a certain comparison of two terms [numerical wholes] measured against themselves."[39] It appears as the intellectual comprehension of that which is sensed in sound. Thus, having considered ratios Boethius highlights their connection with sound. He says, "Now we should add the justification given by the Pythagoreans for associating musical consonances with the ratios discussed above."[40] Boethius proceeds to classify the consonances: "The consonance whose property the critical faculty more easily comprehends ought to be classified as the very first and most pleasing consonance. For just as every single thing is in itself, so also is it recognised by the critical faculty."[41]

Hence, the consonance of the diapason is given primacy,[42] equivalent to what is also called the "octave" with a ratio of 2:1. Boethius main-

39. Ibid., 2.12.242.

40. Ibid., 2.18.249.

41. Ibid. Bower translates *sensus* as "critical faculty." He notes that *sensus* has a variety of meanings, ranging from "perception through the senses" to "understanding." However, given the Pythagorean distrust of the senses because of their unreliability Bower elects to use "critical faculty." Ibid., 2.18.249 n. 47.

42. Boethius uses a "natural numerical series" from "unity to 4." Ibid., 2.18.250. Boethius follows the ranking outlined by Nicomachus: "According to Nicomachus, then, this is the ranking of the consonances: first is the diapason; second, diapason-plus-diapente; third, bis-diapason; fourth, diapente; and fifth, diatessaron." Bower points out that the ranking of consonances is not found in any extant work of Nicomachus. Ibid., 2.18.250 n. 49.

tains that it is the most intelligible of the consonances and is therefore the most pleasing. He says: "if that consonance which consists of the duple ratio is easier to know than all the others, then there is no doubt that the consonances of the diapason, since it precedes the others in being known, is the first of all and surpasses the others in merit."[43] In explanation, the ratio 2:1 means that for every single vibration of the lower sound there are two of the higher. This is a simple relation that results in an audible sense of co-operation between the two sounds and, as it were, a complete absence of conflict.[44]

After the diapason Boethius places the diapason-plus-diapente, which has a ratio of 3:1, and the bis-diapason, which is produced by the ratio 4:1.[45] Subsequent to these, Boethius ranks the diapente, equivalent to a "perfect fifth," with a ratio of 3:2. This musical interval is found "by playing or singing the notes do to sol (or re to la, or mi to ti), again progressing rightward."[46] The diatessaron, or "perfect fourth," follows the diapente. It relies upon the ratio of 4:3 and "can be heard by playing or singing do to fa above it (or re to sol, or sol to do)."[47] In short, ratio and sound are mutually dependent: ratio is the intellectual rationale for the consonant blending of distinct sounds.

MOVEMENT

With the Boethian understanding of consonance in mind, as demonstrated in sound and ratio, it is important to comprehend the role of movement that grounds it. Boethius identifies an inter-dependence between sound, movement, and consonance: "Consonance, which governs all setting out of pitches, cannot be made without sound; sound is not produced without some pulsation and percussion; and pulsation and

43. Ibid., 2.18.249.

44. The consonance of the diapason/octave can be illustrated with reference to the opening notes of the song "Over the Rainbow," beginning on the word "somewhere." Isacoff says, "Though a leap separates them, the two *dos* sound so much alike, they share the same name. Listening to them, you might think you are perceiving two reflections of a single object, or two points along the same straight line" (Isacoff, *Temperament*, 36–37).

45. These ratios describe the octave intervals *above* 2:1.

46. Isacoff continues: "As in every musical fifth, the *sol* is vibrating faster than the *do* (and their relative string lengths are) in the proportion 3:2." This interval can be heard in the folk song "Kumbaya." Ibid., 37.

47. Isacoff notes as an example the first two notes of Richard Wagner's famous bridal chorus in "Lohengrin," "Here Comes the Bride." Ibid., 38.

percussion cannot exist by any means unless motion preceded them."[48]
This supposition is apparent from Boethius' differentiation of consonance (wherein discrete notes coalesce and their separate movements are
reconciled and rendered compatible with one another) from dissonance
(wherein distinct sounds refuse blending, tend in different directions,
and therefore cohere only hesitantly). However, it is also evident within
individual sounds themselves, which are comprised of a series of pulsations. In explanation, "If the same string is made tighter, it sounds high,
if loosened, low." This is due to the fact that when a string is tighter "it
produces faster pulsation, recurs more quickly, and strikes the air more
frequently and densely." This contrasts the slackness of a string, which
"brings about lax and slow pulsations, and, being less frequent because
of this very weakness of striking, does not vibrate very long."[49]

Although both distinct sounds and individual sounds are made up
of pulsations they are more evident in the former by virtue of the fact
that within individual sounds multiple pulsations cohere in such a way
that renders them undetectable, forming a single articulation as it were.
Boethius says:

> one should not think that when a string is struck, only one sound
> is produced, or that only one percussion is present in these nu-
> merous sounds; rather as often as air is moved, the vibrating
> string will have struck it. But since the rapid motions of sounds
> are connected, no interruption is sensed by the ears, and a single
> sound, either high or low, impresses the sense. Yet each sound
> consists of many sounds, the low of slower and less frequent
> sounds, the high of faster and more frequent ones.[50]

Boethius illustrates this with the example of a cone or "top" which has
one stripe of red (or another color) painted on it and is then spun as fast
as possible. Whilst the top is spinning, it seems to be entirely red in color,
"not because the whole thing is thus, but because the velocity of the red
stripe overwhelms the clear parts, and they are not allowed to appear."[51]

In sum, for Boethius movement is essential to music in two ways:
first, it characterizes the relationship between different sounds, and sec-

48. Boethius *Fundamentals* 1.3.189.
49. Ibid., 1.3.190.
50. Ibid.
51. Ibid. Boethius restates most of this later in the treatise, cf. 4.1.301.

ond, it refers to the multiplicity of vibrations that underpin individual sounds. In each instance movement is bound up with consonance.

The Threefold Classification of Music

The *That*, *Why*, and *How* of music signal the importance of harmony as the principle of the cosmos and the attraction of humankind to that which is harmonious. As we have seen, Boethius' exposition of consonance gives substance to this: harmony creates consonance, drawing together those things which are dissimilar. Boethius applies the notions of harmony and consonance to the multiplicity of the cosmos, articulating a threefold classification of music. He thus draws out its ontological significance.

Boethius distinguishes between "Cosmic" music (*musica mundana*), "Human" music (*musica humana*), and "Instrumental" music (*musica instrumentalis*).[52] "Cosmic" music forms the grandest example and is concerned with the harmony that results from celestial movement. "Human" music is the smaller counterpart of "Cosmic" music and is the coalescence of sense and reason as well as parts of the body; and "Instrumental" music is the human production of harmony by means of instruments. It is only by virtue of the association that Boethius makes between movement, sound, and consonance that these levels of music exist: each sphere contains a number of movements and thus a plurality of sounded notes that are rendered coherent by means of the principle of harmony. In effect, therefore, consonance is manifested in a two-fold way. First, consonance emerges laterally within the different spheres. It does so by means of the principle of harmony, which draws the individual movements within each sphere of the cosmos into concord. Second, consonance appears cosmically. Each sphere is rendered consonant and is thereby fitted to its cosmic counterparts, joined together harmoniously. We will examine each in turn, highlighting the intimate connection lying between them.

"Cosmic" music (*musica mundana*)[53] involves the consonance that occurs between the celestial bodies; it exists within the binding of

52. The second chapter is famous for its division of music into that of the spheres, man, and instruments. Caldwell notes that the line of demarcation between the two latter classes was often misunderstood by later writers, who equated human music with vocal sounds. Caldwell, "*De Institutione Arithmetica*," 145.

53. Previous references to "cosmic music" include: Plato *Timaeus* 35–36; *Laws* 889b–c. Prior references to the "harmony of the heavens" include Pliny *Naturalis his-*

elements; and obtains in the arrangement of seasons. It is "discernible especially in those things which are observed in heaven itself or in the combination of elements or the diversity of seasons."[54] Boethius argues for the existence of cosmic music by virtue of their movement. He says, "For how can it happen that so swift a heavenly machine moves on a mute and silent course?"[55] In line with the dependence of sound upon movement, Boethius regards it as impossible that:

> such extremely fast motion of such large bodies should produce absolutely no sound, especially since the sources of the stars are joined by such harmonious union that nothing so perfectly united, nothing so perfectly fitted together, can be realised. For some orbits are borne higher, others lower; and they revolve with such equal energy that a fixed order of their courses is reckoned through their diverse inequalities. For that reason, affixed sequence of modulation cannot be separated from this celestial revolution.[56]

Significantly, Boethius draws upon what he is shortly to classify as "Instrumental" music (*musica instrumentalis*) in order to illustrate how the music of the cosmos arises, thereby indicating both the concurrent similarity and difference of the three classes of music. To explain, harmony is the fundamental congruency within the three levels of music. Hence, by virtue of their common reliance upon ratio and the harmonious blending of notes they implicitly offer each other mutual elucidation. Thus, in talking about "Cosmic" music Boethius uses the example that "Instrumental" music provides:

> just as, on the one hand, adjustment of pitch in lower strings is such that lowness does not descend into silence, while, on the other hand, adjustment of sharpness in higher strings is carefully monitored lest the excessively stretched strings break because of the tenuity of pitch, but the whole corpus of pitches is coherent and harmonious with itself, in the same way we discern in cosmic

toria 2.22(20).84; Cicero *De re publica* 6.18.18; Plutarch *De musica* 1147; Nicomachus *Enchiridion* 3; Censorinus *De die natali* 12; Macrobius *In somnium Scipionis* 2.1.2 and 6.1–6; Ptolemy *Harmonica* 3.10–16, 104–11. Previous references to "harmony of the elements" include Plato *Symposium* 188a; *Timaeus* 32c; Macrobius *In somnium Scipionis* 1.5.25. References to the "harmony of the seasons" are found in Plato *Symposium* 188a.

54. Boethius *Fundamentals* 1.2.188.

55. Ibid.

56. Ibid.

music that nothing can be so excessive that it destroys something
else by its own intemperance.[57]

Further on in the book, Boethius relates the relationship between
the tetrachords to the "celestial order" and its "specification" of which it
is an "exemplar." Thus, "The hypate meson is assigned to Saturn, whereas
the parhypate is like the orbit of Jupiter. The lichanos meson is entrusted
to Mars. The sun governs the mese. Venus holds the trite synemmenon.
Mercury rules the paranete synemmenon. The nete is analogous to the
orbit of the moon."[58]

However, although sharing the fundamental congruency that harmony provides, the three classes are differentiated according to their
nature. Boethius alludes to this again in his use of "Instrumental" music,
this time speaking about the distinctness of "Cosmic" music. The introduction makes it clear that "Cosmic" music exemplifies the harmony
towards which all other types of music aspire. It is set over and against
the other classes of music, is thereby set apart from them and, perhaps
for this reason, cannot be heard in and of itself by the human sense of
hearing.[59] It is for this reason that "Instrumental" music features within

57. Ibid.

58. Ibid., 1.27.219. Boethius also outlines a different order drawn up by Marcus
Tullius. For Tullius, "Nature is so disposed that low sound emanates from its one extreme part, whereas high sound emanates from its other. Therefore that high celestial
orbit, that of the stars, the revolution of which is faster, moves with a high and shrill
sound, whereas the weak orbit of the moon moves with a very low sound. The earth, in
ninth place, remaining immobile, is alone always fixed in place." Thus the earth according to Tullius is silent. Boethius continues, "Next after the earth he assigns the lowest
sound to the moon, which is closest to silence, so that the moon is proslambanomenos,
Mercury the hypate hypaton, Venus parhypate hypaton, the sun the lichanos hypaton,
Mars the hypate meson, Jupiter the parhypate meson, Saturn the lichanos meson, and
the highest heaven the mese" (ibid.).

59. Aristotle considers absurd the Pythagorean belief that the planets emit sounds:
"Since, however, it appears unaccountable that we should not hear this music, they explain this by saying that the sound is in our ears from the very moment of birth and is
thus indistinguishable from its contrary silence, since sound and silence are discrimi-
nated by mutual contrast, what happens to men, then, is just what happens to copper-
smiths, who are accustomed to the noise of the smithy that it makes no difference to
them. But, as we said before, melodious and poetical as the theory is, it cannot be a true
account of the facts. There is not only the absurdity of our hearing nothing, the ground
of which they try to remove, but also the fact that no effect other than sensitive is produced upon us. Expressive noises, we know, shatter the solid bodies even of inanimate
things: the noise of thunder, for instance, splits rocks and the strongest of bodies. But if
the moving bodies are so great, and the sound which penetrates to us is proportionate

Boethius' account of "Cosmic" music, for it can be heard and, by virtue of the fact that it is grounded in the same set of ratios, creates an aspiration within humanity towards (and may even give a limited awareness of) "Cosmic" music.

"Human" music (*musica humana*)[60] is the harmony of the cosmos embodied within humankind, in the consonance of body and soul, in the joining of the parts within the soul itself, of the rational and irrational parts, and in the mixing of the elements and the fixed proportioning of members within the body alone.[61] The principle of harmony and consonance remains the same in "Human" music as it is in "Cosmic" music. It is for this reason that Boethius says, "what united the incorporeal nature of reason with the body if not a certain harmony and, as it were, a careful tuning of low and high pitches as though producing one consonance"[62] and maintains that "whoever penetrates into his own self perceives human music."[63]

Again, although similar, "Human" and "Cosmic" music are different. "Human" music follows the paradigm of cosmic harmony but has less scope. To explain, Boethius identifies two types of voice, "continuous" (συνεχής) and "sustained" (διαστεματική).[64] A continuous voice occurs when "we hurry over words," as "in speaking or reciting a prose oration."[65] Herein, the voice "hastens not to get caught up in high and

---

to their size, that sound must needs reach us in an intensity many times that of thunder, and the force of its action must be immense. Indeed the reason why we do not hear, and show in our bodies none of the effects of violent force, is easily given: it is that there is no noise" (Aristotle *De caelo* ii, 9, 290b–291a). However, given the emphasis upon intellect in the Greek tradition, it may be possible to make a case for the idea that "Cosmic" music cannot be heard because it is beyond our grasp.

60. Previous references to human music include: Plato *Phaedrus* 86; *Laws* 653b; *Republic* 442–43; Cicero *Tusculanae disputations* 1.10; Plutarch *De musica* 1140b; Ptolemy *Harmonica* 3.5–7.

61. Boethius *Fundamentals* 1.2.189.

62. Ibid., 1.2.188.

63. Ibid.

64. Ibid., 1.12.199. Cf. Nicomachus *Enchiridion* 2, concerning these classifications and descriptions. Boethius chooses the word *suspense* (*suspendo*) to contrast with *continua* (*continuo*); *suspendo* implies both interrupting and suspending, supporting or hovering, as in the case of a melody which is both sustained and interrupted by intervals. *Suspensa* has been translated as "sustained" by Bower.

65. Boethius *Fundamentals* 1.12.199.

low sounds, but to run through the words very quickly."[66] Its "impulse" arises from a preoccupation with "pronouncing and giving meaning to words."[67] The sustained voice stands in contrast. It is that "which we sustain in singing, wherein we submit less to words than to a sequence of intervals forming a tune."[68] Boethius is clear, each and every voice is either continuous or sustained and in itself knows no limit either through the "flowing through words" or via "rising to high pitches or sinking to low ones." The only limitations result from the condition of the human body: "The human breath places a limit on the continuous voice, which it cannot exceed for any reason, for every person speaks continuously as long as his natural breath permits." Likewise human nature places a limit on the sustained voice and "puts bounds on a person's high and low pitch, for a person can ascend just so high and descend just so low as the range of his natural voice allows."[69] This is important. Although "Human" music and "Cosmic" music are identified through the principle of harmony, "Human" music is limited by comparison to the scope of "Cosmic" music.

"Instrumental" music (*musica instrumentalis*) is implicit within Boethius' discussion of the other classes of music and explicit in his discussion of "Cosmic" music. However, in definition it is that music which rests in various instruments: "This music is governed either by tension, as in strings, or by breath, as in the aulos or those instruments activated by water, or by certain percussion, as in those which are cast in concave brass, and various sounds are produced from these."[70]

In sum, the threefold classification of music exemplifies the importance of music to the existence of the cosmos, for without music (which is the active principle of harmony) the world would not form an ordered whole. The classification of "Cosmic," "Human," and "Instrumental" music serves to demonstrate the extent of music's remit and implicitly reveals the degree to which consonance permeates the created order. In this way, it amplifies the notion of likeness: "Cosmic" music stands paradigmati-

66. Ibid.

67. Ibid.

68. Ibid.

69. Ibid., 1.13.200. Cf. Nicomachus *Enchiridion* 2.

70. Boethius *Fundamentals* 1.2.189. "*ut in cithara vel tibias ceterisque, quae cantilenae famulantur.*" Instrumental music refers to music that "rests on certain instruments, such as the kithara or the aulos or other instruments which serve melody" (ibid., 1.2.187).

cally, as the largest instance of harmony. "Human" music ideally reveals the same pattern as its cosmic counterpart. However, as we shall see in the *Consolation of Philosophy*, the embodiment of harmony is jeopardized by humankind's free will which can lead to an internal dissonance between body and soul. By virtue of the tendency toward imbalance within "Human" music, "Instrumental" music offers a more fragile embodiment of harmony: due to the fact that it is performed by humans, it implicitly depends upon the internal harmony of the performer for its own harmony.

Given, the priority of number, which the *Arithmetic* made clear was to be understood as an exemplar of God's thought, it is natural to interpolate a notion of "Divine" music within Boethius' thought, especially given the tiered character of music's instantiation and, more crucially, the fact that the world is created by God and therefore bears some imprint of Him.[71] The inter-relationship between these four types of musical instantiation will become explicit in the *Consolation* where they structure Boethius' recovery.[72]

Music, Sense, and Reason

The cosmic span of music, which is integral to the createdness of the cosmos by means of the principle of harmony, is clear. It is in virtue of this, as well as the mutual interaction of body and soul, that music has a potent effect upon the mind by means of the body and effects "radical transformations." Moreover, it is for this reason that Boethius suggests that the mind is particularly receptive through hearing: "no path to

71. Cassiodorus alludes to this: "As we have mentioned above, it is said that the heavens themselves rotate in accord with the sweetness of music. In short, whatever design there is in the heavens and on earth which accords with the governance of the Creator Himself occurs only through this discipline (music)" (Cassiodorus *Institutiones* Bk. II, Ch. V, IX).

72. Chamberlain notes that Boethius goes even further than the *Fundamentals* in the *Consolation*. Herein Boethius embodies a fourth species of music, *divina musica*, that which exists in God and by which He first creates and thereafter maintains world music. It is implicit in the *Consolation* by unavoidable deduction from Boethius' exemplarism. It is explicit in later writers, especially Jacobus of Liège who adds divine music as a fourth species to Boethius' other three and includes in its functions those that it has implicitly in the *Consolation*. Boethius deductively requires that divine music exist: "If God holds the pattern of all created things within Himself, then He must possess the perfect forms of world, human, and instrumental music." Cf. Chamberlain, "Philosophy of Music in the *Consolatio* of Boethius," 95–96.

the mind is as open for instruction as the sense of hearing. Thus, when rhythms and modes reach an intellect through the ears, they doubtless affect and reshape the mind according to their particular character."[73]

It is due to the impact of the senses upon the mind that Boethius advocates the involvement of the intellect. In doing so, Boethius proceeds according to the general aim of the *quadrivium*, which by means of the intellect examines sense and advances towards the true nature of things. At the beginning of the introduction, Boethius says: "it is indisputable that we use our senses to perceive sensible objects. But what is the nature of these very senses according to which we act? And what is the property of the sensible objects? Answers to these questions do not come easily to anyone; nor can they become clear unless appropriate inquiry has guided one in reflection concerning truth."[74] Thus, "When someone sees a triangle or a square, he recognises easily that which is observed with the eyes. But what is the nature of a triangle or a square? For this you must ask a mathematician."[75]

In fine, the intellect introduces a reasoned understanding to sensory experience. It is for this reason that the involvement of the intellect is required, "For just as in seeing it does not suffice for the learned to perceive colors and forms without also searching out their properties, so it does not suffice for musicians to find pleasure in melodies without also coming to know how they are structured internally by means of ratio of pitches."[76] Music affects body and mind, each one offering a level of understanding. Boethius says, "the sense of hearing is capable of apprehending sounds in such a way that it not only exercises judgement and identifies their differences, but very often actually finds pleasure if the modes are pleasing and ordered, whereas it is vexed if they are disordered and incoherent."[77] However, intellect is emphasized over sense.

73. Boethius *Fundamentals* 1.1.181.

74. Ibid., 1.1.179.

75. Ibid.

76. Ibid., 1.1.187. Bower notes in his translation, that "pitch" renders the Latin *vox*, Boethius' rendering of the Greek φθόγγος. He also notes that *vox* is a term with a wide spectrum of meanings, even in musical contexts, for it can mean the human voice, sound in general or musical pitch. However the most common usage in the treatise is the last of these. For the Pythagoreans, pitch is an expression of quantity in music and knowing the ratios of pitches is the goal of the first four books of this treatise. Ibid., 1.1.187 n. 34.

77. Ibid., 1.1.179.

Hence, the rest of the treatise gives a reasoned reflection upon and exposition of what is heard through sense.

In fact, this accords with who Boethius understands the true musician (*musicus*) to be: "How much nobler, then, is the study of music as a rational discipline than as composition and performance! It is as much nobler as the mind is superior to the body; for devoid of reason, one remains in servitude. Reason exercises authority and leads to what is right; for unless the authority is obeyed, an act, lacking a rational basis, will falter."[78] It is thus that Boethius distinguishes three classes of those who are engaged in the "musical art." The first consists of "those who perform on instruments," the second comprises "those who compose songs," and the third involves "those who judge instrumental performance and song."[79] Those of the first class "are excluded from comprehension of musical knowledge" since they are "totally lacking in thought." Those of the second class are led "not so much by thought and reason as by a certain natural instinct" and are also therefore "separated from music." It is only the third class, who are "totally grounded in reason and thought," that are "esteemed as musical." They have "an ability for judging" so that they "can carefully weigh rhythms and melodies and the composition as whole."[80]

Summary of the Fundamentals of Music

The *Fundamentals of Music* makes a number of key points clear. First, order is essential to the cosmos. Second, consonance, as the mixture of diversity, is the process by which the cosmos is aligned. Third, as the discipline that actively reveals and encourages consonance, music is the active principle of harmony and the harbinger of change.

---

78. Ibid., 1.34.224. Boethius continues, "a musician is one who has gained knowledge of making music by weighing with the reason, not through the servitude of work, but through the sovereignty of speculation" (ibid.).

79. Ibid.

80. Ibid., 1.34.225. Christopher Page notes that Boethius' antipathy towards the practical musician results from his desire to distance from the musician of the secular realm. Page also traces the transposition and development of the term *musicus* within the monastic setting in relation to *cantor* from 800. Here, "a term that which originally denoted the essential occupation of every monk, *cantor*, sank until it became almost a term of abuse. It was an insult to be thought of as a mere *cantor* or 'singer', one who did not have the intellectual power or curiosity to understand the theory of chant" (Page, "Musicus and Cantor," 77).

In short, within the Boethian framework music is of ontological and epistemological importance. It is thus grounded "ethically," exercising a direct effect upon the human person. It is for this reason that its significance becomes existential in character. Music comprises the cosmos (including humankind) and stands integral to humankind's self-understanding. However, although music as sound is important, it is the formal basis of music that constitutes the ultimate location of musical meaning due to its foundation in number. These points will be disclosed further through an examination of *The Consolation of Philosophy*. Specifically, the existential dimension of music will be elucidated through its transformative impact upon Boethius, as will the ultimate prioritization of intellect over sense.

3

Know Thyself—
The Place of Humankind within Created Beauty

An Examination of The Consolation of Philosophy

I N THE LIGHT OF those aspects of music set forth in the *Fundamentals of Music*, I now turn to *The Consolation of Philosophy*.[1] Herein, the ontological and epistemological dimensions identified in the former are expanded upon, the *Consolation* drawing out the existential significance of music through the notion of likeness.[2] Music provides a means of transformation.

The *Consolation* is Boethius' last work. It is written from a prison cell where he awaits execution[3] and as such is a window onto crippling disappointment and anguish. It therefore illustrates particularly well the existential dimension that music acquires by virtue of its cosmic presence (originating in God). For, on the one hand, it testifies to Boethius' predicament and recovery, wherein having lost sight of the remit of God's order he comes to reaffirm his inclusion and, on the other hand, it pays witness

---

1. On the debt of the *Consolation* to Consolation literature, see O'Daly, *Poetry of Boethius*, 23; Crabbe, "Literary Design in *De Consolatione*," 238–41.

2. Chamberlain notes the fact that in the *Fundamentals* Boethius promises to say more about *musica mundana* and *musica instrumentalis* but does not do so therein. He believes that this omission is rectified in the *Consolation*: "Boethius does more, however, than simply carry out his early promises. He permeates the *Consolatio* with ideas about music. Indeed, the work may be said to have a main theme that is musical and to embody a more complete philosophy of music than *De Musica* itself" (Chamberlain, "Philosophy of Music in the *Consolatio* of Boethius," 80).

3. Text references are to book, section, verses (where appropriate) and page number of the edition I have used. For further information about the context that gave rise to Boethius' situation see his own account in *Consolation* I.IV, 8–15. Cf. also Chadwick, *Boethius: The Consolations of Music*, chap. 1, especially 46–56.

to the active role of music. Music encourages Boethius to re-examine the divine createdness of the cosmos, which the study of the *quadrivium* led him to accept in earlier days, by calming his anxiety, preparing his mind to accept the truths that Lady Philosophy presents to him through the action of harmony, and refreshing his mental weariness.[4]

As well as building upon the premises outlined in the *Fundamentals*, the *Consolation* makes two significant contributions to the Boethian account of music: first, it takes the notions of harmony and order present within the *Fundamentals* and implicitly frames them with the notion of beauty. Second, it places the notion of beauty, and thus of harmony and order, explicitly within the context of likeness. We shall see the significance of this: Boethius' journey centers upon the acknowledgement of beauty and thereby the realization of his true likeness, likeness to God. Music is dynamic herein. Before we consider the *Consolation* in detail and the significance of music, however, I will briefly outline the principle of self-discovery underlying the work.

"KNOW THYSELF"

The Delphic recommendation to "know thyself" is a significant feature of philosophical and theological life. Hence, the paradigmatic status of Socrates who, by means of dialogue, exposed the ignorance underlying claims to certain knowledge and thereby encouraged self-reflection upon the soul and knowledge of right conduct so that one might attempt to live a good life. Hence, in Plato's *Apology* we are told that Socrates believed his divine mission to be a "gadfly," provoking everyone he met into a deeper mode of thinking.[5]

---

4. John Marenbon notes that although there is no good reason to suppose that the circumstances of the *Consolation*'s composition are other than presented in the work itself, "this is not to say that the states of mind attributed to the character Boethius need ever have been those of the real Boethius. Boethius the character is a persona, very possibly fictional in many of his thoughts and feelings, although sharing in events of the author's life." Thus, in his own writing on the *Consolation* Marenbon clearly distinguishes between Boethius "the character" and Boethius "the author." Marenbon, *Boethius*, 99. It has also been suggested that, due to the influence of the dialogue form on the *Consolation* (including Augustine's *Soliloquia*), the work actually takes the form of an inner dialogue. In effect, therefore, Lady Philosophy is Boethius' own reason. In this respect, some (including Lerer and O'Daly) choose to refer to the central character as "the prisoner," using "Boethius" to refer to the writer. See O'Daly, *Poetry of Boethius*, 22–23.

5. "I was attached to this city by the god—though it seems a ridiculous thing to

The quest for self-knowledge is universal and it is of no surprise to find the theme within the work of Boethius. Indeed, embodying the journey of self-knowledge, and thus the Delphic injunction, Boethius becomes a paradigmatic example, for although the *Consolation* reflects Boethius' very particular situation it is written in such a way to identify Boethius with humankind more generally. Boethius stands as a pattern for humankind. Thus, when Philosophy attends to Boethius she attends to all, directing them towards God. Examples of this synonymy extend throughout the *Consolation*: Boethius' injustice is equated with that suffered by others who in their pursuit of good have also been brought to death;[6] Boethius' arbitrary treatment and consequent losses are universalized;[7] and in her discussion of happiness, Philosophy considers man in the plural, speaks of the "pursuits of men" and concludes that "the only thing men desire is happiness."[8] Moreover, Philosophy commences her address to Boethius: "*You earthly creatures*, you also dream of your origin, however faint the vision"[9] and later on, in her juxtaposition of Providence and Fate, states: "It is because *you men* are in no position to contemplate this order that everything seems confused and upset."[10] The most powerful presentation of this connection appears in the implicit parallel made between Boethius and "evil people." Boethius is keen to distinguish himself from those who are evil but cannot do so completely since he shares with them the burden of self-forgetfulness. Nevertheless, the identification is not complete, since Boethius' condition is temporary. He can recover himself by building upon his fundamental belief

---

say—as upon a great and noble horse which was somewhat sluggish because of its size and needed to be stirred up by a kind of gadfly" (Plato *Apology* 30e).

6. "This is hardly the first time wisdom has been threatened with danger by the forces of evil. In olden times, too, before the time of my servant Plato, I fought many a great battle against the reckless forces of folly. And then, in Plato's own lifetime, his master Socrates was unjustly put to death—a victorious death won with me at his side" (Boethius *Consolation* I.III, 7).

7. "You must surely have been aware of my ways. You must have heard of Croesus, king of Lydia, who was once able to terrorise his enemy Cyrus, only to be reduced to misery and be condemned to be burnt alive: only a shower of rain saved him. And you must have heard of Aemilius Paulus and how he wept tears of pity at all the disasters that had overwhelmed his prisoner, Perses, the last king of Macedonia." (Ibid., II.II, 25–26).

8. Ibid., III.II, 49.

9. Ibid., III.III, 51. My italics.

10. Ibid., IV.VI, 106. My italics.

in the order of the world and the recognition of God as its Source and Originator. He thus stands in contrast to those who are evil for their loss of identity is severe, stemming from a more permanent amnesia. Evil people, according to Philosophy, fail even to acknowledge the order of the world and therefore do not look beyond themselves. They are guided and motivated only by their own desires.[11]

In brief, the *Consolation* provides a tale of self-remembering and is universal to one degree or another. Before tracing its narrative, however, we will sketch the tradition of self-knowledge out of which it emerges. This will allow us to understand the primarily intellectual nature of the act. We will first turn to the *First Alcibiades*,[12] which stands in the Platonic tradition, and thereafter outline its later development within Neo-Platonism, specifically, within Plotinus and Augustine.

Plato

In the *First Alcibiades* the theme of self-knowledge is bound up with Socrates' effort to win over Alcibiades' affection. In his attempt to do so Socrates makes a case for his own indispensability. For Alcibiades is keen to impress the Athenians.[13] To this end, Socrates questions Alcibiades' ability to demonstrate his importance, asking what skill or knowledge he will use to do so. Alcibiades is unsure and it is at this point that Socrates asserts his own value for he considers himself crucial to Alcibiades' success.[14] He establishes the importance of self-cultivation and its pre-

11. Ibid., I.IV, 15.

12. It is generally agreed that Plato is not the author of *First Alcibiades*. Hutchinson notes that "The clearest argument against Plato's authorship is probably that Plato never wrote a work whose interpretation was as simple and straightforward as that of *Alcibiades*" (Plato *Alcibiades* 557). However, the work remains important, emphasizing self-knowledge and for this reason featuring significantly within the study of Platonic philosophy. Hutchinson notes that *Alcibiades* held pride of place in later antiquity as the ideal work with which to begin the study of Platonic philosophy: there are extensive commentaries from Olympiodorus (complete) and Proclus (first half only) and fragments of commentaries by Iamblichus, Damascius, and others. Cf. also Chadwick, "Philosophical Tradition and the Self," 60–81.

13. Socrates says: "You think that as soon as you present yourself before the Athenian people—as indeed you expect to in a very few days—by presenting yourself you'll show them that you deserve to be honoured more than Pericles or anyone else who ever was" (Plato *Alcibiades* 105a–b).

14. "I'm hoping for the same thing from you as you are from the Athenians: I hope to exert great influence over you by showing you that I'm worth the world to you and

cedence over all other forms of knowledge. Socrates asks Alcibiades: "could we ever know what skill makes us better if we didn't know what *we* were?"[15] He concludes: "Whether it's easy or not, nevertheless this is the situation we're in: if we know ourselves, then we might be able to know how to cultivate ourselves, but if we don't know ourselves, we'll never know how."[16] It is through self-knowledge that one is able to self-improve.

Within the Platonic corpus more generally, it is clear that "knowing oneself" is equivalent to knowing one's origin. This links with our earlier discussion of Plato: the intelligible realm of the "forms" is distinguished from the visible realm, and the educational system advocated within the *Republic* encourages an attention to the unchangeable rather than the changeable (the disciplines of arithmetic, geometry, astronomy, and harmonics are instrumental to this end). Importantly, within the *Republic* the form of the Good stands above all other "forms" in the intelligible realm since knowledge of it imparts "the most complete account" of the nature of reality.[17] It is, thus, the "most important thing to learn about" since it imbues the cosmos and everything therein with meaning.[18] However, paradoxically, it resists definitive circumscription and is virtually impossible to grasp. Socrates himself deliberately avoids speaking about what he thinks the Good is and maintains that no one, except the philosophers, has such knowledge.[19] It is for this reason that he recommends that one talk about the "offspring" of the Good rather than the Good itself. In this way, one can examine that which bears most resemblance to it, and offers most insight into its nature.[20] Beauty becomes the means by which knowledge is attained.

that nobody is capable of providing you with the influence you crave, neither your guardian nor your relatives, nor anybody else except me—with the gods' help of course" (ibid., 105e).

15. Ibid., 128e.

16. Ibid., 129a.

17. Plato *Republic* VI, 504d.

18. Ibid., VI, 504e.

19. Socrates insists that although people claim to know what the Good is, they are merely confused: some think that knowledge is the Good and some that pleasure is the Good. Ibid., VI, 506d–e. As we shall see later, this resonates within the *Consolation*: humankind desires goodness and happiness but most are mistaken about what constitutes this.

20. Ibid. Socrates demonstrates this with three examples: the image of the sun (ibid., VI, 507a–509c); the divided line (ibid., VI, 509d–513e); and the allegory of the cave

The elusiveness of the Good and the clarity of Beauty is confirmed in the *Phaedrus*: souls are separable from the body, and the pre-incarnate sight of the "forms" is contrasted with the images that are afforded in the "murkiness" of the sensual state in which we are locked "like an oyster in its shell."[21] Beauty is unique in this regard. In contrast to other forms, which do not "shine out" through their visible images and thus do not draw people unequivocally to their "original,"[22] Beauty defies obfuscation in its sensual existence. It is the form that is grasped "sparkling through the clearest of our senses"[23] and most easily points beyond itself to its source.[24] In this way, Beauty stands centrally within the recommendation to 'know thyself.'" It is a means of reaching that which is unchangeable and, as such, is a means of attaining self-knowledge, which is not of the body but of the soul.

Thus, returning to *First Alcibiades* and the Delphic recommendation in which Alcibiades must trust,[25] Socrates summarizes: "So the command that we should know ourselves means that *we should know our souls*."[26] He therefore maintains a distinction between knowledge of body and knowledge of self: "So no doctor, to the extent he's a doctor, knows himself, and neither does any trainer, to the extent he's a trainer."[27] Socrates illustrates further (thereby securing Alcibiades' affection):

(ibid., VII, 514a–518b). All three illustrate the difficulty involved in reaching the Good, which is the "last thing to be seen." However, importantly, when the Good is glimpsed one realizes that "it is the cause of *all that is correct and beautiful* in anything, that it produces both light and its source in the visible realm, and that in the intelligible realm it controls and provides truth and understanding" (ibid., VII, 517b–c. My italics).

21. Plato *Phaedrus* 250c.

22. Ibid., 250b.

23. Ibid., 250d.

24. It is beauty's transparent visibility that explains the apparent madness of the philosopher: the philosopher "sees the beauty we have down here and is reminded of true beauty." His soul "takes wing and flutters in his eagerness to rise up," but he is unable to do so. ('Wings' are symbolic in the *Phaedrus* for perception of the forms. The pre-incarnate soul is 'winged' and is thus able to follow the gods and catch a glimpse of the forms. Ibid., 246e–248b. In earthly existence the wings sprout when images remind a person of their authentic counterpart. Ibid., 249c). He thus "gazes aloft, like a bird, paying no attention to what is down below." It is not madness but possession by the gods that is perceptible in the philosopher's behavior. Ibid., 249d. Beauty is the "most clearly visible and the most loved" of the forms. Ibid., 250e.

25. Plato *Alcibiades* 124a–b.

26. Ibid., 130e. My italics.

27. Ibid., 131a.

"Now if there was someone who loved Alcibiades' body, he wouldn't be loving Alcibiades, only something that belonged to Alcibiades." Hence, if someone loves only the body of Alcibiades, "Wouldn't someone who loves your body go off and leave you when your beauty is no longer in full bloom?"[28] This contrasts with the person who loves Alcibiades' soul: "someone who loves your soul will not leave you, as long as you are making progress."[29] Socrates claims himself to be this person: "I was your only lover—the others were only lovers of what you had. While your possessions are passing their prime, *you* are just beginning to bloom."[30]

Plotinus

The emphasis of *First Alcibiades* upon the soul is clear and it continues within the tradition that follows. Thus, in the philosophy of the Neo-Platonist Plotinus it is knowledge of the soul that determines the manner of a person's conduct. To explain briefly, the Plotinian framework consists of the *One*, *Noûs*,[31] *Soul*, and *Material World* and proceeds by emanation:[32]

> It [the outgoing process] must unfold from some concentrated central principle as from a seed, and so advance to its term in the varied forms of sense. The prior in its being will remain unalterably in the native seat; but there is the lower phase, begotten to it by an ineffable faculty of its being, native to soul as it exists in the Supreme.[33]

Herein, the material world stands furthest away from its source and is thus antithetical to it, and the *Soul*, which consists of three parts (one of which retains union with the *Noûs*)[34] aims to achieve union with the

28. Ibid., 131c.

29. Ibid., 131d.

30. Ibid., 131e.

31. The relationship between *One* and *Intellect* is characterized thus, "We are to proclaim one Intellectual-Principle unchangeably the same, in no way subject to decline, acting in imitation, as true as its nature allows, of the Father" (Plotinus *Enneads* II.9, 2).

32. For further explanation of this, see Copleston, *History of Philosophy*, 463–70; Rist, *Plotinus*, 21–37.

33. Plotinus *Enneads* IV.8, 6. It is also like a spring that never runs dry but always remains exactly as it was despite the stream of water that eternally flows from it. Ibid., III.8, 10.

34. Plotinus affirms an intimate and original link between *Soul* and *Noûs*, one not destroyed or lost when the soul became embodied: "The Souls of men, seeing their im-

One, and thus attain self-knowledge.[35] To this end, sense is a distraction and self-knowledge is achieved by the soul turning away from flesh towards the superior incorporeal mind,[36] thereby achieving liberation from the constraints of the body.[37]

Beauty features also within the Plotinian account of self-knowledge. Unlike the Platonic account, however, wherein memory of the intelligible realm is lost upon the soul's incarnation and only remembered thereafter when prompted, Plotinus maintains that through continued association with *Noûs*, the *Soul* retains knowledge of the intelligible realm and therein recognition of "beauties of sense."[38] It is this that allows them to be perceived as such. However, one must proceed beyond these and, thus, beyond the sensible for there are "earlier and loftier beauties than these. In the sense-bound life we are no longer granted to know them, but the Soul, taking no help from the organs, sees and proclaims them. To the vision of these we must mount, leaving sense to its own low place."[39]

---

ages in the mirror of Dionysius as it were, have entered into that realm in a leap downward from the Supreme: yet even they are not cut off from their origin, from the divine Intellect; it is not that they have come bringing the Intellectual Principle down in their fall; it is that though they have descended even to earth, yet their higher part holds for ever above the heavens" (ibid., IV.3, 12). Thus, "as to our own Soul we are to hold that it stands, in part, always in the presence of the Divine Beings, while in part it is concerned with the things of this sphere and in part occupies a middle ground" (ibid., II.9, 2).

35. Ibid., IV.7, 10, 19; VI.5, 7. For Plotinus, the ordinary embodied soul has powers, some of which are exalted and admirable, and others that are inferior. All of them however are "the soul's possessions rather than its being. It has them and uses them. Beyond and above them, however, lies something which is more than the skills acquired by a good liberal education. This is the true self" (Chadwick, "Philosophical Tradition and the Self," 64).

36. Ibid., 62. Plotinus has no hesitation in labeling the body as an evil on the ground of its materiality, whereas the incorporeal soul is free of evil. *Enneads* I.8, 1, 4. The temporal successiveness of bodily existence, created by our physical needs and external circumstances, drags the soul in all directions. Ibid., IV.4, 17.

37. Ibid., VI.8, 6–7. Proclus and Iamblichus concurred in thinking that it must be impossible to assert that "our soul" can be placed on an equality with the gods, identical in being (*homoousios*) with divine souls and on the same level with mind and indeed the One itself, leaving the lower world wholly behind it and by virtue of the union becoming "established." Chadwick, "Philosophical Tradition and the Self," 63.

38. Plotinus *Enneads* I.6, 3.

39. Ibid., I.6, 4. However, Rist notes that for Plotinus, the *One* is not equated with the Beautiful, only the Good: the *One* is the source of Beauty. Rist, *Plotinus*, 53–65.

Augustine

The emphasis upon the soul rather than the body is clear also in the early Christian tradition, appearing significantly in Augustine.[40] Although Augustine's attitude towards the body is a matter of dispute among scholars, it is nonetheless clear that self-knowledge concerns the identification of the soul with God, not the body. Hence, union with God is achieved by leaving the body and all material things behind, the soul thereby ascending towards God. In the *Confessions*, Augustine says of his first union with God: "I was caught up to you by your beauty and quickly torn away from you by my weight. With a groan I crashed into inferior things. This weight was my sexual habit."[41] The body is a hindrance to the soul's ascent to God and it is for this reason that the ascent is made in stages. First, Augustine proceeds "from bodies to the soul which perceives through the body," moving "from there to its inward force, to which bodily senses report external sensations." Thereafter, he finds this mutable power within himself raised "to the level of its own intelligence" so that his thinking is led "out of the ruts of habit."[42] It is thus that Augustine is able to declare that "the unchangeable is preferable to the changeable." He is able to attain union with God "in the flash of a trembling glance" but only fleetingly, due to his physical condition.[43]

Again, in the experience of God that Augustine shares with his mother Monica, the senses are transcended: "The conversation led us towards the conclusion that the pleasure of the bodily senses, however delightful in the radiant light of this physical world, is seen by comparison with the life of eternity to be not even worth considering. Our minds were lifted up by an ardent affection towards eternal being itself."[44] Augustine and Monica arrive at the summit of their minds and transcend this also. Once again, as previously, it is the materiality of existence

40. Chadwick notes that self-knowledge also became "the ultimate ground of religious awareness" (Chadwick, "Philosophical Tradition and the Self," 61). For information on the relationship between Augustine and Boethius (Augustine standing as one of Boethius' sources) see Crabbe, "Literary Design in *De Consolatione*," 251–63.

41. Augustine *Confessions* VII, 23.

42. Ibid., VII, 23.

43. Augustine writes, "to keep my gaze there was beyond my strength. I was forced back through weakness and returned to my familiar surroundings, bearing with me only a loving memory, one that yearned for something of which I had caught the fragrance, but could not yet feast upon" (ibid.).

44. Ibid., IX, 24.

that cuts the ascent short: "we touched it in some small degree by a moment of total concentration of the heart. And we sighed and left behind
us 'the first-fruits of the Spirit' (Rom. 8:23) bound to that higher world,
as we returned to the noise of our human speech where a sentence has
both a beginning and an ending."[45]

Within the context of the Delphic tradition, it is unsurprising to
find a similar emphasis in Boethius. In the *Fundamentals of Music*,
Boethius is clear to maintain some sort of balance between sense and
reason for sense is the origin of the data of music upon which reason
reflects and therefore implicitly relies. Reason, however, is ultimately of
greater value than sense. In *The Consolation of Philosophy* the journey of
self-knowledge is constructed similarly. Although the order of the world
is manifested in and detected through the senses and the sensible, in
the event, self-knowledge is a mental act. Hence, Philosophy promises
Boethius: "I will show you the path that will bring you back home. I will
give your mind wings on which to lift itself; all disquiet shall be driven
away and you will be able to return safely to your homeland."[46]

THE *CONSOLATION OF PHILOSOPHY*
AND THE ROLE OF MUSIC

It is in the light of the tendency to abstract from the sensible in this tradition of self-knowledge that I turn to the *Consolation* and in particular
the role of music. Music is pivotal to both the recognition of God's order
and the redirection of the human gaze that occurs as part of Boethius'
journey, appearing both implicitly and explicitly. Implicitly, music figures in two ways. First, within Boethius' allusion to the *quadrivium*, of
which music is a part: the *quadrivium*, and thus music, lead Boethius to
observe order and conclude that God is its Source. Second, music also
appears within the order and harmony of the movement of the spheres
and the pattern of the seasons that Boethius observes in the world and
which in the *Fundamentals* is termed "Cosmic" music. Explicitly, music
is actively present throughout the various stages of Boethius' recovery,
preparing Boethius' mind for the changes that lie ahead. This involvement relies upon the principle of harmony, which extends throughout

45. Ibid.

46. Boethius *Consolation* IV.I, 86. This of course resonates with the wings mentioned
earlier in relation to the *Phaedrus*. For further information on the notion of "path" (*via*)
see Lerer, *Boethius and Dialogue*, 106–12.

the cosmos, impacting upon the mind by means of the body and thereby enabling Boethius to recognize his place within God's created order. In this way, the soul and the body resonate harmoniously, resulting in what is classed in the *Fundamentals* as an aspect of "Human" music. Let us examine these in more detail.

Implicit Role of Music

Music is one of the four disciplines of the *quadrivium* and is therefore implicitly alluded to in Boethius' recognition that the world is ordered. Soon after her entrance, Lady Philosophy makes it clear that formerly Boethius spent a great deal of time studying the *quadrivium*.[47] In her first poem she remembers how Boethius, who is now downcast, used to walk as a free man under the open sky, contemplating the course of sun, stars, and the other natural phenomena: "Astronomer once used in joy / To comprehend and to commune / With planets on their wandering ways."[48] Boethius' study of the movement of the sky implicitly invokes "Cosmic" music, arising from the order and harmony of the celestial bodies and the earthly seasons. There are many poems throughout the *Consolation* that confirm this association:

> The world in constant change
> Maintains a harmony,
> And elements keep peace
> Whose nature is to war.
> The sun in car of gold
> Draws forth the rosy day,
> And evening brings the night
> When Luna holds her sway.
> The tides in limits fixed
> Confine the greedy sea;
> No waves shall overflow
> The rolling field and lea.[49]

Moreover, both Boethius and Philosophy recall how in the past he rendered the secrets of nature intelligible. Contrasting Boethius' pres-

---

47. On the figure of Philosophy, see Marenbon, *Boethius*, 153–54.

48. Boethius *Consolation* I.II, vv. 10–12, 5. The poem continues: "He sought the reason why spring hours / Are mild with flowers manifest, / And who enriched with swelling grapes / Ripe autumn at the full of year" (ibid., I.II, vv. 18–21, 6).

49. Ibid., II.VIII, vv. 1–12, 45.

ent state to his former one, Philosophy remarks, "Now see that mind that searched and made / all Nature's hidden secrets clear."[50] Moreover, Boethius, in his indignant reply to Philosophy's request that he reveal his "wound," compares his current situation to that in which Philosophy and Boethius used to meet and study together:

> Surely the severity of Fortune's attack on me needs no further mention; it is self-evident. Look at the mere appearance of this place. Is it the library of my house which you chose yourself as a place of sure repose and where you so often used to sit with me discussing all topics of philosophy? Are my clothes the same and my face the same as when I used to probe the secrets of nature with you, and you used to describe the various paths of the planets with your stick and relate human ethics and the whole of human life to the patterns of the celestial order?[51]

ORDER AND ACKNOWLEDGING GOD AS THE SOURCE OF THE WORLD

Importantly, recognizing the regularity and harmony of the created order that the study of the *quadrivium* facilitates leads Boethius to derive God as its Source. It is thus, in response to the question whether or not regularity is due to merely random chance, that Boethius says: "I could never believe that events of such regularity are due to the haphazards of chance. In fact I know that God the Creator watches over His creation."[52] Hence, having identified the order of the world, the poem continues: "And all this chain of things / In earth and sea and sky / One ruler holds in hand."[53]

In short, God's creation of the world is inextricable from its ordering.[54] It is for this reason that frequently within the *Consolation* a

50. Ibid., I.II, vv. 22–23, 6.

51. Ibid., I.IV, 9. For Uhlfelder the meaning is clear: the study of astronomy had revealed the orderly arrangement and movement of heavenly bodies, and that perception of this order had served as an *exemplum* for Boethius in developing a principle of order for his own life. "Role of The Liberal Arts in Boethius' *Consolatio*," 24.

52. Boethius *Consolation* I.VI, 19.

53. Ibid., II.VIII, vv. 13–15, 45.

54. "Fixed laws" are mentioned consistently alongside the order of the world: "Creator of the starry heavens, / Lord on thy everlasting throne, / Thy power turns the moving sky / And makes the stars obey fixed laws" (ibid., I.V, vv. 1–4, 15). It is through this fixed order that seasons involve specific tasks. "For God has fixed the seasons' tasks / And each receives its own" (ibid., I.VI. vv. 15–16, 18). The order is divinely ordained and cannot be altered: "No power is free to disarray / The order God has shown" (ibid., I.VI,

given aspect of the world's order accompanies the mention of creation. Examples extend from the organization of celestial bodies[55] to the patterns of the season[56] and to the place of humankind within that order. As we shall see, it is the place of humankind within the order that Boethius acknowledges which proves vital, for it is this that enables him to recover:

> From one beginning rises all mankind;
> For one Lord rules and fathers all things born.
> He gave the sun his light, the moon her horns,
> And men to earth and stars to deck the sky;
> He closed in bodies minds brought down from on high,
> A noble origin for mortal men.[57]

To summarize, the disciplines of the *quadrivium*, including music, lead Boethius to acknowledge God as the Beginning of creation and thus posit Him as its End. This is demonstrated after Boethius initially acknowledges that God is the Source of all things.[58] Philosophy says to him: "How can it be then, that you know the beginning of things but don't know their end?"[59] The connection between the two is assumed and it is this realization that serves as the beginning point of Boethius' recovery, this "tiny spark" now blazing with the "fire of life."[60] Significantly, it is from the implicit role of music and the central premise that results, the divine creation of a harmonious world, that the *Consolation* proceeds

---

vv. 17–18, 18). If one attempts to do this, to perform a task ill-fitted to the arrangement of the seasons, it will only fail: "If when summer solstice brings / The Crab with parching heat, / In furrows that refuse to seed / The farmer sows his wheat, / No crops will spring to glad his hopes / And acorns he shall eat" (ibid., I.VI, vv. 1–6, 18).

55. "Thou makest lesser stars grow dim / Before the Moon's reflected rays / When opposite her kinsman bright: / Then closer to the Sun she moves / And loses all her borrowed light" (ibid., I.V, vv. 5–9, 15). Later on also: "My pleasure is to sing with pliant strings / How mighty Nature holds the reins of things, / And how she frames her laws in providence / Which keep in motions fixed the globe immense / How all things singly she doth bind and curb / With such a bond that nothing can disturb" (ibid., III.II, vv. 1–6, 50).

56. Of the pattern of seasons: "Thy power rules the changing year: / The tender leaves the North wind stole / The spring West wind makes reappear, / The seeds that Winter saw new sown / The Summer burns as crops full-grown" (ibid., I.V, vv. 18–22, 15).

57. Ibid., III.VI, vv. 1–6, 59.

58. Ibid., I.VI, 19.

59. Ibid., I.VI, 20.

60. Ibid.

and constructs its framework. It is on this basis that music features explicitly.

Explicit Role of Music

Music is present throughout the entire movement of the *Consolation* and Boethius' recovery. This explicit use of music is grounded in the principle of harmony, which is established by means of the *quadrivium* more generally and understood more clearly by means of the distinction made in the *Fundamentals* between "Cosmic," "Human," and "Instrumental" music. "Cosmic" music manifests the order of God in an unparalleled way and stands in contrast both to "Human" music and "Instrumental" music, the harmony of both "Human" and "Instrumental" music being susceptible to upset and change. Thus, the notions of "order" and "ordering" are integral to the structure of the *Consolation* and the recovery of Boethius, legitimizing the role of music. Music is bound up with cosmic order, and is thus granted the capacity to bring about change as the embodiment of the principle of harmony, as we shall now see.

THE "MUSICAL" STRUCTURE OF THE *CONSOLATION*

One can distinguish six sections in the *Consolation:* the first acts as an introduction to the work, and the five that follow trace the movement within which Boethius' health is rekindled. Music is pivotal throughout. A brief overview: the work begins (Section One: I.I–I.II) by introducing Boethius' situation to the reader. Importantly, music signals his change in fortune, for Boethius "once wrote songs with joyful zeal" but is now "driven by grief to enter weeping mode."[61] At this point, Philosophy makes her appearance: she reflects upon Boethius' decline and proceeds to diagnose Boethius' condition (Section Two: I.III–I.VII). It is striking that Boethius experiences great fluctuations of emotion at this time. Philosophy observes that in Boethius' present state of mind a "great tumult of emotion" has fallen upon him so that he is "torn this way and that by alternating fits of grief, wrath and anguish."[62] It is for this reason that Philosophy is obliged to begin her treatment of him by first applying "gentler" remedies that will "temper" Boethius so that he is "ready to

---

61. Ibid., I.I, vv. 1–2, 3.
62. Ibid., I.V, 18.

receive the strength of a sharper medicament"[63] (Section Three: II.I—II.
IV). Significantly, the gentle remedies consist of music and rhetoric, selected for their capacity to promote moderation and stability. Having
employed these Philosophy moves on to "stronger" ones (Section Four:
II.V—II.VIII), countering Boethius' belief that Fortune has turned
against him by arguing that inconstancy is Fortune's nature, and showing him that he has not lost anything of value for Fortune's blessings
are only transitory. Implicitly herein, the instability and disorder of
Fortune is contrasted with the stability and order of God. Philosophy
argues that even if Fortune's gifts were not transitory they would not
be valuable, for they are blessings external to humankind. Only at this
point does Philosophy introduce "bitter" remedies, turning attention
away from partial goods and happiness towards perfect good and happiness (Section Five: III.I—III.XII). After this point the final obstacles
to Boethius' recovery are removed (Section Six: IV.I—V.VI). In these
last three sections the deliberate use of music to encourage Boethius'
recovery is clear. Thus in the final section, when Boethius is a great deal
stronger, the reliance upon music diminishes to the extent that it merely
acts as a "refreshment" from the exercise of reason. We will examine each
stage in turn, giving particular attention to the changing role of music.

Section One (I.I—I.II)—Fortune's Abandonment of Boethius

The initial stage of the *Consolation* makes the nature of Boethius' predicament clear, sets forth the role of Lady Philosophy, and presents key
elements of the Boethian understanding of music. In the first instance,
therefore, the state of affairs is plain: Boethius' desolation stems from
God's abandonment. However Philosophy is unambiguous, the abandonment that Boethius feels is self-imposed. It is for this reason that
Philosophy speaks in terms of self-estrangement. Philosophy states this
clearly in her diagnosis of Boethius:

> The moment I saw your sad and tear-stained looks, they told me
> that you had been reduced to the misery of banishment; but un-
> less you had told me, I would still not have known how far you
> had been banished. However, it is not simply a case of your hav-
> ing been banished far away from your home; *you have wandered*

63. Ibid.

away yourself, or if you prefer to be thought of as having been banished, *it is you yourself that have been the instrument of it.*[64]

It is clear that self-estrangement results from a compressed understanding of the world. This is evident in the lament with which the work begins. Here, Boethius implicitly expresses the alienation he feels from both God and His order: he seeks the comfort of the Muses rather than God, vents his sorrow "with the help of my pen," and thereby indulges in despair. It is thus noteworthy that one of first things that Lady Philosophy does upon arriving is to banish the Muses who encourage Boethius to remain blinkered: "'Who,' she demanded, her piercing eyes alight with fire, 'has allowed these hysterical sluts to approach this sick man's bedside? They have no medicine to ease his pains, only sweetened poisons to make them worse.'"[65]

This episode demonstrates the nature of Boethius' illness. He suffers from a sickness of mind since, according to Philosophy, the Muses "habituate men to their sickness of *mind* instead of curing them."[66] It is for this reason that Philosophy understands Boethius' illness as the result of a deterioration of vision whereby light fades, darkness prevails, and knowledge becomes obscured:

> So sinks the mind in deep despair
> And sight grows dim; when storms of life
> Inflate the weight of earthly care,
> The mind forgets its inward light
> And turns in trust to the dark without.[67]

It is also in virtue of this that Philosophy recollects a previous and contrasting scenario: "This man, this man sought out the source / Of storms that roar and rouse the seas."[68] Likewise, "Now see that mind that

64. Ibid., I.V, 16–17. My italics.

65. Ibid., I.I, 4. The muses encourage Boethius to write elegy. Philosophy sets herself over and against them: "poetry plays the painted whore to Philosophy's virtuous woman" (Crabbe, "Literary Design in De Consolatione," 250). Crabbe continues, "The stress in the *De Musica* on the inherent tendency of certain types of music to produce demoralizing 'affectus' is closely parallel to Philosophy's analysis of harm done by the Muses" (ibid.). For background on the Muses see O'Daly, *Poetry of Boethius*, 59–60.

66. Boethius *Consolation* I.I, 4. My italic. The text continues: "These rebukes brought blushes of shame into the Muses' cheeks, and with downcast eyes they departed in a dismal company" (ibid., I.II, 5).

67. Ibid., I.II, vv. 1–5, 5.

68. Ibid., I.II, vv. 13–14, 5.

searched and made / All Nature's hidden secrets clear / Lie prostrate prisoner of night. / His neck bends low in shackles thrust, / And he is forced beneath the weight / To contemplate – the lowly dust."[69] It is plain that Boethius' gaze is inverted, directed to the earthly. His cosmic vision has caved in and he has enchained himself mentally and spiritually.

The role of Lady Philosophy is apparent throughout: Philosophy arrives, dismisses the Muses, performs a diagnosis of Boethius' condition, and thus positions herself as physician: she will encourage Boethius to re-evaluate his situation and thereby illuminate his darkened vision.[70] Hence, music's appearance at this point in the *Consolation* is important. It develops the premise introduced in the *Fundamentals* that music is an expression of the soul: within this section music powerfully exemplifies the effect that Boethius' demise has had upon him.[71] Moreover, having granted music the capacity to express Boethius' feelings, grounds are established for developing the idea of music as a means of transformation. Once again this is supported by the *Fundamentals*, wherein the power of music upon the mind is made clear. As we shall see, this is pivotal to the *Consolation* and Boethius' recovery. Finally, the way in which music is employed within Boethius' treatment reveals an important aspect of its character: music leads to change rather than demands it. It creates a response rather than commanding action.[72]

69. Ibid., I.II, vv. 22–27, 6.

70. Chamberlain suggests that Philosophy is the "complete *musicus*" since she fulfils the criteria of the perfect music (instrumental skills, creative, judgment of rhythms, melodies). Chamberlain, "Philosophy of Music in the Consolation of Boethius"; O' Daly, *Poetry of Boethius*, 55. However, one can perhaps go further and suggest that Philosophy is the complete embodiment of music as the perfection of 'human' music, the consonance of body and mind. Thus, it is music rather than Philosophy that stands as the true physician.

71. Interestingly, Lerer views Boethius' situation and recovery through the loss, recovery, and retrieval of language. One can relate this to Boethius' incapacity to reason: he is thus rendered speechless (the muses dictate to Boethius) and it is music that attends to him in the first instance. Lerer, *Boethius and Dialogue*.

72. Hence, in Boethius' telling of the Orpheus myth, Orpheus uses music to woo Eurydice's captors and yet is unable to change his own state of mind.

Section Two (I.III—I.VII)—Diagnosis of Problem[73]

Boethius' recognition of Philosophy occurs alongside his acknowledgment of her as his "physician."[74] Accordingly, Boethius' display of grief allows Philosophy to reach a diagnosis of his condition, thereby enabling her to bring him to a point where he might begin treatment. Within this process, it becomes apparent that Boethius upholds God as the Creator of the world, as "the source from which all things come."[75] Philosophy asks Boethius outright whether he believes that life consists of "haphazard and chance events" or if it is "governed by some rational principle." In response, Boethius insists that the regularity of nature arises from God's creation of the world, emphatically asserting that "The day will never come that sees me abandon the truth of this belief."[76]

Thus, it seems that *in spite of* his despair Boethius maintains belief in God and the created order. In contrast, however, it is exactly *because* he understands God as the Source of the world that Boethius' desolation arises. For how does the injustice he has suffered fit into God's order? Boethius reminds Philosophy that he has led a good life and makes his distress clear:[77] "now you see the outcome of my innocence—instead of

73. Although within these chapters Philosophy says that she will use gentle remedies she does not do so until II.I: "Will you first then let me discover your state of mind and test it with a few simple questions? That way I can discover the best method of curing you" (Boethius *Consolation* I.IV, 19).

74. Ibid., I.III, 7.

75. Ibid., I.VI, 19.

76. Ibid. Uhlfelder draws attention to the strength of this assertion. She views the Latin, *verum operi suo conditorem praesidere deum scio nec umquam fuerit dies qui me ab hac sententiae veritate depellat,* and notes the strength of Boethius' conviction: Boethius does not talk about "belief or unqualified opinion" but uses "the strongest possible verb '*scio,*' 'I know.'" Thus, she continues, "although the noun 'sententia'—'view'—may suggest opinion rather than knowledge, the 'veritate'—'truth'—upon which the 'sententia' depends syntactically, leaves no doubt that in this case the opinion is correct, and is regarded by Boethius as the equivalent of truth" (Uhlfelder, "Role of The Liberal Arts in Boethius' *Consolatio,*" 23).

77. In outlining his plight to Philosophy, Boethius presumes her knowledge of his goodness: he says "You remember, I am sure, since you were always present to give me your guidance when I was preparing a speech or some course of action—you remember how at Verona a charge of treason was made against Albinus and how in his eagerness to see the total destruction of the Senate the king tried to extend the charge to them all in spite of their universal innocence; and you remember how I defended them with complete indifference to any danger, and you know that I am telling the truth and have never boasted of any merit of mine" (Boethius *Consolation* I.IV, 13).

reward for true goodness, punishment for a crime I did not commit."[78] The unfairness of Boethius' situation forces him to conclude that although God orders the world he does not reign over humankind:[79]

> All things obey their ancient law
> And all perform their proper tasks;
> All things thou holdest in strict bounds,—
> To human acts alone denied Thy fit control as Lord of all.[80]

In short, it must be the case that God's order does not extend to humankind. Otherwise Boethius would not find himself in his current situation.

The quandary facing Boethius is marked. However, so is the two-fold edge of belief in the world's creation. Although belief in God's order is in some sense responsible for Boethius' despair it proves crucial to his recovery, since it is only by means of it that Philosophy can undertake her treatment of him.[81] She says: "In your true belief about the world's government—that it is subject to divine reason and not haphazards of chance—there lies our greatest hope of rekindling your health."[82] Thus, Boethius' belief in the created order and its origin in God stands as the starting point of Philosophy's treatment. However, emotional turmoil envelops Boethius: "It is as if you had become swollen and calloused under the influence of these disturbing passions."[83] Here, the close partnership between body and mind is unequivocal. Philosophy observes that "no sudden change of circumstances ever occurs without some upheaval in

78. Ibid.

79. Boethius elaborates: "I seem to see the wicked haunts of criminals overflowing with happiness and joy; I seem to see all the most desperate of men threatening new false denunciation; I seem to see good men lying prostrate with fear at the danger I am in while abandoned villains are encouraged to attempt every crime in the expectation of impunity or even in the hope of reward for its accomplishment; and I seem to see the innocent deprived of peace and safety and even of all chance of self defence" (ibid., I.IV, 14–15).

80. Ibid., I.V, vv. 23–27, 16. Boethius continues: "O Thou who bindest bonds of things / Look down on all earth's wretchedness; / Of this great work is man so mean / A part, by Fortune to be tossed?" (ibid., I.V, vv. 42–45, 16).

81. Uhlfelder rightly notes that had this premise not been established as such, the therapy would necessarily have taken a different course. "Role of The Liberal Arts in Boethius' *Consolatio*," 23.

82. Boethius *Consolation* I.VI, 20.

83. Ibid., I.V, 18.

the mind; and that is why you, too, have deserted for a while your usual calm."[84] It is for this reason that Philosophy begins treatment not with strong remedies but with "gentler" ones that will assuage Boethius' upset and prepare the ground for "sharper medicament."[85]

Section Three (II.I—II.IV)—"Gentler" remedies

The classification of the gentle remedies is extremely important for an understanding of music within the *Consolation* for it is here that music appears along with rhetoric and, thus, that Boethius' understanding of music is largely revealed.[86] As we have seen, Boethius is too weak to be prescribed any strong remedies. It is for this reason that Philosophy prepares him by employing more gentle ones. As will become clear later in the work the stronger remedies rely upon the use of reason, and it is thus that the understanding of music within the *Consolation* presents itself: music is a preparation for reason. Philosophy says, "It is time, then, for you to take a little mild and pleasant nourishment which by being absorbed into your body will prepare the way for something stronger."[87]

Philosophy treats Boethius initially with the gentle action of music and rhetoric, taking his belief in God as the Source of the created order as her oblique starting point. Philosophy examines Boethius' complaint that he has been stripped of all possessions and abandoned by Fortune. She tries to show him that in Fortune Boethius "did not have and did not lose anything of value"[88] since Fortune is inconstant by nature and thus cannot lead towards happiness. In doing so, Philosophy implicitly contrasts the inconstancy of Fortune with the constancy of God.[89] It is by

84. Ibid., II.I, 22.

85. Ibid., I.V, 18.

86. Philosophy uses "the persuasive powers of sweet-tongued rhetoric, powers which soon go astray from the true path" unless they follow Philosophy's instruction, and music, "the maid-servant" of Philosophy's house, who will sing "melodies of varying mood" (ibid., II.I, 22).

87. Ibid.

88. Ibid.

89. Philosophy broadly demonstrates the inconstancy of Fortune to Boethius. It is not the case that Fortune has changed towards him. On the contrary, she has merely revealed her true character: "Change is her normal behavior, her true nature. In the very act of changing she has preserved her own particular constancy towards you" (ibid., II.I, 23). Philosophy continues the discussion "by using Fortune's own arguments." Fortune tells Boethius, "You have been receiving a favor as one who has had the use of

means of this comparison that Boethius' focus begins to sharpen since God is the proper end through which all things are understood. Fortune cannot stand as such an end as we will see later when the juxtaposition between Fortune and God re-emerges.

Elucidating the classification of gentle remedies further, there are three points that must be noted about Boethius' treatment of music. First, Philosophy uses sung melody.[90] This confirms that music is more than a metaphor explaining the coherence and order of the world. Rather, it is an active force which, in its sounded embodiment, has a direct impact upon humankind.[91] Second, the music used employs "melodies of varying mood."[92] This discloses the existential dimension of music. In reaction to the weeping modes that have taken hold of Boethius Philosophy will make use of different varieties and will thereby effect his initial transformation. This capacity for transformation derives from the principle of harmony established in the *Fundamentals* and the interrelationship of "Cosmic," "Human," and "Instrumental" music outlined there. Philosophy will use modes that promote order and harmony and will thereby draw the body and soul into a consonant relationship, orientating Boethius within the cosmos. In doing so, it seems that, through the body's effect upon the mind, the mind will become more receptive to those at present unpalatable truths that subsequent stronger treatment and the use of reason will reveal. Third, the action of music is intrinsically connected to the pleasure that it evokes in Boethius. Philosophy uses music to present truths in an appealing fashion and Boethius responds accordingly. It is

another's possessions, and you have no right to complain as if what you have lost was fully your own" (ibid., II.II, 25). It is for this reason that Boethius has not lost anything of importance, for the happiness that Fortune offers is transitory, and that Philosophy is able to ask Boethius "Do you really hold dear that kind of happiness that is destined to pass away?" (Ibid., II.I, 23). Philosophy contrasts the transient happiness offered by fortune with the true blessings that lie in the constancy and love of Boethius' family: Symmachus, Boethius' father-in-law, "disregards his own sufferings and weeps for yours," and Boethius' wife is "still alive and in her disgust with this life draws every breath for you alone" (ibid., II.IV, 30).

90. Ibid., II.I, 22.

91. "Unlike the music and the muses of the prisoner's open lament, it [Philosophy's music] will be both comforting and meaningful. Like *De Trinitate*'s spark of intelligence, this native music comes from within. It somehow belongs to us and resides in us" (Lerer, *Boethius and Dialogue*, 113). This supports Chamberlain's reading and goes against that of O'Daly, who says that human music "is no more than a metaphor for the body-soul structure" (O'Daly, *Poetry of Boethius*, 56).

92. Boethius *Consolation* II.I, 22.

thus that the authentic music of Philosophy is contrasted with that of Fortune: "While Philosophy's music held an inner sweetness, Fortuna's is sugar-coated."[93]

However, two implicit criticisms emerge from this understanding of music's "action." One, despite the fact that music implicitly introduces harmony to Boethius it acts largely as a preparation for reasoned meaning. Hence, its capacity to convey truth in and of itself is limited. Two, the transience of sounded music means that the pleasure that it produces is temporary: Boethius states that "it is only while one is actually listening that one is filled with pleasure, and for the wretched, the pain of suffering goes deeper. So as soon as your words stop sounding in our ears, the mind is weighed down again by its deep seated melancholy."[94] This seems to diminish the harmony that music establishes as sound, as the embodiment of harmony. Philosophy agrees with Boethius: "'It is true,' she rejoins, 'for none of this is meant to be a cure for your condition, but simply a kind of application to help soothe a grief still resistant to treatment. When the time comes I will apply something calculated to penetrate deep inside.'"[95]

Section Four (II.V—II.VIII)—"Stronger" Remedies

Philosophy moves on to "rather stronger" remedies, having soothed Boethius' grief a little by means of music and rhetoric.[96] She sets aside the transitory nature of Fortune's gifts outlined to Boethius and takes a different approach: "So then, if the gifts that Fortune offers are not transitory and short-lived, tell me, which is there among them that can ever belong to you or whose worthlessness is not revealed by a moment's thoughtful consideration?"[97] She asks this in order to prove that, even if the gifts of Fortune were not transitory, they would still not bring true happiness. Once again Fortune is implicitly contrasted with God—God is the true Source of happiness. In arguing this, Philosophy reaffirms to Boethius that he is "weeping over lost riches" and reminds him that, on

93. Lerer, *Boethius and Dialogue*, 113. See Boethius *Consolation* II.III, 27.

94. Ibid.

95. Ibid.

96. Ibid., II.V, 33.

97. Ibid.

the contrary, he has found "the most precious of all riches—friends who are true friends."[98]

Significantly, beauty appears amongst the external blessings and riches that Philosophy calls into question (others considered include wealth and fame).[99] She asks "What makes riches precious, the fact that they belong to you or some quality of their own?" Of beauty Philosophy enquires: "If Nature gives them their beauty, how does it involve you? They would still have been pleasing by themselves, even if separated from your possessions. It isn't because they are part of your wealth that they are precious, but because you thought them precious that you wanted to add them to the sum of your riches."[100] In fine, the value of beauty is objective. It is this that renders it desirable. That it is God that grounds the value of beauty will be made explicit shortly but that this is the case is intimated by the poem concluding this section which explicitly expresses the link between creation, order, harmony, and beauty.[101] Here, a conjunction of different forms of music transpires: the poem about cosmic music is sung by Philosophy. This arrests Boethius' attention and instills in him a desire to hear more: "She has stopped singing, but the enchantment of her song left me spellbound. I was absorbed and wanted to go on listening."[102] Music thus presents truths through the content it conveys by means of the poem but also in virtue of the physical manifestation of harmony of which it speaks. By this means, Boethius' recovery advances.[103]

---

98. Ibid., II.VIII, 45.

99. It is clear from Philosophy's argument how "poor" and "barren" wealth is: "it is impossible for many to share them undiminished, or for one man to possess them without reducing all the others to poverty." For Philosophy, although fame is allied with a desire for immortality, immortality can never be achieved by means of it: "When you think of your future fame you think you are creating for yourself a kind of immortality. But if you think of the infinite recesses of eternity you have little cause to take pleasure in any continuation of your name" (ibid., II.VII, 42).

100. Ibid., II.V, 35.

101. Ibid., II.VIII, 44–45.

102. Ibid., III.I, 47.

103. Chamberlain notes, "World music appears primarily in the poems or songs of the work, where figurative meanings can most justly be expected; and where, fittingly, it is actually *instrumental* music that offers ideas about *world* music" ("Philosophy of Music in the *Consolatio* of Boethius," 86). This affirms the close relationship between the three spheres of music observed in Boethius' *Fundamentals*.

Section Five (III.I—III.XII)—"Bitter" Remedies

With the enchantment of Philosophy's song leading Boethius forth, he declares his readiness for even stronger treatment: "You were talking of cures that were rather sharp. The thought of them no longer make me shudder; in fact I'm so eager to hear more, I fervently beg you for them."[104] It is interesting at this point to note Boethius' thoughts on the manner of the treatment he has received. He regards Philosophy as "the greatest comfort for exhausted spirits" and importantly has been helped by the "weight" of her "tenets" and the "delightfulness" of her "singing." In effect, he implicitly pits the pleasure of music against the content of reason and thus draws attention to the tenor of subsequent remedies which rely upon reason. In contrast to those that have gone before, which are sweet and palatable, the next batch of remedies "taste bitter to the tongue, but grow sweet once they are absorbed."[105] The idea of absorption here reinforces the fact that music acts only superficially and that, by contrast, reason penetrates more deeply. Hence the preparatory use of music of which Philosophy has taken advantage, using it to create eagerness in Boethius and to instill in him the desire to hear more and to progress further. She says: "Once you began to hang on my words in silent attention, I was expecting you to adopt this attitude—or rather, to be more exact, I myself created it in you."[106]

Significantly, the myth of Orpheus finds articulation at the end of Philosophy's use of bitter remedies. At this point, Boethius is nearing a full recollection of his self-identity.[107] Philosophy comments to Boethius: "I think little remains for me to do before you acquire happiness and return safe and sound to your true homeland."[108] This acknowledgement is significant in two ways. First, the Orpheus myth supports Philosophy's use of music, the sweetness and pleasure of which, as she has admitted, have been used to influence Boethius. In the myth, the power of music is startling. Music effects creation:

---

104. Boethius *Consolation* III.I, 47.

105. Ibid. "The tongue that first has tasted bitter food / Finds honey that the bees have won more sweet" (ibid., III.I, vv. 5–6, 48).

106. Ibid., III.I, 47.

107. Ibid., III.XII, 82–84.

108. Ibid., III.XII, 79.

> Once when Orpheus sad did mourn
> For his wife beyond death's bourn,
> His tearful melody begun
> Made the moveless trees to run,
> Made the rivers halt their flow,
> Made the lion, hind's fell foe,
> Side by side with her to go,
> Made the hare accept the hound
> Subdued now by the music's sound.[109]

Moreover, music secures the release of Eurydice from the under-world:[110] "At last the monarch of the dead / In tearful voice, "we yield," he said: / "Let him take with him his wife / *By song redeemed* and brought to life."[111] Importantly, in both instances the power of music does not operate by precipitating action. Rather it attracts the listener and thereby creates a response, bringing about sympathy to change. This is evident both in the changes that Orpheus brings about, and in the treatment that Philosophy employs. In both cases music achieves momentous results. Significantly, the myth is delivered in song by Philosophy. This is apparent from the beginning of the next book, which tells us that "Philosophy delivered this sweet and gentle song with dignity of countenance and gravity of expression."[112]

Second, the location of the myth at this transitional point forms a didactic parallel between the myth of Orpheus and Boethius' recovery:[113] Boethius is almost free from the gloom that has held him prisoner and the myth stresses to Boethius that he must maintain his upward ascent if he is hold secure all that he has achieved thus far:

---

109. Ibid., III.XII, vv. 5–13, 82–3.

110. "There on sweetly sounding strings / Songs that soothe he plays and sings; / All the draughts once drawn of song / From the springs the Muses throng, / All the strength of helpless grief, / Give their weight then to his weeping, / As he stands the lords beseeching / Of the underworld for grace" (ibid., III.XII, vv. 20–28, 83).

111. Ibid., III.XII, vv. 40–43, 83. My italics.

112. Ibid., IV.I, 85.

113. On how Boethius re-writes the Orpheus myth see Lerer, *Boethius and Dialogue*, 159–64; O'Daly, *Poetry of Boethius*, 188–207. Lerer observes: "When Philosophy notes that her fable itself *respicit* she means two things. First, she implies that the narrative looks back over the prisoner's progress to this moment. The poem itself points backwards to the worldly concupiscence which enslaved him, and forward to the higher day towards which he must direct his mind" (Lerer, *Boethius and Dialogue*, 159).

> For you the legend I relate,
> You who seek the upward way
> To lift your mind into the day;
> For who gives in and turns his eye
> Back to darkness from the sky,
> Loses while he looks below
> All that up with him may go.[114]

The bitter remedies aim to lead Boethius towards "true happiness." Thus, by means of reasoned argument Philosophy sketches an idea of "the cause of happiness." This will enable Boethius to turn his gaze in a different direction and recognize "the pattern of true happiness," that is, God.[115]

To this end, Philosophy first examines examples of "false happiness" and, in doing so, returns to beauty (as well as wealth and fame). This time she places it within its proper order.[116] Importantly, in doing so she does not declare its complete falsity. Rather, she maintains that the happiness it offers is only partially true since humankind treats it as an absolute apart from God: "In spite of a clouded memory, the mind seeks its own good, though like a drunkard it cannot find the path home."[117] Humankind tends to pursue goods as if they are self-sufficiently so, as if they are bearers of absolute happiness. However, as Philosophy notes, such goods, "because they can neither produce the good they promise nor come to perfection by the combination of all good, these things are not the way to happiness and cannot by themselves make people happy."[118] The crux of the problem is plain: humankind has a faint vision of its origin and instinctive desire to pursue absolute happiness and goodness but is misguided in various ways and led astray.[119] Elucidating the partial goodness of those things pursued by humankind, Philosophy signals

114. Boethius *Consolation* III.XII, vv. 52–58, 84.

115. Ibid., III.I, 47.

116. Ibid., III.II, 49–50. The rest of III.III, 52–53, deals with wealth; ibid., III.IV, 54–56, deals with appointments of high office; ibid., III.V, 56–58, deals with power; ibid., III.VI, 58–59, deals with fame; ibid., III.VII, 59–60, deals with bodily pleasure.

117. Ibid., III.II, 49.

118. Ibid., III.VIII, 62. So Philosophy asks Boethius, "Are all the many things we see included under the word happiness like parts combining to form a single body, yet separate in their variety, or is there any one of them which can fully supply the essence of happiness and under which the others may be classed?" (ibid., III.X, 71).

119. Ibid., III.III, 51–52.

their source, self-sufficient goodness, and iterates that it is "human per-
versity" that divides that "which by nature is one and simple" and, "in
attempting to obtain part of something which has no parts, succeeds in
getting neither the part, which is nothing—nor the whole, which they
are not interested in."[120]

Philosophy informs Boethius that if he turns his "mind's eye in the
opposite direction" he will see the "true happiness" that Philosophy has
promised. To demonstrate this, she proceeds from effect to cause and
thereby locates perfect goodness and happiness in God: "The natural
world did not take its origin from that which was impaired and incomplete, but issues from that which is unimpaired and perfect and then
degenerates into this fallen and worn out condition."[121] From imperfect
happiness (*imperfecti boni*) Philosophy infers the existence of perfect
happiness (*perfecti boni*): "there can be no doubt that a true and perfect
happiness exists." She identifies perfect goodness with God: "Since nothing can be conceived better than God, everyone agrees that that which
has no superior is good." She continues: "Reason shows that God is so
good that we are convinced that His goodness is perfect. Otherwise He
couldn't be the author of creation. There would have to be something
else possessing perfect goodness over and above God."[122]

Philosophy clarifies the discussion by contrasting perfect and imperfect goodness and perfect and imperfect happiness, focusing on the
contrast between unity and multiplicity, and the striving of all things for
unity.[123] In short, Philosophy maintains that everything strives towards

120. Ibid., III.IX, 64.

121. Ibid., III.X, 68–69.

122. Ibid., III.X, 69. There are three additional assertions that ground this intrinsic
association of God and goodness. First, the notion that goodness must be "natural property" of God rather than something "logically distinct"; if the latter were the case, "an
able mind might be able to imagine the existence of a power responsible for bringing
together the two that were separate." Second, "that which by its own nature is something
distinct from supreme good, cannot be supreme good; but this is something we may not
hold about Him to whom we agree there is nothing superior." Third, the impossibility
of two "supreme goods" that exist in separation from the other: "For it is clear that if the
two goods are separate, the one cannot be the other, so that neither could be perfect
when each is lacking to the other. But that which is not perfect is obviously not supreme. It is therefore impossible for there to be two separate supreme goods. However,
we deduced that both happiness and God are supreme goodness, so that it follows that
supreme happiness is identical with supreme divinity" (ibid., III.X, 70–71).

123. Before showing how all things strive towards unity, Philosophy justifies the
equation of unity and goodness. Philosophy reminds Boethius that the "various things

unity: "Now, whatever seeks to subsist and remain alive desires to be one; take unity away from a thing and existence too ceases."[124] The underlying assumption is that unity is identical with goodness and that, therefore, it is true that everything desires goodness.[125] This realization is pivotal to Boethius' recovery, confirming to him the order of the world. Philosophy says: "No truer conclusion could be discovered. For either all things are inclined to no one thing and will wander about aimlessly as though destitute of any head or helmsman to guide them, or if there is something to which all things are inclined, it will be the sum of all good."[126] She continues: "I am very happy, my son, for you have fixed in your mind the very mark of the central truth. And in this you have revealed the very thing you were just saying now you did not know," that is, the "end of all things." Philosophy clarifies: "For certainly it is the same as that which all things desire; we have deduced that that is goodness, and so we must agree that the end of all things is the good."[127]

This prepares the way for the confirmation that is shortly to follow, namely, that Boethius has travelled far in his recovery. Boethius confirms his belief in God as Creator, which he articulated at the beginning of

---

that the majority of men pursue are not perfect and good, for the reason that they differ from one another, and because they are lacking to one another and cannot confer full and perfect good," stating that "unless all are one and the same thing they have no claim to be included among worthwhile objects of pursuit" (ibid., III.XI, 74). She summarizes: "When these objects differ, they're not good, but when they begin to be one they become good; so it comes about that it is through the acquisition of unity that these things are good" (ibid.). In this way, by saying that all strives for unity, Philosophy maintains that everything strives for goodness. Of living creatures Philosophy says "when soul and body come together and remain united, we speak of a living being, but when this unity breaks up through the separation of either component, it is clear that the living being perishes and no longer exists. The body, too, so long as it remains in one form through the combination of its members, you see a human figure; but if the parts are divided up and separated and the body's unity destroyed, it ceases to be what it was. You may run through every other thing and it will be clear beyond a shadow of a doubt that everything subsists as long as it is one, but perishes when its unity ceases" (ibid., III.XI, 75). Philosophy also extends her example to nature and the principle is even extended, tenuously, to inanimate objects (ibid., III.XI, 75–76).

124. Ibid., III.XI, 77.

125. Cf. ibid. The main reason for seeking all things is goodness: "For it is quite impossible for that which contains no good in itself whether real or apparent, to be an object of desire. On the other hand, things which are not good by nature are sought after if they nevertheless seem as if they were truly good" (ibid., III.X, 72).

126. Ibid., III.XI, 77.

127. Ibid.

his journey. However, this time Boethius substantiates it with reasons. Philosophy says to him: "Just now you thought it was beyond doubt that this world was ruled by God." He responds: "I still do think it is beyond doubt, and will always think so. *I will briefly explain the arguments which convince me in this matter.*"[128] Boethius cites three arguments: first, the unification of the diverse elements of the world into a whole: "The world would never have coalesced into one form out of such diverse and antagonistic parts had there not been one who could unify such diversity." Second, the necessity of a power that holds together the unity of diverse elements: "Their very diversity in turn would make them break out into dissension and tear apart and destroy the unity of the world unless there were a power capable of holding together what he had once woven." Third, following from the first, the necessity of a stable power which maintains the order of unstable elements: "Nature's fixed order could not proceed on its path and the various kinds of change could not exhibit motions so orderly in place, time, effect, distance from one another, and nature, unless there was one unmoving and stable power to regulate them." It is, thus, that Boethius concludes: "For this power, whatever it is, through which creation remains in existence and in motion, I use the word which all people use, namely God."[129]

All that has gone before has led Boethius to this *re*-cognition, this re-acknowledgement that God is the source of everything. Boethius claimed to know this at the beginning of the *Consolation*. At this point, however, he is able to set forth reasons that support his conviction. Philosophy acknowledges the significance of this progression: "Since this is your opinion, I think little remains for me to do before you acquire happiness and return safe and sound to your true homeland."[130]

However, to complete the final leg of Boethius' recovery, Philosophy prepares an answer to Boethius' continuing conviction that although God orders creation, his order excludes humankind. She does so by echoing her former assertion that knowing God as the Beginning of creation is to know him as its End. She argues that all things, including humankind, strive towards unity and therefore goodness, that God is supreme, and that all things thus strive towards God through their own nature and accord and not by means of some imposition. Philosophy

128. Ibid., III.XII, 79. My Italics.
129. Ibid.
130. Ibid.

says: "Since we are right in thinking that God controls all things by the helm of goodness, and all things, as I have said, have a natural inclination towards the good, it can hardly be doubted, can it, that they are willingly governed and willingly obey the desires of him who controls them, as things that are in harmony and accord with their helmsman."[131] Hence, Philosophy concludes, "there is nothing, therefore, which could preserve its own nature as well as go against God."[132]

Section Six (IV.I—V.VI)—Clearing the Path

Although this insight is momentous, Boethius' dismay is intensified and attention returns to the problem at hand, such that Boethius cuts Philosophy short, "You have spoken of things I had forgotten because of the pain of what I had suffered, but before this they were not entirely unknown to me." However, he says, "the greatest cause of my sadness is really this—the fact that in spite of a good helmsman to guide the world, evil can still exist and even pass unpunished."[133] Addressing this major obstacle gives impetus to the last phase of Boethius' recovery, such that Philosophy says to him: "when we have run through all that I think we should clear out of the way beforehand, I will show you the path that will bring you back home."[134] The rest of the *Consolation* responds to related concerns, dealing with the existence of evil people amidst a good ordering of creation, and knowledge of God's plan, in explanation introducing a distinction between Providence and Fate. It finishes with the related question of the compatibility of Providence and Divine Foreknowledge.

Philosophy explores possible explanations of why humankind turns from "virtue" to "vice." She is clear that all humankind strives towards that which is good and on this basis concludes that the actions of evil men "depend on the belief that they are going to obtain the good they desire through the things that give them pleasure. But they do not

131. Ibid., III.XII, 80. Boethius confirms this conclusion: "It is necessarily so, for it would hardly seem a happy government if it were like a yoke imposed upon unwilling necks instead of a willing acceptance of salvation" (ibid.).

132. Ibid.

133. Ibid., IV.I, 85. Boethius continues, "there is something even more bewildering. When wickedness rules and flourishes, not only does virtue go unrewarded, it is even trodden underfoot by the wicked and punished in the place of crime. That this can happen in the realm of an omniscient and omnipotent God who wills only good, is beyond perplexity and complaint" (ibid.).

134. Philosophy will be his "guide," his "path" and his "conveyance" (ibid., IV.I, 86).

obtain it, because evil things cannot reach happiness."[135] However, this does not alleviate Boethius' concern but rather accentuates it, for evil is more tolerable if the world is without a God who oversees it. Boethius says: "I would be less surprised if I could believe that the confusion of things is due to the fortuitous operations of chance. But my wonder is only increased by the knowledge that the ruling power of the universe is God. Sometimes He is pleasant to the good and unpleasant to the bad, and other times He grants the bad their wishes and denies the good."[136] The question that follows is vital: "since He often varies between these two alternatives, what grounds are there for distinguishing between God and the haphazards of chance?"[137]

It is at this point that the intimately related distinction between Providence and Fate is set in place in order to set Boethius further in the right direction, substantiating the idea that "even if you don't know the reason behind the great plan of the universe, there is no need for you to doubt that a good power rules the world and that everything happens aright."[138] For Providence (*providentia*) is the plan which comes from the mind of God whilst Fate (*fatum*) is its outworking in time.[139] Philosophy

135. Ibid., IV.II, 92. Philosophy offers three explanations for the existence of evil, addressing Boethius. First, "If you say it is because they do not know what is good, I shall ask what greater weakness is there than the blindness of ignorance." Second, "if you say that they know what they ought to seek for, but pleasure sends them chasing off the wrong way, this way too, they are weak through lack of self control because they cannot resist vice." Third, "if you say they abandon goodness and turn to vice knowingly and willingly, this way they not only cease to be powerful, but cease to be at all. Men who give up the common goal of all things that exist, thereby cease to exist themselves" (ibid., IV.II, 90–91). It is for this reason that wickedness itself is self-inflicted punishment, for it is removed from goodness and happiness (ibid., IV.III, 93–94). Hence Philosophy notes an interesting corollary, one in line with Boethius' own sickness of mind: "it is clear that when someone is done an injury, the misery belongs not to the victim but to the perpetrator." For the guilty "ought to be brought to justice not by a prosecution counsel with an air of outrage, but by a prosecution kind and sympathetic, *like sick men being brought to the doctor, so that their guilt could be cut back by punishment like a malignant growth*" (ibid., IV.IV, 100. My italics). On this basis Philosophy concludes that "the wicked are happier if they suffer punishment than if they are unrestrained by any just retribution" (ibid., IV.IV, 96; also IV.IV, 98).

136. Ibid., IV.V, 102.

137. Ibid.

138. Ibid.

139. "The generation of all things, the whole progress of things subject to change and whatever moves in any way, receive their causes, their due order and their form from the unchanging mind of God. In the high citadel of its oneness, the mind of God

uses the example of a craftsman who anticipates in his mind the plan of the thing he is going to make and then sets about executing the work, carrying out in time "the construction of what he has seen all at one moment present to his mind's eye." Thus God, in his Providence, "constructs a single fixed plan of all that is to happen, while it is by means of Fate that all that He has planned is realized in its many individual details in the course of time."[140]

The distinction between Providence and Fate underpins the notion of appropriate knowledge, that is, knowledge appropriate to the human capacity. The poem that follows is based on this assumption. Philosophy maintains that just because the causes of human action are not as evident as the causes of the world, it does not mean that the human sphere is chaotic. Rather, simply put, it is that the cause remains unrevealed to the human mind. It is the light of this distinction that the problem faced by Boethius and all of humankind becomes apparent. Humankind cannot contemplate the order completely and it is this that is the source of many problems.[141]

---

has set up a plan for the multitude of events. When this plan is thought of as in the purity of God's understanding, it is called Providence, and when it is thought with reference to all things, whose motion and order it controls, it is called by the name the ancients give it, Fate" (ibid., IV.VI, 104). Hence, as Philosophy makes clear, everything that comes under Fate "is also subject to Providence." However, "certain things which come under Providence are above the chain of Fate." Such things "rise above the order of change ruled over by Fate in virtue of the stability of their position close to the supreme Godhead." Philosophy is clear that the distinction between Providence and Fate is not clearly defined, but graduated. She illustrates this by imagining a "set of revolving concentric circles": "The inmost one comes closest to the simplicity of the centre, while forming itself a kind of centre for those set outside it to revolve round. The circle furthest out rotates through a wider orbit and the greater its distance from the indivisible centre point, the greater space it spreads through. Anything that joins itself to the middle circle is brought close to simplicity, and no longer spreads out widely . . . The relationship between the ever-changing course of Fate and the stable simplicity of Providence is like that between reasoning and understanding, between that which is coming into being and that which is, between time and eternity, or between the moving circle and the still point in the middle" (ibid., IV.VI, 105).

140. Ibid., IV.VI, 104–5.

141. Philosophy says: "It is because you men are in no position to contemplate this order that everything seems confused and upset. But it is no less true that everything has its own position, which directs it towards the good and so governs it. There is nothing that can happen because of evil or because engineered by the wicked themselves, and they, as we have most amply demonstrated, are deflected from their search for the good by mistake and error, while the order which issues from the supreme good at the centre of the universe cannot deflect anyone from his beginning" (ibid., IV.VI, 106).

Yet no one wonders when the north west wind
Sweeps in the roaring waves to beat the shore,
Or when the frozen mass of hard-packed snow
Dissolves before the sun's aestival heat.
The causes in this case are clear to view,
But hidden cause confounds the human heart,
Perplexed by things that rarely come to pass,
For unexpected things the people dread.
Then let the clouds of ignorance give way
And these events will no more wondrous seem.[142]

It is clear that Providence extends throughout creation and includes humankind: "the protector of the good and scourge of the wicked is none other than God, the mind's guide and physician. He looks out from the watch-tower of Providence, sees what suits each person, and applies to him whatever He knows is suitable. This, then, is the outstanding wonder of the order of fate; a knowing God acts and ignorant men look on with wonder at his actions."[143] Thus, according to God's ordering everything has a purpose, even the evil amongst humankind:

> some, when they think they suffer injustice at the hands of the worst of men, burn with hatred for evil men, and being eager to be different from those they hate, have reformed and become virtuous. It is only the power of God to which evils may also be good, when by their proper use He elicits some good result. For a certain order embraces all things, and anything which departs from the order planned and assigned to it, only falls back into order, albeit a different order, so as not to allow anything to chance in the realm of Providence.[144]

Hence, "Evil is thought to abound on earth. But if you could see the plan of Providence, you would not think there was evil anywhere."[145]

Having established the inclusion of humankind within the God's order, the final section of the *Consolation* deals with questions related to Providence,[146] specifically the compatibility of freedom with the alleged

142. Ibid., IV.V, vv. 13–22, 103.

143. Ibid., IV.VI, 106.

144. Ibid., IV.VI, 109.

145. Ibid., IV.VI, 110.

146. Philosophy pursues this at the insistence of Boethius. She thinks that "useful as it is to know about these matters, they are somewhat aside from our proposed path" and that Boethius "may be so worn out by digressions" that he will be "unable to complete the journey." Nevertheless, she does as Boethius wishes. Ibid., V.I, 116.

necessity involved in God's foreknowledge.[147] Within this final stage, the importance of reason is clear. The *Consolation* has demonstrated the growing strength of Boethius, such that he can now tackle questions such as the existence of evil, and problems such as providence and foreknowledge, without the sweetening of rhetoric and music. Rather it is pure reason that aids the remainder of Boethius' recovery. Hence Philosophy says to Boethius, "You anticipate correctly. As the doctors like to think, it is a sign of a constitution strong and fighting back. *But seeing you are so quick of understanding, I will pile the arguments on.*"[148] As a result the sweetness and pleasure of music that coaxed Boethius through the earlier stages of his treatment now provide a temporary relief to the application of reason: "You are worn out by the prolixity of the reasoning and have been looking forward to the sweetness of song. So take a draught that will refresh you and make you able to apply your thoughts more closely to further matters."[149]

HARMONY, CONSONANCE, AND BEAUTY

Beauty and Likeness

As we have seen, the *Consolation* traces the re-ordering and re-orientation of Boethius (herein Boethius becomes aware of the "fittingness" between himself and the world), implicitly drawing upon the notions of harmony and consonance set out in the *Fundamentals*. However, in contrast to the *Fundamentals*, in the *Consolation* they are placed in the context of the notion of beauty.

---

147. Philosophy resolves the tension between freedom and necessity by delineating two types of necessity. The first is simple: the example Philosophy gives is "all men are mortal." The second is conditional: the example is, "if you know someone is walking, it is necessary that he is walking." The second does not exist in virtue of its nature "but in virtue of a condition that is added." Philosophy explains: "No necessity forces the man to walk who is making his way of his own free will, although it is necessary that he walks when he takes a step" (ibid., V.VI, 135). In the same way, "if Providence sees something as present, it is necessary for it to happen, even though it has no necessity in its own nature. God sees those future events which happen of free will as present events; so that these things when considered with reference to God's sight of them do happen necessarily as a result of the condition of divine knowledge; but when considered in themselves they do not lose the absolute freedom of their nature" (ibid., V.VI, 35–36).

148. Ibid., IV.II, 90. My italics. Later Boethius says to Philosophy: "I do beg you to *tell me your teaching* on this point" (ibid., IV.VI, 103. My italics).

149. Ibid., IV.VI, 110.

The *Consolation* is clear: beauty is integral to the world and humankind pursues beauty because of its objective and, therefore, inherent value.[150] This results from three points of belief: one, beauty has its origin in God and is an intrinsic aspect of Him; two, the created order is an outpouring of God and for this reason beauty is an essential feature of it; three, by pursuing beauty within the created order one attains an understanding of the world, moves towards God, and becomes more like Him. I will elaborate upon each point in turn.

It is apparent throughout the *Consolation* that God is the Source of the world and everything therein. Indeed, it is the recognition of this that rehabilitates Boethius. Thus, God is the Source of Beauty, for if the world derives from God then it follows that so do all beautiful things therein. The *Consolation* confirms this by attributing beauty to God: He is the "high archetype" and the "height of beauty," and the beauty of the world and humankind arises from Him.

Therefore, in order to speak about the character of beauty, one turns to the created order in the first instance. It is thus that one discerns beauty as order and harmony. The *Consolation* is clear: the cosmos and everything therein is ordered and harmonious. The term harmony is used throughout, referring to the co-operation that exists between the diverse elements of the world. In this respect, the unity of the cosmos is of great importance: it is necessary for the existence of the cosmos as the creation of God, which as such stands in His likeness. In explanation, as Perfection, God necessarily exists in unity rather than diversity, for unity is better than diversity.[151] In this way, through the manifestation of harmony and participation therein, the cosmos bears the likeness of God:

150. Ibid., II.V, 35.

151. Ibid., III.XI, 75. Boethius' emphasis upon the unity of God in the *Consolation* is clear. However, there are five theological tractates transmitted by manuscripts, often in association with the *Consolation*, which recent scholars attribute to Boethius. Marenbon, *Boethius*, 66–67; Chadwick, *Consolations of Music, Logic, Theology and Philosophy*, 174–75. The first two tractates, probably the latest to be composed, deal with the Trinity. Ibid., 211. For an outline of their argument and sources cf. ibid., 211–22. Chadwick accounts for the absence of anything specifically Christian in the *Consolation* thus: "The work's intention is given by its title. Boethius is not in quest of consolation from divine grace in the remission of sins and the promise of eternal life to those redeemed through Christ. His doctrine of salvation is humanist, a soteriology of the inward purification of the soul. The *Consolation* is a work written by a Platonist who is also a Christian, but is not a Christian work" (ibid., 249). For English translations of the tractates, cf. *The Theological Tractates*, 3–129. For further information on these, see Mair, "Text of

> All things Thou bringest forth from Thy high archetype:
> Thou, height of beauty, in Thy mind the beauteous world
> *Dost bear, and in that ideal likeness shaping it,*
> *Dost order perfect parts a perfect whole to frame.*
> The elements by harmony Thou dost constrain
> That hot to cold and wet to dry are equal made,
> That fire grow not too light, or earth too fraught with weight.[152]

It is for this reason that Boethius understands God as the power that holds together created diversity[153] and that Philosophy maintains that everything strives for unity rather than multiplicity.[154] God is Unity: He is the Source of the world and creates the world to be beautiful, so that it is united and bears His likeness.

In sum, beauty is a feature of God and He is its paradigmatic example. In the cosmos, therefore, which is created in His likeness by means of order and harmony, beauty is an intrinsic and invaluable dimension. For this reason, beauty is infused with existential importance for it is constitutive of human nature and its likeness to God. It comprises both subject and object and thus intimately relates the two.

The "End" of Self-Knowledge

It is on this basis, knowing God as the End of all creation, that self-knowledge comes to the fore. Boethius' misery is bound up with the question of self-knowledge since he is created by God, made in His likeness, and yet faces apparent abandonment. Hence, the movement of the *Consolation* traces Boethius' recovery of likeness to God, which occurs by his acknowledging humankind as part of the order of the cosmos. Music, as the active principle of harmony, leads Boethius forth and encourages the internal harmony between body and soul. Thus, at the beginning

---

the Opuscula Sacra," 206–13; Gibson, "Opuscula Sacra in the Middle Ages," 214–34; Marenbon, *Boethius*, 66–95.

152. Boethius *Consolation* III.IX, vv. 6–9, 66. My italics. "*Forma boni livore carens, tu cuncta superno / Ducis ab exemplo, pulchrum pulcherrimus ipse / Mundum mente gerens similique in imagine formans / Perfectasque iubens perfectum absolvere partes.* Elsewhere: And all this chain of things / In earth and sea and sky / One ruler holds in hand: / If Love relaxed the reins / All things that now keep peace / Would wage continual war / And wreck the great machine / Which unity maintains / With motions beautiful. (*pulchra*)" (ibid., II.VIII, vv. 13–21, 45).

153. Ibid., III.XII.

154. Ibid., III.XI.

Boethius' lack of self-knowledge leads him to concentrate upon the world rather than God.[155] The association of loss of self-understanding with a concern for earthly things is confirmed by Philosophy when she appears: "Now I know the other cause, or rather the major cause of your illness: *you have forgotten your true nature*."[156] Indeed, Boethius suffers from a "touch of amnesia," a temporary loss of identity and, as a result, is preoccupied solely with earthly matters. For this reason he dwells upon the loss of material treasures. However, as Philosophy notes, the real loss that Boethius has suffered does not involve the loss of worldly posses-sions: "it is not the sight of this place which gives me concern but your own appearance, and it is not the walls of your library with their glass and ivory decoration that I am looking for, *but the seat of your mind*."[157]

The problem is clear to Philosophy, it is because Boethius is con-fused as a result of losing his memory that he weeps, speaking of banish-ment and loss of possessions.[158] Hence, Philosophy's attempt to show the partial worth of earthly blessings such as wealth and fame: humankind has forgotten that its nature is molded to resemble God and it therefore seeks happiness elsewhere. Thus Philosophy complains: "Their eyes are used to the dark and they cannot raise them to the shining light of truth. They are like birds whose sight is sharpened by night and blinded by day. So long as they look only at their own desires and not the order of creation, they think freedom to commit crimes and the absence of punishment as happy things."[159]

Becoming reacquainted with the truth that humankind is part of God's order allows Boethius to re-evaluate human nature and focus on true goodness and happiness: "Why then proclaim your kin and ancestry? / Look whence you came and see who made you, God. / No man is base except through sin he quit / His proper source to cherish meaner things."[160] Hence, his gaze is drawn away from earthly concerns

155. Ibid., I.II, vv. 1–5, 5; ibid., I.II, vv. 22–27, 6.

156. Ibid., I.VI, 20. My italics. Boethius "has forgotten for a while who he is" (ibid., I.II, 6).

157. Ibid., I.V, 17. My italics. Philosophy continues: "That is the place where I once stored away—not my books, but—the thing that makes them have any value, the phi-losophy they contain" (ibid., I.V, 17).

158. Ibid., I.VI, 20.

159. Ibid., IV.IV, 99.

160. Ibid., III.VI, 59.

towards God and, in order that they follow the right path, Philosophy and Boethius pray:

> Grant, Father, that our minds thy august seat may scan,
> Grant us the sight of true good's source, and grant us light
> That we may fix on Thee our mind's unblended eye.
> Disperse the clouds of earthly matter's cloying weight;
> Shine out in all thy glory; for Thou art rest and peace
> To those who worship Thee; to see Thee is our end,
> Who art our source and maker, lord and path and goal.[161]

The "Chain of Being"

The tradition of self-knowledge that Boethius presumes is grounded in the "chain of being."[162] This makes a connection between beauty and likeness, identifying God as the End of creation. According to this scheme, everything within the created order has its place, with God, the Supreme Being, as its End. In the case of humankind, as demonstrated in the case of Boethius, one can turn away from God, thereby disrupting the chain of being. In the first instance, humankind becomes blind to God as its End and pursues mediate goods and ends as if they were

161. Ibid., III.IX, vv. 22–28, 67.

162. Arthur O. Lovejoy traces the development of the "chain of being." He notes the origin of the idea in Plato, wherein the mutable world is contrasted with "otherworldliness" Lovejoy, *Great Chain of Being*, 25. Moreover, he notes that grounding mundane reality in the Good, which stands as its "replica," gives rise to the "principle of plenitude." This principle "insists upon the necessarily complete translation of all the ideal possibilities into actuality" in order that the world constitutes the best possible image of the intelligible. Ibid., 50. Lovejoy observes that although in the Platonic dialogues there are intimations that the "Ideas" and therefore their sensible counterparts are not all of "equal metaphysical rank or excellence" the idea of a hierarchy is only a "vague tendency." He suggests that it was Aristotle who instantiated a "principle of continuity" wherein all animals are arranged in a single graded *scala naturae* according to their degree of perfection (even though Aristotle recognized the multiplicity of possible systems of classification). Ibid., 58. Lovejoy summarizes: "The result was the conception of the plan and structure of the world which, through the Middle Ages and down to the late eighteenth century, many philosophers, most men of science, and, indeed, most educated men, were to accept without question—the conception of the universe as a 'Great Chain of Being,' composed of an immense, or—by the strict but seldom rigorously applied logic of the principle of continuity—of an infinite, number of links ranging in hierarchical order from the meagerest kind of existents, which barely escape non-existence, through 'every possible' grade up to the *ens perfectissimum*" (ibid., 59). For responses to Lovejoy's seminal work, and for further explorations of concepts of hierarchy cf. Leathers Kuntz and Grimley Kuntz, *Jacob's Ladder and the Tree of Life*.

ultimate, in effect ejecting God from the mind of the individual. In the second instance, and as a result, the divine likeness of humankind becomes clouded, leading to, in the third instance, the disruption of the divinely ordained order of the cosmos. Herein, humankind becomes more "animal" than "human."

It has been demonstrated that God, for Boethius, is the Creator and Source of the cosmos and therefore is the End of humankind. Accordingly, God is the ultimate source of Goodness and Happiness to which all action and thought is directed.[163] Thus, when a human person recognizes God as Creator and is ordered correspondingly a harmony obtains between body and soul, creating "Human" music. This harmony signals the achievement of goodness and happiness by humankind, and in effect involves what might be called divinization. Philosophy explains, "Goodness is happiness, and therefore it is obvious that all good men obtain happiness in virtue of their being good. But we agree that those who attain happiness are divine. The reward of the good, then, a reward that can never be decreased, that no-one's power can diminish, and no-one's wickedness darken, is to become gods."[164] By contrast, when humankind loses sight of God as its Source it directs itself towards other created things and pursues them as if they were the ultimate. Hence Philosophy says to Boethius, "Why then do you mortal men seek after happiness outside yourselves, when it lies within you? You are led astray by error and ignorance."[165] By pursuing goodness and happiness in external things, true goodness and happiness are not realized and a shift within the created order occurs.

It is no accident that beauty provides a key example for, as we have seen, beauty constitutes likeness to God. Hence failing to acknowledge God as the Source of the cosmos leads humankind to pursue other beautiful objects which, accordingly, are classed as "side-tracks." They lead away from rather than towards true happiness. Philosophy is unambiguous, worldly beauty is impermanent: it is "fleeting and transitory, more

163. "The proper way of looking at it is to regard the goal of every action as its reward, just as the prize for running in the stadium is the wreath of laurels for which the race is run" (Boethius *Consolation* IV.III, 93).

164. Ibid.

165. Ibid., II.IV, 31. Philosophy continues: "If I ask you whether there is anything more precious to you than your own self, you will say no. So if you are in possession of yourself you will possess something you would never wish to lose and something Fortune could never take away" (ibid.).

ephemeral than the blossom in spring."[166] It is not a source of authentic beauty in and of itself. Philosophy says: "If, as Aristotle said, we had the piercing eyesight of the mythical Lynceus and could see right through things, even the body of Alcibiades, so fair on the surface, would look thoroughly ugly once we had seen the bowels inside."[167] She continues: "Your own nature doesn't make you look beautiful. It is due to the weak eyesight of the people who see you. Think how excessive this desire for the good of the body is, when, as you know, all that you admire can be reduced to nothing by three days of burning fever."[168]

In short, created beauty is transitory and true beauty is only appropriately applied to God, the Source of all things. Hence, pursuing beauty for its own sake throws humankind into confusion and, ultimately, leads away from God. For this reason, Philosophy says of "precious stones" that such things may be "works of the Creator and may draw some minimal beauty from their own ornamental nature," but are of "an inferior rank to you as a more excellent creature, and cannot in any way merit your admiration."[169] Moreover, it is because of the misdirection of the human gaze that Philosophy, whilst acknowledging the beauty of creation (observing that "Creation is indeed very beautiful, and the countryside a beautiful part of creation"),[170] notes the tendency of humankind to pursue it to excess, as if a possession. Philosophy is brutally to the point: "The fact that flowers blossom in spring confers no distinction on you, and the swelling fullness of the autumn harvest is no work of yours, You are, in fact, enraptured with empty joys, embracing blessings that are alien to you as if they were your own."[171] Philosophy's case is clear, beauty is inherently valuable and it is so because it belongs to God. It is for this

166. Ibid., III.VIII, 61.
167. Ibid., III.VIII, 61–62.
168. Ibid.
169. Ibid., II.V, 34.
170. Ibid.

171. Ibid. Philosophy emphasizes humankind's desire to possess beautiful things, their consequent denial of the source of beauty, and the empty possession that results. Thus, for example, attention is not drawn to the person who wears the beautiful garment but to the garment's intrinsic beauty. Philosophy declares: "Perhaps you think that beauty means being resplendent in clothing of every variety: but if the clothing catches my eye, my admiration will be directed at either the quality of the material or the skill of the tailor" (ibid.).

reason that humankind desires it and not because it becomes beautiful upon possession.[172]

The case of beauty accords with Philosophy's diagnosis of Boethius' predicament. Not only is beauty something which humankind is attracted to and which imparts knowledge of the nature of the world, it is intrinsically bound up with modes of existence. Boethius has lost his sense of identity, which is bound to God and His order, and which is thus intrinsically valuable. For this reason, he seeks value and goodness away from God. Philosophy comments: "It seems as if you feel a lack of any blessing of your own inside you, which is driving you to seek your blessings in things separate and external."[173]

As we have seen the pursuit of mediate ends is a symptom of the disharmony within the human person who, having overlooked its relationship to God, seeks its end in other created things. However, the pursuit of mediacy instead of ultimacy is more than symptomatic: it furthers the disharmony within the human person and further conceals divine likeness, encouraging a life outside of that which God has ordained. This causes upset within the chain of being, which spans the entire cosmos and the range of existence. In explanation: humankind has its foundation in God. Hence Philosophy says, "There is nothing, therefore, which could preserve its own nature as well as go against God."[174] The nature of humanity is to be turned towards God its Creator. In effect, therefore, when a human person pursues things apart from God, he becomes denatured, more like an animal than a human. Philosophy explains:

> when a being endowed with a godlike quality in virtue of his rational nature thinks that his only splendor lies in the possession of inanimate goods, it is the overthrow of the natural order. Other creatures are content with what is their own, but you, whose mind is made in the image of God, seek to adorn your superior

172. Philosophy notes that beauty is that which has individual worth which "she immediately transfers to whoever possesses her" and that, "as public offices cannot do this, it is clear that they have no beauty (*pulchra*) or worth of their own" (ibid., III.IV, 55). This is interesting in the light of the *First Alcibiades*, and Socrates' desire to help Alcibiades in achieving importance amongst the Athenians.

173. Boethius *Consolation* II.V, 35. "What an obvious mistake to make—to think that anything can be enhanced by decoration that does not belong to it. It's impossible. For if there is anything striking in the decoration, that is what is praised, while the veiled and hidden object continues just the same in all its ugliness" (ibid., II.V, 35–36).

174. Ibid., III.XII, 80.

nature with inferior objects, oblivious of the great wrong you do your Creator. It was His will that the human race should rule all earthly creatures, but you have degraded yourself to a position beneath the lowest of all.[175]

Hence, "If every good is agreed to be more valuable than whatever it belongs to, then by your own judgment when you account the most worthless of objects as goods of yours, you make yourself lower than those very things, and it is no less than you deserve."[176] For human nature "towers above the rest of creation" only as long as it recognizes its own nature. Once the human person forgets this "he sinks lower than the beasts." For, Philosophy says, ignorance of one's nature is natural to other living things but not natural to the human person for whom it is a defect.[177]

In short, the ability of humankind to recognize its true nature privileges it within the chain of being. Thus, when humankind fails to do so, it is denatured. This is evident in the case of Boethius but features more strongly in the case of evil people. The difference is one of degree: Boethius acknowledges the order of God's creation but has temporarily forgotten his place therein and thus forgets what it means to be human. By contrast, evil people do not even acknowledge the order of creation. As a result their amnesia is permanent. Thus, they cease to be human, no longer rise to a divine condition, and sink to the level of being an animal.[178] Hence, Philosophy says: "You could say that someone who robs with violence and burns with greed is like a wolf." Moreover, "the man who is lazy, dull and stupid, lives an ass's life." Likewise, "a man wallowing in foul and impure lusts is occupied by the filthy pleasures of a sow."[179] Boethius agrees with Philosophy: "I see the justice of saying that though they retain the outward appearance of the human body, wicked people change into animals with regard to their state of mind."[180] Again

175. Ibid., II.V, 35.

176. Ibid., II.V, 35–36.

177. Ibid., II.V, 36.

178. Ibid., IV.III, 94.

179. Ibid.

180. Ibid., IV.IV, 96. It is important to iterate that although evil exists in the world, Philosophy does not see this as evidence counting against God's order. Rather God incorporates evil into His order. Philosophy says, "let it be enough that we have seen that God, the author of all natures, orders all things and directs them towards goodness. He is quick to hold all that He has created in His own image, and by means of the chain

the emphasis is clear, likeness to God occurs not in the body but in the soul. In terms of the *First Alcibiades*, the body is merely the soul's vessel, and cannot tell us anything about the human person. Only the soul can do this. If a person does not acknowledge God then he denies that element that marks out humans as unique.

Philosophy explores the existential implications of this: she builds upon the assumption that "all that exists is in a state of unity and that goodness itself is unity" and infers from this that "we must see everything that exists as good." Evil people turn away from goodness and as a result cease to exist. This is doubtless because they are dissonant, no longer comprising unity and exemplifying human music. They cease to be beautiful. Thus, "the wicked cease to be what they once were." She clarifies: "That they used to be human is shown by the human appearance of their body which still remains. So it was by falling into wickedness that they also lost their human nature. Now, since only goodness can raise a man above the level of human kind, it follows that it is proper that wickedness thrusts down to a level below humankind those whom it has dethroned from the condition of being human."[181]

Hence, the question of *existence* is tied up with human nature, beauty, and likeness to God. Philosophy explains:

> Some may perhaps think it strange that we say that wicked men, who form the majority of men, do not exist; but that is how it is. I am not trying to deny the wickedness of the wicked; what I do deny is that their existence is absolute and complete existence. Just as you might call a corpse a dead man, but couldn't simply call it a man, so I would agree that the wicked are wicked, but could not agree that they have unqualified existence. A thing exists when it keeps it proper place and preserves it own nature. Anything which departs from this ceases to exist, because its existence depends on the preservation of its nature.[182]

By claiming that evil people cease to exist, Philosophy does not suggest a physical death, which happens when the union between soul and body disintegrates, but a spiritual death. To explain: God is the source of the universe and creates it so that everything therein tends towards goodness and unity. Therefore order and harmony, and beauty, are con-

---

of necessity presided over by Fate banishes all evil from the bounds of His commonwealth" (ibid., IV.VI, 110).

181. Ibid., IV.III, 94.

182. Ibid., IV.II, 91.

stitutive of human nature. Hence, evil people go both against God and human nature. As a result they cease to be truly human and in this sense cease to exist.[183]

CONCLUSION

In line with the Greek tradition that Boethius is so concerned to mediate, order and harmony ground the world and beauty stands therein as a property, leading the human subject forth to knowledge of the self and the world-in-itself. It thus bridges the distinction between subject and object. More than this, it provides the ground for their interrelationship. For beauty extends cosmically, integrating subject and object. Significantly, it does so by means of sensible expression as well as intellectual comprehension. Within this context, music is unique: it is intrinsically bound up with the order of the cosmos and stands as an active principle that communicates the harmony resounding therein. It does so both as sound and ratio, drawing diverse elements into a coherent whole. In this sense, Boethius values the materiality of music. However, intellect is prioritized over sense, and thus the formal basis of music is set over and against music as sound. This is in virtue of the fact that the location of beauty ultimately originates with God and is exhibited in creation as a result. Hence, the meaning of the physical world, beauty, and music is located in a prior, underlying, non-material ground.

The priority of intellect over the physical is present in the *Fundamentals*, leading Boethius to assert the true musician as the person who judges music rather than performs it. However, it is most strikingly apparent in the *Consolation*: Boethius' recovery is a movement that traces the re-cognition of his place within the order of creation. Herein, acknowledging God as not only the Source of humankind but also its End allows the true resonance of the created order to reveal itself. However, although sounded-music steers Boethius through the initial stages of his recovery (his experience of it allowing a re-ordering of his body and mind and thereby a progression towards God) it ultimately

183. It is because good turns towards God and fulfils human nature, and evil turns away from God and becomes denatured, that Philosophy considers good and evil to be their own rewards and punishment. She says: "let us see what is decreed by everlasting law: if you have turned your mind to higher things, there is no need of a judge to award a prize; it is you yourself who have brought yourself to a more excellent state: but if you have directed your zeal towards lower things, do not look for punishment from without; it is you yourself who have plunged yourself into the worse condition" (ibid., IV.IV, 99).

acts as a preparation for reason, which is better able to pursue objective and absolute meaning. Thus, when Boethius is altogether stronger and in control, he is able to speed forth with the use of reason.

Two caveats are perhaps significant with regard to the priority of reason over sense. First, the *Consolation* does not end with Boethius' unification with God: it appears that even reason does not take Boethius all the way he needs to go.[184] Second, the fact that everything derives from God implies that harmony is not only the means by which the created order is brought into an image of God but as part of God Himself, is also part of the End. On this basis it might be maintained that music, whether understood intellectually or felt physically, allows the subject to engage with God.[185]

In sum, although Boethius values the material, he does so only to a certain extent and only to the degree that it coincides with reason. It is thus, that sounded-music is characterized with epithets such as "sweet" and "palatable," bringing about only "temporary" relief, and serving as "refreshment."[186] We will now turn to Kant where God is not invoked in order to ground meaning and validate the information secured through the material world. Such speculation would be beyond the scope of reason. Thus, as we shall see, beauty is once more constructed through a pre-existing understanding of the epistemological relationship between subject and object, self and world. However, this time, the ground occurs within the subject and, more specifically, is positioned within its intellectual powers.

184. Weighing up the arguments of Gruber and Tränkle, O'Daly concludes that on balance Gruber's arguments for the symmetrical structure of the work suggest completeness. He also warns against reading the abrupt ending through the lens of Boethius' imprisoned status, thereby presuming that his opportunity to write was cut short. *Poetry of Boethius*, 28–29. Reason's inability to proceed further may be a result of the breakdown of human language when attempting to speak about God. See Lerer, *Boethius and Dialogue*, 209–12.

185. This links with the idea of *divine music*, mentioned earlier, implicit within Boethius' cosmic understanding of music.

186. These descriptions may exemplify the non-coercive nature of music mentioned earlier, that which renders music a gentle remedy as opposed to a 'bitter' one, and underpins its contrast with reason. For in contrast to reason, sounded-music is *non*-propositional and cannot be expected to be so. It is perhaps this indeterminacy that makes sounded-music uniquely attractive. Importantly, one might note that the non-coercion of music mirrors the human attraction towards God, as its End, the response evoked in each case arising naturally. As Boethius notes, God is goodness itself, and this requires the non-coercion of order, which is the willing reconciliation of contraries. Boethius *Consolation* III.IX, vv. 6–9, 66.

4

The Kantian Understanding of the World, the Role of Beauty, and the Value of Music

Those who have recommended the singing of spiritual songs as part of the domestic rites of worship have not considered that by means of such a *noisy* (and precisely for that reason usually pharisaical) form of worship they have imposed a great inconvenience on the public, for they have forced the neighbourhood either to join in their singing or to give up their own train of thought.

—Immanuel Kant, *The Critique of Judgment*, §53, 5:330, n. 1, 207.[1]

T HE TYPE OF MUSIC which Kant had in mind is one harmonically rather than melodically conceived. However, it features little in his actual treatment of music (Kant does not anchor his discussion with musical technicalities). The dominant attitude of the *Critique of Judgment* is that music intrudes upon thought. It equates music primarily with sound rather than with tonal organization, thus classifies it as mere sensation, and denies its contribution to cognition. As we shall see, for Kant the contribution of fine art to cognition stems from the connection, via reflection, between pure aesthetic judgment and cognition in general. By denying that music is anything but sensory Kant denies its involvement with reflection, disallows its connection with pure aesthetic judgment and thereby cognition in general, and precludes its inclusion amongst the fine arts. It is for this reason that Kant even refers to music as noise, distracting the mind from thought.

---

1. Hereafter, referred to as *CJ*. The last number of each reference to the *Critique* indicates the edition page number.

To tease out the elements of this argument we must begin by considering two interrelated issues underpinning Kant's view of music. The first is the distinction, permeating and shaping Kant's philosophy, between that which can and that which cannot be known. The second is the consequent emphasis upon the subjective form of beauty. Kant invokes various terms to convey the distinction between that which can and that which cannot be known. These include the phenomenal and the noumenal, the empirical and the transcendental, and appearance and thing-in-itself. The notion of the supersensible substrate encompasses these, denoting at a general level that which lies beyond the bounds of knowledge.[2]

As we shall see, within the Kantian scheme one can only know that which appears through a priori conditions within the subject. Thus, the idea of God and also the idea of self (those notions which we saw are not only accepted by Boethius but are formative to his account) cannot be known or demonstrated by reason. However, they are necessary to provide a degree of coherence and are therefore invoked. According to Kant, one must assume the existence of God as designer, for "without assuming an intelligent author, no comprehensible ground for design and order can be stated without falling into patent absurdities."[3] Likewise with the existence of a self: "Consciousness of self according to the determinations of our state in inner perception is merely empirical, and always changing. No fixed and abiding self can present itself in this flux of inner appearances." However, one must assume such an abiding consciousness. If one does not, "There can be in us no modes of knowledge, no connection or unity of one mode of knowledge with another."[4] The notions of God and self are tolerable postulates.

Reason is circumscribed, discussing only that which is within its limits: it cannot attain absolute and unconditional knowledge. However, it is reason's pursuit of exactly this that gives rise to the antinomies of pure reason at the heart of Kant's philosophy. The antinomies aim to

2. Roger Scruton draws attention to a bridging passage between the analytic and the dialectic in *Critique of Pure Reason* that suggests this. Cf. Kant, *Critique of Pure Reason* (referred to as *CPR* hereafter), especially A 288–89; B. 344–46. Scruton notes that many scholars do not accept this interpretation, *Kant: A Very Short Introduction*, 58.

3. Kant, "What Is Orientation in Thinking?" 298.

4. Kant calls this "transcendental apperception," the "pure original unchangeable consciousness." *CPR*, A 107, 136; also B 155–56, 167; cf. also Kant, *Anthropology*, §7, Remark, 26.

confine the use of reason to that which can be known through experience.[5] To explain: in general terms one can define an antinomy as a fallacy enabling both a proposition and its negation to be derived from the same premise. The contradiction, however, is only apparent and not genuine, the inconsistency arising from a false assumption.[6] Kant employs the antinomy in all three of his *Critiques*, considering it a "decisive experiment" that necessarily exposes "any error lying hidden in the assumptions of reason."[7] Through their contradiction antinomies "force reason to give up the otherwise very natural presupposition that holds objects of the senses to be things in themselves" and, in doing so, guide it "to count them as appearances, and ascribe to them an intelligible substratum (something supersensible, the concept of which is only an idea and permits no genuine cognition)."[8]

It is the tension between the world-as-it-appears and the world-in-itself that frames Kant's discussion of beauty (*das Schöne*), by means of the paradoxical nature of the antinomy of taste, and affects Kant's understanding of music. Hence, I will attend to Kant's understanding of beauty in the first instance and thereafter view its relation to music. As we shall see, Kant's conception of beauty is fundamentally descriptive: beauty results from the discussion about aesthetic judgment rather than being a central presupposition of it, elucidating that which Kant places at the core of aesthetic experience, the harmony of the free play of the cognitive powers. As such, beauty is a means by which one understands the process of aesthetic appreciation rather than a quality of the world itself, and meaning is located in the intellectual powers of the subject rather than the material object. The implications of this will be demonstrated in the case of music. Music is an arrangement of tones that is experienced by means of the sense of hearing: it has physical foundations. However, Kant's emphasis upon the subject and its intellectual powers cannot take

5. Scruton states: "antinomies result from the attempt to reach beyond the perspective of experience to the absolute vantage point from which the totality (and hence the world "as it is in itself") can be surveyed" (*Kant: A Very Short Introduction*, 64).

6. Ibid., 62. "Antinomy" is a rhetorical form of presentation cited by Quintilian (35–100) in his *Institutio oratoria* of 92–5 (bk. VIII, ch. 7) in which arguments are presented side-by-side with each other. The form was widely used in seventeenth century jurisprudence to point to differences between laws arising from clashes between legal jurisdictions. Caygill, *Kant Dictionary*, 75.

7. Kant, *Prolegomena*, §52b, quoted in Caygill, *Kant Dictionary*, 76.

8. Kant, *CJ*, §57, Remark II, 5:344, 219.

full account of this. Thus, in order to talk about musical meaning Kant is forced to abstract from the physical features of music, regarding only its formal presentation.

THE ANTINOMY OF TASTE, THE PROBLEM OF BEAUTY, AND EMPIRICISM AND RATIONALISM

In the *Critique of Judgment*, with regard to taste, the first commonplace of the antinomy maintains that "Everyone has his own taste" and the second asserts, "There is no disputing about taste."[9] Most importantly, the antinomy boldly presents the paradoxical nature of taste (and therein the claim of beauty) which acknowledges that my taste is my own and yet assures me that everyone ought to concur with my judgment. However, it implicitly illustrates the main debate of the Enlightenment period, the context within which Kant develops his ideas.[10] Is it the power of reason itself, located in the subject, which is to be valued apart from any outcome it may have, or is the value of reason attributable to its foundation in absolute truth? The antinomy embodies the empiricist and rationalist positions and, specifically, conveys their attitudes towards beauty. The first commonplace reflects the reliance of beauty upon a principle given "*a posteriori* by means of the senses"[11] and the second alludes to its dependence upon an "*a priori* ground."[12] I will examine each commonplace in turn, setting the context of Kant's discussion of beauty.

9. Ibid., §56, 5:338, 214.

10. The Enlightenment is commonly thought of as the *Age of Reason*. In general terms this characterization indicates the shift of emphasis away from *deduction* towards *analysis*. The former, the method of deduction, stems from the Cartesianism of the seventeenth century where philosophical system is the norm and inference proceeds from first principles to sensible phenomenon. Herein, reason is bound to that which holds true eternally, frames the sensible world and thereby gives it meaning. Reason is a bridge between the divine and the human: the exercise of reason allows one to attend to matters of truth, participate in the divine, and thereby gain access to the intelligible realm. The latter, analytic method, patterns itself upon Newtonian methodology. This gained popularity in the eighteenth century: a priori principles no longer provided an adequate and unambiguous starting point for reason. Rather, experience and observation were its ground and reason was considered as a tool for analysis, rather than tied to an eternal given. Cf. Cassirer, *Philosophy of the Enlightenment*, 8; Gardner, *Kant and the Critique of Pure Reason*, 2–12; Anderson, *Europe in the Eighteenth Century*, 337–57.

11. Kant, *CJ*, §58, 5:346, 221.

12. Ibid.

"Everyone has his own taste"[13]

The first commonplace suggests that taste is subjective with no grounds for proof. This broadly reflects the empiricist position, which denies the possibility of knowledge through reason on the grounds that reason cannot operate without ideas, the acquisition of ideas being tendered only through the senses. Thus, it is only my experience that confirms anything for me. David Hume (1711–1776) is representative of the empiricist approach and Kant had acquaintance with some of his work, Hume awaking him from his "dogmatic slumber."[14] His essay *Of the Standard of Taste*[15] expounds the affirmation of the first commonplace, wherein knowledge is bound to the subjective conditions of the knower.

Hume anchors beauty in sentiment,[16] which itself is located in the relation of the object to the subject. It is thus subjective. Hume says: "no sentiment represents what is really in the object. It only marks a certain conformity or relation between object and the organs or faculties of the mind."[17] For this reason it is neither necessary nor binding. Sentiment cannot command the agreement of anyone else: "every individual ought to acquiesce in his own sentiment, without pretending to regulate those of others."[18]

13. Ibid., §33, 5:284–85, 164–66.

14. Kant says, "I freely admit it: it was David Hume's remark that first, many years ago, interrupted my dogmatic slumber and gave a completely different direction to my enquiries in the field of speculative philosophy" (*Prolegomena*, 9). This was with regard to the notion of causality: "The question was not whether the concept of cause is correct, useful, and in respect of all knowledge of nature indispensable, for this Hume had never held in doubt; but whether it is thought *a priori* by reason, and in this way has an inner truth independent of all experience, and hence also has a more widely extended usefulness, not limited merely to objects of experience" (ibid., 7–8. Cf. Gardner, *Kant and the Critique of Pure Reason*, 10). It is clear that Kant had almost certainly made acquaintance with Hume's *Enquiry Concerning Human Understanding* (1748) in the 1750's. Having said this, it is not clear that Kant had read *Of the Standard of Taste*. Cf. Pluhar, "Translator's Introduction," li.

15. Hume, "Of the Standard of Taste," 133–54.

16. The conflation of sentiment and beauty is suggested by the similarity of the way in which Hume talks about them. Just as sentiment does not represent anything about the object but is located in the relation of subject and object, so "Beauty is no quality in things themselves: it exists merely in the mind which contemplates them" (ibid., 136–37).

17. Ibid., 136.

18. Ibid., 137.

Although for Hume the subjective nature of taste precludes it from
universality it does admit of generalizations about both sentiment and
"catholic and universal beauty."[19] It does so through the cultivation of
taste in the subject and the observation of those objects which cause
pleasure and displeasure. To elucidate: for Hume the capacity for taste is
akin to a sensible organ. He says, "To seek the real beauty, or real defor-
mity, is as fruitless an enquiry, as to pretend to ascertain the real sweet
or real bitter. According to the disposition of the organs, the same object may be both sweet and bitter."[20] As a capacity, the conditions under
which it operates can be optimized, yielding a delicacy of taste. Hume
attributes delicacy to those organs of taste that are "so fine, as to allow
nothing to escape them; and at the same time so exact as to perceive
every ingredient in the composition."[21] Thus cultivation of taste depends
upon several things. First, a subject must attend to an object a number of times before making a judgment,[22] for only then can the subject
see past the "flutter or hurry of thought which attends the first perusal
of any piece, and which confounds the genuine sentiment of beauty."[23]
Second, a subject must compare different objects of taste[24] since it is only
through comparison that "we fix epithets of praise or blame, and learn
how to assign the due degree of each."[25] Third, the mind of the subject
must be "free from prejudice" so that nothing enters the consideration of
the subject save the object under examination.[26]

The cultivation of taste grounds generalizations about particular
objects and their capacity to evoke pleasure or displeasure. Hume concedes that there are "certain qualities in objects, which are fitted by nature" to produce the feeling of pleasure associated with taste,[27] and that

19. Ibid., 139.

20. Ibid., 137.

21. Ibid., 141.

22. Hume says: "before we can give judgment on any work of importance, it will
even be requisite, that that very individual performance be more than once perused by
us, and be surveyed in different lights with attention and deliberation" (ibid.).

23. Ibid., 144.

24. "It is impossible to continue in the practice of contemplating any order of beauty,
without being frequently obliged to form *comparisons* between the several species and
degrees of excellence, and estimating their proportion to each other" (ibid., 141).

25. Ibid., 144.

26. Ibid., 145.

27. In illustration of this Hume has recourse to a story in Don Quixote. Sancho
speaks of two of his kinsmen who were once called to give their opinion of a "hogshead"

these instances can be observed in order to produce "established models" and patterns. In this way he assumes some level of communicability but does not guarantee it: beauty is only ever latent within the relationship of subject and object, relying upon the optimization of conditions within the subject, on the one hand, and upon the existence of certain stimuli in the object, on the other. Hume summarizes: "Strong sense, united to delicate sentiment, improved by practice, perfected by comparison, and cleared of all prejudice, can alone entitle critics to this valuable character; and the joint verdict of such, wherever they are to be found, is the true standard of taste and beauty."[28]

In sum, for empiricism, beauty is not given a priori but emerges from experience, from within the partnership of subject and object. It is not a matter of judgment but of sentiment that arises in response to certain stimuli. Hume summarizes: "Some particular qualities, from the original structure of the internal fabric are calculated to please, and others to displease; and if they fail of their effect in any particular instance, it is from some apparent defect or imperfection in the organ."[29] Thus, beauty is not universal but general and therefore is only contingently communicable. Accordingly, in the case of music it pleases by means of its action upon the senses: beautiful music is music that pleases me.

"There is no disputing about taste" [30]

The second commonplace acknowledges the quasi-objectivity of taste and beauty and implies that there are grounds to command the assent of everyone. The rationalism to which Kant refers is an amalgamation of thought proceeding from Gottfried Wilhelm Leibniz (1646–1716)

---

which "was supposed to be excellent, being old and of a good vintage." One man tastes it and "pronounces the wine to be good, were it not for a small taste of leather which he perceived in it." The other man also favors the wine "but with the reserve of a taste of iron, which he could easily distinguish." They were both ridiculed for their judgment until, upon emptying the hogshead, "there was found at the bottom an old key with a leathern thong tied to it" (ibid.).

28. Ibid., 147. Hume notes two variations of taste which elude such a standard. The first is the "different humours of particular men" and the second are the "particular manners and opinions of our age and country." Hume says, "where there is such a diversity in the internal or external situation as is entirely blameless on both sides" then "a certain degree of diversity in judgment is unavoidable, and we seek in vain for a standard, by which we reconcile the contrary sentiments" (ibid., 149–50).

29. Ibid., 140.

30. Kant, *CJ*, §32, 5:281–83, 162–64.

and Christian Wolff (1679–1754),[31] by means of others, to Alexander
Gottlieb Baumgarten (1714–1762). Significantly, Leibniz formulates a
fundamentally intellectual understanding of beauty: taste is located in
sensory cognition and is understood as an imperfect form of intellectual
cognition.

In explanation: for Leibniz a "distinct" idea is an idea that is clear in
all its parts and in their combination. It can abstract from sensible detail,
receive definition, and, therefore, be explicitly distinguished from other
ideas. Leibniz writes: "such is the knowledge of the assayer who discerns
the true and false by particular tests or marks comprising the definition
of gold."[32] "Distinct" ideas are allied with intellectual cognition. "Clear"
ideas stand in contrast, and are connected with sensory cognition. A
"clear" idea is distinguishable from other ideas only in an in-definable
way: we cannot say what characteristics in particular distinguish it from
other ideas. Leibniz states:

> When I can recognize one thing among others without being able
> to say in what its *differentiae* or properties consist, my knowledge
> is *confused*. Thus it is that we sometimes know *clearly* without
> being in any doubt at all whether a poem or picture is well or
> badly made, because there is an I don't know what that satisfies
> or shocks us.[33]

In accordance with these two types of ideas, Leibniz proposes a
hierarchy in which different types of idea supply a distinct degree of
knowledge: the ideas proceeding from "adequate," "distinct," and "clear,"
to "confused" and "obscure." For Leibniz, confused knowledge is associated with sensory cognition, consisting of "minute perceptions" that
make up the "je ne sais quoi, those flavours, those images of sensible
qualities, vivid in the aggregate but confused as to the parts."[34] Thus, he
states, in order to hear "the roaring or noise of the sea which impresses
itself on us when we are standing on the shore" we must "hear the parts

31. Leibniz had an indirect influence on the Enlightenment. His main work on the
theory of knowledge was *New Essays on the Human Understanding*. This was not known
until 1765 when the evolution of the Enlightenment thought was all but complete. It was
through its transformation in the work of Wolff that it came to attention; the Leibniz-
Wolffian System was the staple for the first part of the eighteenth century in Germany.

32. Leibniz, "Discourse on Metaphysics," 24, 68. Cf. also Pluhar, "Translator's Introduction," xlviii.

33. Ibid.

34. Leibniz, *New Essays on Human Understanding*, Preface, 55.

which make up this whole." That is, we must hear "the noise of each wave, although each of these little noises makes itself known only when combined confusedly with all the others, and would not be noticed if the wave which made it were by itself."[35] The confusion of sensory cognition can achieve clarity but is not able to grasp "distinct" ideas, which belong to the realm of intellectual cognition.[36]

In short, for Leibniz, sense knowledge is not qualitatively different from clear intellectual knowledge. It is merely imperfect and can attain clarity only as confused and obscure. Thus, appreciation of beauty is the subconscious appreciation of the formal features that comprise a beautiful object. Notably in the case of music, therefore, Leibniz says: "Music charms us, although its beauty only consists in the harmonies of numbers and in the reckoning of the beats or vibrations of sounding bodies, which meet at certain intervals, reckonings of which we are not conscious and which the soul nevertheless does make. The pleasures which sight finds in proportions are of the same nature; and those caused by the other senses amount to almost the same thing, although we may not be able to explain it so distinctly."[37]

Baumgarten substantially develops the Leibnizian account of beauty.[38] He coins the term "aesthetics" and in doing so forms a parallel to intellectual knowledge within aesthetic experience. Herein, aesthetic experience is perceptual rather than conceptual and in its sensory perfection is called beautiful.[39] According to Baumgarten, there are two

35. Ibid., 54. Leibniz continues, "we must be affected slightly by the motion of this wave, and have some perception of each of these noises, however faint they may be; otherwise there would be no perception of a hundred thousand waves, since a hundred thousand nothings cannot make something" (ibid., 55).

36. Ibid., bk. II, "Of Ideas," ch. XXIX, §§2–16, 254–63.

37. Leibniz, "Principles of Nature and of Grace" (1714), §17, 306–7; quoted in Beardsley, *Aesthetics from Classical Greece to The Present*, 154.

38. Baumgarten, *Reflections on Poetry* (1735), and *Aesthetica* (1750–58); cf. Beardsley, *Aesthetics from Classical Greece to The Present*, 156.

39. Aesthetics is "the science of sensory cognition" (*scientia cognitionis sensitavae*). Baumgarten, *Aesthetica*, §1; cf. Bearsdley, *Aesthetics from Classical Greece to The Present*, 157. Aesthetics bridges the gap between the general and the particular: truth is not in opposition to concrete qualities but is realized in virtue of them. The degree of clarity in an idea is called "intensive clarity," and "extensive clarity" is when an idea contains more ideas within it, so long as they are clear (though confused). Baumgarten, *Aesthetica*, §16; cf. Beardsley, *Aesthetics from Classical Greece to The Present*, 159. In short, there is no conceptual reduction or concentration. Rather the artist encompasses both the centre and the periphery in one glance.

types of ideas. On the one hand, there are ideas that do not depend on sensibility, operate logically and can be distinct. On the other, there are ideas that do depend on sensibility, function demonstratively and cannot be distinct.[40] Although, like Leibniz, Baumgarten maintains the distinctiveness of sense and intellect he admits a discrete logic to the senses. Sensible phenomena yield confusion, but this confusion is understood as a richness of content and vividness of appearance.[41] It is necessary that sensible knowledge is indistinct and confused.[42] For only thus can its ideas be fused together, rather than explicitly distinguished, and sensible experience offered a perfection of its own.[43]

In sum, for the rationalists as a whole, beauty lies beyond the immediate pleasure of an object: it is grounded in formal rules and principles. It is thus that beauty is objective, universal, and therefore absolutely communicable both unconsciously by virtue of its form and consciously through the exercise of the mind. In the case of music in particular, beauty lies beyond the immediate pleasure that it induces: it is discernible in order and pattern, in rules and principles.[44]

SUMMARY OF THE ANTINOMY OF TASTE

The antinomy is crucial to the consideration of taste and, according to Kant, demands to be confronted. The empiricist position is encapsulated

40. Baumgarten, *Aesthetica*, §123; cf. Kemal, *Kant's Aesthetic Theory*, 16–19.

41. Baumgarten, *Aesthetica*, §§6, 19, 22.

42. On the role of confusion, see ibid., §§14, 15.

43. Vividness attaches best to particular representations rather than to abstract concepts and ideas: the latter are not determinable in every respect and cannot sustain any great vividness. Ibid., §19; Kemal, *Kant's Aesthetic Theory*, 18; cf. also Cassirer, *Philosophy of the Enlightenment*, 341.

44. The rationalist approach lies also behind the doctrine of *affections* in music, wherein a discernible congruence of tonal and emotional patterns is maintained and music has the capacity to portray emotions. As we shall see later, Kant offers an understanding of music based on the theory of affect. Bowman, *Philosophical Perspectives on Music*, 73; Beardsley, *Aesthetics from Classical Greece to The Present*, 155. An example of "Affect Theory" (*Affectenlehre*) is to be found in Mattheson, *Der vollkommene Capellmeister* (1739); it also grounds the harmonic theory of Jean-Philippe Rameau, who maintains the lawful derivation of chords from the harmonic series and sets out rules for common-practice harmonic progression. Rameau also maintains that music's patterns of consonance and dissonance, stability and instability, derive from innate propensities shared by all human minds. Bowman, *Philosophical Perspectives on Music*, 73; cf. also Beardsley, *Aesthetics from Classical Greece to The Present*, 156.

by the first commonplace: it eliminates the distinction between the object of our delight and what Kant shall call the "agreeable" (*das Angenehme*), regarding beauty as primarily sensory. The rationalist position is contained within the second commonplace: it obliterates the object's distinction from what Kant calls the "good" (*das Gute*), understanding beauty as fundamentally intellectual. Kant maintains that both positions deny the place of beauty in the world and reduce it to a "special name, perhaps for a certain mixture of the two previously mentioned kinds of satisfaction."[45] Thus, if one accepts one or other premise either one is forced to "deny that any *a priori* principle lies at the basis of the aesthetic judgement of taste" or is given to suppose that the judgment of taste "is in fact a disguised judgment of reason on the perfection discovered in a thing and the reference of the manifold in it to an end." According to the first, "all claim to the necessity of a universal consensus of opinion is an ideal and empty delusion" and a judgment of taste is correct only to the extent "that *it so happens* that a number share the same opinion." According to the second, a judgment of taste is only called aesthetic "on account of the confusion that here besets our reflection, although fundamentally it is teleological."[46] For Kant both conclusions are unacceptable. It is therefore on the basis of the antinomy that Kant constructs his own distinctive understanding of beauty.

---

45. Kant, *CJ*, §58, 5:346–47, 221.

46. Ibid., Remark 2, 5:346, 220. The "teleology" of something is its "end." We will see this explicitly when we discuss logical judgment.

5

The Play of Harmony—
The Subjective Powers in Relation

An Examination of the Critique of Judgment

AIM AND STRUCTURE OF THE THIRD CRITIQUE

GIVEN THE IMPORTANCE OF the antinomy to the question of beauty in particular and knowledge more generally, its central position within Kant's account is no surprise. The antinomy supplies the general terms of the discussion. The rationalist-empiricist debate about the nature of taste is conducted in terms of beauty. As we have seen, for the rationalist beauty is a recognizable property whilst for the empiricist it is the subjective capacity for appreciation of an object partnered with certain stimuli within the object itself. Kant takes the notion of beauty up as part of the *lingua franca*. Moreover, the positions of the antinomy furnish Kant's examination with a structure: the commonplaces provide a backdrop against which Kant articulates his own understanding of beauty, responding to the issues that they raise. Thus, Kant formulates a response to the commonplaces of taste, the empiricist and rationalist positions and to their implicit concern with universality, necessity, and communicability. In the third *Critique* Kant asks whether beauty is a feeling located within the subject or a quality possessed by an object. In doing so, he explores the tension that lies between taste (understood as the individual experience of an object) and beauty (understood as an a priori concept to which an object corresponds). Finally, in line with rationalism and empiricism, Kant uses beauty as the distinguishing characteristic of what he calls pure aesthetic judgment. However, he does so in a distinct way since he uses the conception of beauty to clarify aspects of the process of aesthetic judgment, thereby contrasting it with other types of judgment.

Beauty describes pure aesthetic judgment and key instants within its process. This is implicitly evident in the *Analytic of the Beautiful*, which identifies four "moments" that attend pure aesthetic judgment and uses beauty to refer to the object of these moments.[1] It is explicitly apparent in the *Deduction of the Beautiful*, which clarifies and develops the *Analytic*. Herein, beauty refers to "disinterested pleasure" and the "expression of aesthetic ideas," definitions that describe the "harmony" (*Harmonie*) of the free play of the cognitive powers upon which pure aesthetic judgment is based. Disinterested pleasure refers to the satisfaction that accompanies the harmony of the free play, and the expression of aesthetic ideas signals the exhibition of the supersensible substrate of humanity which is thereby manifested.[2]

The Analytic of the Beautiful

The *Analytic* identifies four "moments" of a judgment of taste[3] and derives four definitions of the beautiful from them. All judgments of taste consider the "quality," "quantity," "relation," and "modality" of an object: it is only thus that one can call an object beautiful. The "quality" of a judgment refers to the ways in which a predicate may be predicated of a subject;[4] the "quantity" of a judgment is determined by whether a predicate may be predicated of a subject;[5] the "relation" involves the manner in which predicates may be related to a subject;[6] "modality" specifies the

---

1. Henry Allison states: "In spite of its title, the Analytic of the Beautiful is concerned not with the nature of beauty *per se*, but rather with the *judgement* through which the beauty (or lack thereof) of a particular object of nature or art is appraised" (*Kant's Theory of Taste*, 68).

2. As mentioned earlier, the supersensible substrate belongs to the noumenal realm, underpinning all experience.

3. In doing so Kant adopts the strategy used in the *CPR*: "In seeking the moments to which this power of judgment attends in its reflection, I have been guided by the logical functions for judging (for a relation to the understanding is always contained even in the judgment of taste)" (*CJ*, §1, 5:203 n. 1, 89). The relation of the judgment of taste to the understanding of which Kant speaks will become apparent further on in our examination of his account and will prove to be quite significant.

4. Ibid., §§1–5, 5:204–11, 89–96.

5. Ibid., §§6–9, 5:211–19, 96–104.

6. Ibid., §§10–17, 5:219–36, 105–20.

relation of the judgment to the conditions of thought in general.[7] The characteristics of beauty follow from these. Beauty is the object of "disinterested satisfaction;"[8] it is "universal" (but not by means of a concept);[9] it is "purposive" and yet without purpose;[10] and it is "necessary."[11]

It will become apparent in the *Deduction*, of which the definitions form the skeleton, that the four definitions of beauty are clarified by pairing the first with the third and the second with the fourth. The first pairing highlights the dependence of the disinterested nature of beauty upon its purposeless purposiveness, since a particular end of an object does not stimulate the satisfaction of beauty. The second pairing indicates the interconnectedness of the universal nature of beauty and the necessity of its satisfaction.[12] This will become clear as we proceed, especially when we come to deal with "common sense" (*sensus communis*).

The Deduction of the Beautiful

The definitions of beauty in the *Analytic* implicitly distinguish the Kantian understanding of beauty from both empiricism and rationalism. This differentiation is also evident in the method of the *Deduction*

---

7. Ibid., §§18–22, 5:236–44, 121–27.

8. "*Taste* is the faculty for judging an object or a kind of representation through a satisfaction or dissatisfaction *without any interest*. The object of such a satisfaction is called *beautiful*" (ibid., §5, 5:211, 96).

9. "That is *beautiful* which pleases universally without a concept" (ibid., §9, 5:219, 104).

10. "*Beauty* is the form of the *purposiveness* of an object, insofar as it is perceived in it *without a representation of an end*" (ibid., §17, 5:236, 120).

11. "That is *beautiful* which is cognized without a concept as the object of a *necessary* satisfaction" (ibid., §22, 5:240, 124).

12. The standard reading of the four moments, initially propounded by Paul Guyer, is that the second and fourth, and the first and third moments "constitute two functionally distinct groups of criteria" (Guyer, *Kant and the Claims of Taste*, 123; cf. Allison, *Kant's Theory of Taste*, 79). Thus, universality and necessity are analytic criteria for distinguishing a judgment of taste from a merely first-person report of a response to an object, and disinterestedness and purposiveness, referring to the 'form of finality,' are the "justificatory criteria" stating the "facts" on the basis of which the claim of universality and necessity is supposedly made. Hence, Guyer denies that the second and fourth moments impose distinct conditions on the judgment and claims therefore that there is really only a single analytic criterion which may be expressed in terms of either universality or necessity. Guyer, *Kant and the Claims of Taste*, 160–64. In contrast, Allison disagrees with the non-inference of universality from disinterestedness. *Kant's Theory of Taste*, ch. 5.

of the Beautiful,[13] which proceeds by means of a "logic of negation."[14] Here, beauty is defined in terms of what it is *not*. Thus, taste, which Kant defines as "the faculty for the judging of the beautiful,"[15] is placed in contrast to logical judgment and sensation. Kant argues that aesthetic judgment is distinct from both sensation, which acts upon us and is merely agreeable, and logical judgment, which subsumes a particular object under either a concept or a purpose or end. Beauty stands between the absolute subjectivity of sensation, the determinate objectivity of logical judgment, and the so-called "interest" of both. Kant thus steers a course between the first and second commonplace (and empiricism and rationalism) by means of a unique understanding of beauty which acts as a third conciliatory possibility.

THE SEARCH FOR AN A PRIORI AND INDETERMINATE "PRINCIPLE OF TASTE"

The antinomy of taste appears twice in the *Critique of Judgment*,[16] in both instances illustrating the two "logical peculiarities" of taste that I have outlined: its "universality" (*Allgemeinheit*) and "necessity" (*Notwendigkeit*).[17] In order to resolve it Kant calls for a principle that is both a priori and indeterminate. Only thus can he maneuver his argument between empiricism and rationalism, assuage their incongruity, and construct an understanding of pure aesthetic judgment and thence beauty.

Interestingly, as we shall see, Kant offers an apparently distinct solution each time the antinomy appears. We will look at each in turn. Before we begin, however, it is important to stress the task at hand, which is to evaluate the function of Kant's conception of beauty. We must ask whether or not there is something intrinsic to beauty that enables it to mediate between the paradoxical commonplaces of taste and the two Enlightenment positions. It will become apparent that beauty functions to describe central aspects of the principle of taste rather than contribut-

13. The deduction is a "guarantee of the legitimacy" of the necessity of judgments of taste. Kant, *CJ*, §31, 5:280, 161.

14. This term is from Crowther, "Significance of Kant's Pure Aesthetic Judgment," 112.

15. Kant, *CJ*, §1, 5:203 n.1, 89.

16. The first appears in ibid., §§32, 33, 5:281–85, 162–66; the second in §56, 5:338–39, 214–15.

17. Ibid., §31, 5:281, 162.

ing anything inherently unique *qua* beauty. Thus, it is more superficial than essential to Kant's account of taste. This will prove vital to our reflection upon Kant's account of the arts in general and music in particular.

The First Solution: The Harmony of the Free Play

Crucial to Kant's first solution is the idea of a "common sense" (*Gemeinsinn*) or *sensus communis* underpinning all aesthetic judgment.[18] This is, as Henry Allison notes, "literally a sense for what is common or shared" and is distinguished from the everyday understanding of common sense by which Kant means the common or ordinary human understanding (*Gemeinen Menschenverstand*).[19] It first appears in the fourth moment of the *Analytic of the Beautiful* where it is introduced to support the necessity alleged by a judgment of taste:[20] "One solicits assent from everyone else because one has a ground for it that is common to all."[21] This common ground rests upon "a subjective principle, which determines what pleases or displeases only through feeling and not through concepts, but yet with universal validity."[22] The notion of a common sense is articulated again in the solution to the first antinomy, this time referring to the ability to think beyond individual judgment, holding it up against the judgment of "human reason as a whole."[23] Once again this supposes

18. I suggest that Kant holds two conceptions of common sense. This is in line with Donald Crawford's reading of Kant, identifying common sense first, as a "universally communicable mental state or feeling," and second, as "a principle underlying the faculty of judgment; it is a principle we all have in common, or must have in common, for there to be objective knowledge or judgments at all" (Crawford, *Kant's Aesthetic Theory*, 128–29). This is in contrast to Guyer, who identifies three: for Kant "common sense seems to be a shared feeling of pleasure; the faculty for judging that such a feeling is shared; the principle on which the exercise of this faculty rests." These are placed respectively in §20; §20, para. 2; §40. *Kant and the Claims of Taste*, 281.

19. Allison, *Kant's Theory of Taste*, 84. Kant notes, "One could designate taste as *sensus communis aestheticus*, common human understanding as *sensus communis logicus*" (*CJ*, §40, 5:295, 175). The latter, *sensus communis logicus*, "judges not by feeling but always by concepts, although commonly only in the form of obscurely represented principles" (ibid., §20, 5:238, 122).

20. Ibid.

21. Ibid., §19, 5:237, 121–22.

22. Ibid., §20, 5:237–38, 122.

23. Ibid., §40, 5:293–94, 173–74. As a digression to the critique of taste, but as an elucidation of the "fundamental principles" of the common human understanding, Kant offers three maxims: "1) To think for oneself; 2) To think in the position of everyone else; 3) Always to think in accord with oneself." The first is the maxim of the "*unprejudiced*

a common basis, a subjective principle that is common to all, by means of which the individual subject can presume to hold up its judgment to the possible judgment of others. Kant says that the fact that we venture to make judgments of taste proves that we presuppose an "indeterminate norm of a common sense."[24]

COGNITION AND COMMUNICABILITY

To begin to uncover the meaning of what Kant calls "common sense," the subjective principle upon which the universality and necessity of taste depends, we must appreciate the implicit importance of communicability (*Mitteilung*).

For Kant, universal communicability is a pre-requisite of all cognition and judgment. Kant asserts that "Cognition and judgments must, together with the conviction that accompanies them, be able to be universally communicated, for otherwise they would have no correspondence with the object: they would all be a merely subjective play of the powers of representation, just as skepticism insists."[25] More importantly for Kant's account, hinted at in the "fourth moment" which suggests that aesthetic judgment operates with feeling rather than concepts, is the idea that just as cognitions are universally communicable so are the mental states that accompany them, and the proportion that makes cognition out of a given representation of an object.[26] Kant says:

> Now since the disposition itself must be capable of being universally communicated, hence also the feeling of it (in the case of a

---

way of thinking"; the second the maxim of the "*broad-minded* way"; and the third the maxim of the "*consistent* way." Ibid., §40, 5:294, 174. These maxims are reminiscent of the guidelines that Hume sets out for the cultivation of taste.

24. Ibid., §22, 5:239, 124. However, Kant states that it is unclear whether the common sense, taste, is "an original and natural ability" (Kant calls this a "constitutive" principle) or "only a demand of reason to produce such agreement in the way we sense" (Kant calls this a "regulative" principle). Thus, his sole aim is to "resolve the faculty of taste into its elements and to unite them ultimately in the idea of a common sense" (ibid., §22, 5:240, 124).

25. Ibid., §21, 5:238, 122.

26. Ibid., §21, 5:238, 123. Kant suggests that the disposition of the cognitive powers has a different *proportion* "depending on the difference of the objects that are given." A good summary of the problematic nature of proportion is given by Guyer who concludes that by "proportion" Kant refers not to "some mathematically expressible function" but rather to a "psychological variation in the ease with which the unity of a given multiplicity may be detected" (Guyer, *Kant and the Claims of Taste*, 284–97).

given representation), but since the universal communicability
of a feeling presupposes a common sense, the latter must be able
to be assumed with good reason, and indeed without appeal to
psychological observations, but rather as the necessary condition
of the universal communicability of our cognition.[27]

Significantly, this places logical judgment which (as we shall see)
embodies the rationalist position, and aesthetic judgment, for which Kant
is making his case, on a continuum. They are both powers of judgment,
which Kant defines as "the faculty for thinking of the particular as contained under the universal."[28] They therefore rely upon the three faculties of the soul, intuition (*Anschauung*), imagination (*Einbildungskraft*),
and understanding (*Verstand*),[29] which Kant identifies as the condition
of the possibility of all experience.[30] This sharing of powers undoubtedly
contributes to the notion of common sense, for they underlie the capacity for cognition shared by humankind and thereby provide a basis for
the comparison of judgments. Importantly, however, the "disposition"
(*Stimmung*) of the cognitive powers and the satisfaction that results, differs within logical and aesthetic judgment. Therefore, this commonality
alone (the universal possession of the three faculties of the soul) cannot
serve as the foundation of aesthetic judgment. Rather, there must be a
principle underlying the uniqueness of aesthetic judgment, encapsulated
by the notion of beauty.

To pursue this end, the elucidation of the notion of common sense,
I will follow Kant in contrasting his own position with that of empiricism
and rationalism, beginning with an explanation of logical judgment, the
disposition of the cognitive powers that occurs therein, and the type of
feeling or satisfaction that results. I will then proceed to the division
within aesthetic judgment between those judgments that are "pure" and
those that are "empirical." This latter juxtaposition will highlight what

27. Kant, *CJ*, §21, 5:329, 123.

28. Ibid., Published Introduction, IV, 5:179, 66.

29. Kant calls these "sense," "imagination" and "apperception." *CPR*, B 127, 127.

30. Intuition, imagination, and understanding comprise "three subjective sources
of knowledge which make possible the understanding itself – and consequently all
experience as empirical product." (*CPR*, A 97–98, 131). Upon these are grounded "the
synopsis of the manifold a priori through sense" (ibid., B 127, 127, cf. A 98–100, 131–32
for details); "the synthesis of this manifold through imagination" (ibid., B 127, 127, cf.
A100–104, 132–34 for details); and "the unity of this synthesis through original apperception" (ibid., B 127, 127, cf. A104–10, 134–38 for details). Cf. *CJ*, §9, 5:217, 102.

might be called the negative end of the continuum for, in contrast to logical judgment and pure aesthetic judgment, empirical aesthetic judgment is mere sensation. It involves entirely personal satisfaction and does not participate in cognition.

LOGICAL JUDGMENT

Logical judgment is associated with the second commonplace of taste and the rationalist position. Kant defines it as a determining power of judgment wherein "the universal" (*das Allgemeine*, the rule, the principle, the law) is given[31] and intuition is subsumed under the understanding by means of the imagination. In this way, the concepts of the understanding correspond to sensible intuitions and determine them by their predicates.[32] To explain, Kant understands the imagination as a power that intuits even when the object is not present. Within logical judgment, the imagination acts reproductively: it "recalls to mind a previous empirical perception."[33] Herein, with the guidance of the understanding, the imagination places a "preceding perception" alongside a "subsequent perception to which it has passed" and thereby forms a "whole series of perceptions."[34] Thus, the imagination brings "the manifold of intuition into the form of an image."[35] Thus, for example, "our application of the concept [dog] will be informed by expectations based on associations

31. Ibid., Published Introduction, IV, 5:179, 67.

32. Ibid., §57, 5:339, 215; cf. also §41, 5:295–96, 175.

33. Kant, *Anthropology*, §28, 56. Cf. also the *CPR*, B 151–52, 164–65. Crowther explains this well: "The particular act of judgment [logical judgment] involves the subsumption or discrimination of sensible particulars under a concept or concepts. This itself is only possible through the exercise of our imagination's powers of attention, recall, and projection. The generation of images enables us to relate an item to past, present, and possible appearances. It is the basis of a unified temporal horizon which, in tandem with the understanding's application of concepts, stabilizes the manifold, and enables the item to be identified as such and such a thing" ("Significance of Kant's Pure Aesthetic Judgment," 112). Crowther states that imagination, "in its normal highly specific employments," is "tightly directed by a relevant concept and functions in a 'reproductive way.'"

34. Without the faculty of concepts, "this apprehension of the manifold would not by itself produce an image and a connection of the impressions" (Kant, *CPR*, A 121, 144).

35. Ibid., A 120, 144.

between the present creature and our previous experience of dog-type appearances and behaviour."[36]

As the role of the imagination indicates, within logical judgment communication occurs by means of concepts. This is exemplified in the form of attention given to an object within logical judgment. Kant asserts, "In order to find something good, I must always know what sort of thing the object is supposed to be, i.e., I must have a concept of it."[37] Within logical judgment, the concept stands as the "end" (*Zweck*) of logical judgment. It acts as its "cause"[38] and gives an object "purposiveness" (*Zweckmäßigkeit*). It is thus that an object is considered "good." In Kantian terms, objects of logical judgment are objectively purposive. They are judgments of the form "the concept of y is purposive for y" or "the concept of y is one of the causes of y." In this way, the concept forms "part of the real grounds of its possibility."[39] Kant states: "Objective purposiveness can be cognised only by means of the relation of the manifold to a determinate end, thus only through a concept."[40]

There are two ways in which this is so: the end upon which an object is dependent is either internal or external. It is internal when an object is good in itself: the object fulfils a set of conditions laid down by a concept and thus *is* what it is. Herein, as "the ground of the possibility of the object itself" the concept determines its perfection either qualitatively or quantitatively.[41] The qualitative perfection is "the agreement of the manifold in the thing with the concept (which supplies the rule for the combination of the manifold in it)."[42] Distinct from this, quantitative perfection occurs when what a thing is supposed to be is already determined and all that is asked is "whether *everything* that is requisite for it exists."[43] In practical terms, in the case of a dog, its qualitative perfection compares all instances of dogs, abstracting from the

36. Crowther, "Significance of Kant's Pure Aesthetic Judgment," 112–13.

37. Kant, *CJ*, §4, 5:207, 93. "That is good which pleases by means of reason alone, through the mere concept" (ibid., §4, 5:207, 92).

38. Burnham, *Introduction to Kant's Critique of Judgement*, 62.

39. Fricke, "Explaining the Inexplicable," 48. Fricke gives the following example: "A hammer is, for example, a suitable means for banging a nail into a wall—and that means: it is purposive with respect to the purpose of banging a nail into a wall" (ibid., 47).

40. Kant, *CJ*, §15, 5:226, 111.

41. Ibid., §15, 5:227, 112.

42. Ibid.

43. Ibid.

manifold and arriving at the concept of dog. Its quantitative perfection measures a particular dog against the already abstracted concept of dog, determining whether it is to be so-called. The end of an object is external when an object is good for something. In this instance, a dog might be viewed in terms of the companionship it offers to its owner. In both cases of objective purposiveness, internal and external, Kant is clear that the good "pleases by means of reason alone, through the mere concept."[44] In the case of internal purposiveness an object is "immediately good" and in the case of external purposiveness an object is "mediately good."[45]

In sum, the disposition involved in logical judgment is determinative and its universality is achieved by the fulfillment of criteria laid down by an end. It is this objective purposiveness that commands necessity and permits communication, since it can be corroborated. As a result, the feeling involved in logical judgment derives from the fulfillment of an objective end. Logical judgment results in an interested satisfaction for "I am satisfied to the extent that an object *is* or *does* something."

EMPIRICAL AND PURE AESTHETIC JUDGMENT

Despite their fundamental kinship as modes of cognition, the disposition of the cognitive powers in aesthetic judgment differs from that in logical judgment, as does the feeling which results. However, before drawing this out, it is useful to explore the contrast between "pure" and "empirical" aesthetic judgment. The juxtaposition will highlight the central aspect of pure judgments of taste and will take us nearer to an understanding of the subjective principle, the common sense, which lies at its core.

"Empirical" judgments "are those which assert agreeableness or disagreeableness."[46] They underpin the first commonplace (reflecting the empiricist position) and by virtue of being anchored in sensation are another form of interested satisfaction. In explanation: empirical aesthetic judgments are judgments of sense.[47] They are grounded in an interested pleasure that derives from the existence of an object in so far as it relates to me, the subject. Kant maintains: an empirical judgment of taste "excites a desire for objects of the same sort, hence the satisfaction presupposes not the mere judgement about it but the relation of its

44. Ibid., §4, 5:207, 92.
45. Ibid., §4, 5:207–8, 93.
46. Ibid., §14, 5:223, 108.
47. Ibid.

existence to my state as it is affected by such an object."[48] Thus, empirical
aesthetic judgment refers to the action of sensation upon us and our
passive reception of it. It is "agreeable" and simply "gratifies." It is subjective and only ever personal.[49] Kant states, "It is not mere approval that I
give it, rather inclination is thereby aroused; and any judgement about
the constitution of the object belongs so little to that which is agreeable
in the liveliest way that those who are always intent only on enjoyment
(for this is the word that signifies intensity of gratification) gladly put
themselves above all judging."[50]

Empirical aesthetic judgment is connected solely with feeling and
cannot be universal: it does not involve communication. It is for this
reason that empirical aesthetic judgment is distinguished from pure aesthetic judgment and the agreeable differentiated from the beautiful. For
Kant, the taste involved in the agreeable is a "taste of the senses"[51] since
the subject feels and acts upon an object but not in any thoughtful way.
By contrast, the taste involved in the beautiful is a "taste of *reflection*."[52]
It is for this reason that only pure aesthetic judgments stand as "proper
judgements of taste."[53] Kant exemplifies the difference: if a man says
"sparkling wine from the Canaries is agreeable" he is quite content that
someone corrects and reminds him that he should say instead "It is
agreeable *to me*."[54] By contrast, "It would be ridiculous if (the precise
converse) someone who prided himself on his taste thought to justify
himself: 'This object (the building we are looking at, the clothing some-

48. Ibid., §3, 5:207, 92.

49. "With regard to the agreeable, everyone is content that his judgment, which he
grounds on a private feeling, and in which he says of an object that it pleases him, be
restricted to his own person" (ibid., §7, 5:212, 97).

50. Ibid., §3, 5:207, 92.

51. Ibid., §8, 5:214, 99.

52. Ibid. My italics.

53. Ibid., §14, 5:223, 108. "Taste" is an appropriate term to apply to pure aesthetic
judgment in virtue of its private nature: "For someone may list all the ingredients of a
dish for me, and moreover even rightly praise the healthiness of this food; yet I am deaf
to all these grounds, I try the dish with *my* tongue and palate, and on that basis (not on
the basis of general principles) do I make my judgment" (ibid., §33, 5:285, 165).

54. Ibid., §7, 5:212, 97. "To say, 'This flower is beautiful' is the same as merely to
repeat its own claim to everyone's satisfaction. On account of the agreeableness of its
smell it has no claims at all. For one person is enraptured by this smell, while another's
head is dizzied by it" (ibid., §32, 5:281–82, 162).

one is wearing, the poem that is presented for judging) is beautiful *for me*.' For he must not call it *beautiful* if it pleases merely him."[55]

Thus, although Kant concedes that the agreeable gives rise to a measure of agreement and thus universality, he notes that its universality is only comparative and its rules only general. He maintains, "one says of someone who knows how to entertain his guests with agreeable things (of enjoyment through all the senses), so that they are all pleased, that he has taste."[56] For communicability of sensation is not universal: "to someone who lacks the sense of smell, this kind of sensation cannot be communicated; and, even if he does not lack this sense, one still cannot be sure that he has exactly the same sensation from a flower that we have from it."[57] By contrast, the feeling arising from the reflective interaction of the cognitive powers permits of universal communication: "In all judgements by which we declare something to be beautiful, we allow no one to be of a different opinion, without, however, grounding our judgement on concepts, but only in our feeling, which we therefore make our ground not as a private feeling, but as a common one."[58] This common feeling "must necessarily rest on the same conditions in everyone, since they are subjective conditions of the possibility of a cognition in general, and the proportion of these cognitive faculties that is required for taste is also requisite for the common and healthy understanding that one may presuppose in everyone."[59]

PURE AESTHETIC JUDGMENT AND REFLECTION

In reflection we arrive at a key notion, for it is this that gives pure aesthetic judgment its distinctive character. In order to understand it more clearly it is helpful to call upon the contrast between pure aesthetic judgment and logical judgment. As illustrated earlier, logical judgment involves the determinative interplay of the cognitive powers, wherein assent is commanded by means of determinate concepts and the law-bound interaction of imagination and understanding. This requires the reproductive action of the imagination. Pure aesthetic judgment stands in contrast:

55. Ibid., §7, 5:212, 98.

56. Ibid., §7, 5:213, 98.

57. Ibid., §39, 5:291, 171.

58. Ibid., §22, 5:239, 123.

59. Ibid., §39, 5:292–93, 173; cf. First Introduction, VIII, 20:222–23, 25; 20:224–25, 27; and Published Introduction, VII, 20:189–90, 75–76.

the cognitive powers interact reflectively and agreement arises from the feeling of pleasure that results from the "harmony" of the free play.[60] This involves the productive action of the imagination.[61]

In explanation, the absence of determinate concepts from pure aesthetic judgment unbinds the imagination so that intuition is no longer subsumed under concept. Rather, the "*faculty* of intuitions or presentations" (the imagination) is subsumed under the "*faculty* of concepts" (the understanding).[62] This generates a "free play" wherein the imagination *in its freedom* harmonizes with the understanding *in its lawfulness*.[63] This free play is pleasurable and gives pure aesthetic judgment its purposiveness. Kant states:

> since the freedom of the imagination consists precisely in the fact that it schematises without a concept, the judgement of taste must rest upon a mere sensation of the reciprocally animating imagination in its *freedom* and the understanding with its *lawfulness*, thus on a feeling that allows the object to be judged in accordance with the purposiveness of the representation (by means of which an object is given) for the promotion of the faculty of cognition in its free play.[64]

The feeling of pleasure arises from reflection and as a result operates uniquely within pure aesthetic judgment, enacting a form of causality, "namely that of maintaining the state of the representation of the mind and the occupation of the cognitive powers without a further aim."[65] It is for this reason that it is paralleled to a "predicate." Kant writes: "What is strange and anomalous is only this: that it is not an empirical concept but rather a feeling of pleasure (consequently not a concept at all) which, through the judgement of taste, is nevertheless to be expected of every-

60. Kant states, "With regard to the good, to be sure, judgments also rightly lay claim to validity for everyone; but the good is represented as an object of universal satisfaction only *through a concept*, which is not the case either with the agreeable or with the beautiful" (ibid., §7, 5:213, 98).

61. See also Kant, *CPR*, A 118, 142–43.

62. Kant, *CJ*, §35, 287, 167–68.

63. Ibid., §35, 5:287, 168.

64. Ibid., §35, 5:287, 167.

65. Ibid., §12, 5:222, 107. Kant confirms, "it is merely for the sake of perceiving the suitability of the representation for the harmonious (subjectively purposive) occupation of both cognitive faculties in their freedom, i.e., to sense the representational state with pleasure" (ibid., §39, 5:292, 172).

one and connected with its representation, just as if it were a predicate associated with the cognition of a concept."[66]

In short, the only difference between logical and pure aesthetic judgment is that within the former the imagination acts "for the sake of an empirical objective concept" whereas in the latter it operates "for the sake of perceiving the suitability of the representation for the harmonious (subjectively purposive) occupation of both cognitive faculties in their freedom, i.e., to sense the representational state with pleasure."[67] Pure aesthetic judgment is subjectively anchored. Kant affirms this: "The judgement of taste is therefore not a logical one, but is rather aesthetic, by which is understood one whose determining ground *cannot* be *other than subjective*."[68]

At this point it is worth noting Allison's exposition of the distinction between the harmony of the faculties and their free play—free play referring to the relation between imagination and understanding in the act of mere reflection and harmony indicating the pleasurable state that potentially manifests itself there. Allison refers to Kant's *Anthropology* to illustrate.[69] Kant claims that to judge an object by taste is to judge whether freedom in the play of the imagination harmonizes or clashes with the lawfulness of the understanding[70] and, as a result, states that free play can happen with or without harmony. Thus, for Allison it is clear: reflection either succeeds or fails to produce a harmonious relation of the faculties. If harmony is attained, the mental state is pleasurable and the object is deemed beautiful. If a state of disharmony arises, wherein "the faculties hinder rather than help one another in their reciprocal tasks thereby producing a mental state of disinterested displeasure and a negative judgement of taste," then the object is not beautiful.[71]

66. Ibid., Published Introduction, VII, 5:191, 77; cf. also §36, 5:288, 168; §37, 5:289, 169.

67. Ibid., §39, 5:292, 172.

68. Ibid., §1, 5:203, 89.

69. Allison, *Kant's Theory of Taste*, 117.

70. Kant, *CJ*, §35, 5:287, 167–68; *Anthropology*, §67, 143. "The judging of an object through taste is a judgement about the harmony or discord concerning the freedom of play between imagination and the law-abiding character of the understanding" (ibid., §7, 241).

71. Allison, *Kant's Theory of Taste*, 116–17. Hannah Ginsborg notes of *CJ*, §9, 5:217, 102–3 (which Kant says is the "key" to the *CJ* and wherein he notes that pleasure cannot *precede* the judgment) that some concede the involvement of two distinct acts of

Allison substantiates this further, noting that just as there can be a free play without harmony there can also be harmony without free play. This occurs in ordinary cognitive judgment, especially so in judgments of perfection where the determinate concept of an object is involved. The judgment involves pleasure but not the pleasure of taste, for judgments of taste involve the unbound activity of the imagination. This distinction is upheld in the *General Remark* that appends the *Analytic of the Beautiful*. Here it is clear that of the objective and subjective harmony of the faculties only the latter is considered to be a "free harmony."[72]

PURE AESTHETIC JUDGMENT AND DISINTERESTED PLEASURE[73]

To clarify the importance of reflection: pure aesthetic judgment is not determined through concepts but is produced by and is discernible in "the feeling (of inner sense) of that unison in the play of the powers of the mind, insofar as they can only be sensed."[74] Kant is clear, in order to decide whether or not something is beautiful one does not relate the representation by means of understanding to the object for cognition. Rather, one relates it by means of the imagination to the subject and its feeling of pleasure or displeasure. In this way, the subject dwells reflectively upon an object.

---

judging. Herein an object gives rise to an initial feeling of pleasure which, through claiming the universal validity of this pleasure, issues in the judgment of taste proper. Crawford, *Kant's Aesthetic Theory*, 69–74; Guyer, *Kant and the Claims of Taste*, 110–16, 151–60. Ginsborg maintains that Kant rules out this interpretation, summarizing: "The formal and self referential judgment that one's present state of mind is universally valid, precedes the feeling of pleasure in the sense of explaining or accounting for it." She continues, "The pleasure, as Kant puts it, is 'consequent' on the universal validity of my mental state in the sense that it is the consciousness or awareness of my mental state as universally valid" (Ginsborg, "Reflective Judgement and Taste," 73). Pippin supports Ginsborg when he notes that aesthetic pleasure has its foundation in a "sense" of the "general significance" of the aesthetic activity. "Significance of Taste," 562.

72. Kant, *CJ*, §22, 5:240–41, 124–25; Allison, *Kant's Theory of Taste*, 117; cf. also the General Comment attached to the *Analytic of Beautiful*: Kant states that everything manifesting a stiff, almost mathematical regularity runs counter to taste and has the effect of boring us. *CJ*, §5, 5:243, 126.

73. It is important to note that the quality of disinterest relied upon by Kant in the third *Critique* is anticipated by some theorists, for example Shaftesbury and Hutcheson. Cf. Townsend, "From Shaftesbury to Kant," 205–23. However, the view that a judgment or experience of beauty is disinterested was not the prevailing opinion of aestheticians. See Guyer, *Kant and the Experience of Freedom*, 48–93; Allison, *Kant's Theory of Taste*, 85.

74. Kant, *CJ*, §15, 5:228, 113.

The interest involved in pure aesthetic judgment is evoked by an attention to the object *qua* "presentation" (*Vorstellung*) and not qua object. It is concerned only with the form of purposiveness. It is on these grounds that pure aesthetic judgment attends to the singularity of a presentation of an object. They "combine their predicate of satisfaction not with a concept but with a given singular empirical representation."[75] To stress this, Kant contrasts the claim of logical judgment that "all tulips are beautiful" with that of pure aesthetic judgment wherein the claim is to the beauty of a "single given tulip." In the first instance, the satisfaction elicited by a single tulip is placed alongside judgments about other tulips and a predication is thereby made of tulips in general.[76] In the second instance, the pleasure obtained from a single tulip is considered as a single instance.

It is exactly the point of importance that although confined to the beauty of a single tulip, pure aesthetic judgment still commands universal validity. It does so by virtue of the form of purposiveness which is tied in with the powers of cognition and their reflective interplay. In explanation: the end of pure aesthetic judgment is the suitability of an object for the reflective and free play of the cognitive powers. It is based on nothing but the form of purposiveness of an object and herein lies its causality: pure aesthetic judgment regards the representation and the occupation of the cognitive powers "without a further aim."[77] Kant affirms, "We *linger* over the consideration of the beautiful because this consideration strengthens and reproduces itself."[78] Kant associates this with the idea of proportion, which arises in cognition and thereby permits its communication: the free play of the powers involves a proportion in which the inner relationship between the imagination and the understanding "is optimal for the animation of both powers of the mind (the one through the other) with respect to cognition (of given objects) in general."[79]

75. Ibid., §37, 5:289, 169.

76. Ibid., §33, 5:285, 165; cf. also §36, 5:287–88, 168.

77. Ibid., §12, 5:222, 107.

78. Ibid.

79. Ibid., §21, 5:238, 123. Guyer maintains that in aesthetic judgment one is kept in a state of disinterest, and that this implies an interest in the continued existence of that which produces the state. He claims this as an argument against the disinterestedness of a pleasure of taste. Guyer, *Kant and the Claims of Taste*, 182. This assertion misunderstands what Kant attempts to illustrate in the conception of disinterested pleasure. For

The absence of determinate concepts from aesthetic judgment leads Kant to posit the concept of the effect of the object as its cause: "where not merely the cognition of an object but the object itself (its form or its existence) *as an effect* is thought of as possible only through a concept of the latter, there one thinks of an end."[80] In pure aesthetic judgment, therefore, purposiveness is derived from the conceptualization of the aesthetic interplay of powers: "it is an aesthetic judgement and not a cognitive judgement, which thus does not concern any *concept* of the constitution and internal or external possibility of the object, through this or that cause, but concerns only the relation of the powers of representation to each other insofar as they are determined by a representation."[81]

In sum, it is because pure aesthetic judgment acts for the sake of free play and its creativity that its medium of communication is disinterested pleasure. Pure judgments of taste are subjectively purposive: "taste is the faculty for judging *a priori* the communicability of the feelings that are combined with a given representation (without the mediation of a concept)."[82]

It is for this reason that agreement in pure aesthetic judgment is not based in experience and in this way that Kant's account can mediate between the rationalist and empiricist positions: a judgment of taste "does

---

Kant, it is not the case that I consciously pursue an object that facilitates disinterestedness; rather I am drawn towards and into contemplation of that object. In any case, Kant does not deny that an interest can develop incidentally to an object of disinterested pleasure; he merely precludes such an interest serving as part of the determining ground of the liking itself. It is only by virtue of the inherent pleasure involved in beautiful objects that interested pleasure arises, as for example in the development of institutions of art, such as museums and galleries. Cf. Allison, *Kant's Theory of Taste*, 86.

80. Kant, *CJ*, §10, 5:220, 105. My italics. Kant continues, "The representation of the effect is here the determining ground of its cause, and precedes the latter" (ibid.).

81. Ibid., §11, 5:221, 106.

82. Ibid., §40, 5:296, 176. Kant states, "The consciousness of the merely formal purposiveness in the play of the cognitive powers of the subject in the case of representation through which an object is given is the pleasure itself, because it contains a determining ground of the activity of the subject with regard to the animation of its cognitive powers, thus an internal causality (which is purposive) with regard to cognition in general, but without being restricted to a particular cognition, hence it contains a mere form of the subjective purposiveness of a representation in an aesthetic judgment" (ibid., §12, 5:222, 107). Later, Kant states, "Only where the imagination in its freedom arouses the understanding, and the latter, without concepts, sets the imagination into a regular play is the representation communicated, not as a thought, but as the inner feeling of a purposive state of mind" (ibid., §40, 5:295–96, 175–76; cf. also §35, 5:287, 167–68).

not say that everyone *will* concur with our judgement but that everyone *should* agree with it."[83] Its pronouncement is ideal. It is rooted in an idea that is "necessary for everyone" and thereby demands universal assent. Only, that is, if we are "certain of having correctly subsumed under it."[84] Thus for Kant *sensus communis* must be understood as "the idea of *communal* sense." It is "a faculty for judging that in its reflection takes account (*a priori*) of everyone else's way of representing in thought." It abstracts from *my* judgment and holds it up to "human reason as a whole," that is, "not so much to the actual as to the merely possible judgements of others." It thereby attends solely to the "formal peculiarities" of my representation or representational state[85] and avoids "the illusion which, from subjective private conditions that could easily be held to be objective, would have a detrimental influence on the judgement."[86] The faculty abstracts from the limitations that contingently attach to our own judging by "leaving out as far as possible everything in one's representational state."[87] Kant asserts, "in itself nothing is more natural than to abstract from charm and emotion if one is seeking a judgement that is to serve as a universal rule."[88]

It is thus that the thoroughly epistemological use of beauty is revealed. Kant says: "Whether someone who believes himself to be making a judgement of taste is in fact judging in accordance with this idea can be uncertain; but that he relates it to that idea, thus that it is supposed to be a judgement of taste, he announces through the expression of beauty."[89]

REFLECTION AND COMMON SENSE

Having established the contrast of pure aesthetic judgment with empirical aesthetic judgment and logical judgment, it is time to return to the

83. Ibid., §22, 5:239, 123.

84. Ibid., §22, 5:239, 124.

85. Ibid., §40, 5:294, 174.

86. Ibid., §40, 5:293–94, 173–74.

87. Ibid., §40, 5:294, 174.

88. Ibid.

89. Ibid., §8, 5:216, 101. Allison notes the epistemological use of beauty, as that which indicates that an individual believes that he has made a judgment of taste. *Kant's Theory of Taste*, 107. He also draws attention to a misreading of this, ibid., 109, since it is not (as Ted Cohen suggests) that "I falsely believe that I have made a judgment of taste at all" but in claiming that "my *de facto* judgment is pure," cf. Cohen, "Why Beauty is a Symbol of Morality," 231–36.

continuum upon which Kant places all three. We will thereby ascertain what it is that stands uniquely at the basis of pure aesthetic judgment, as its common sense.

Empirical aesthetic judgment lies at one end of the spectrum of the disposition or interplay of the cognitive powers. It does not involve the cognitive powers and therefore does not seek to make sense of nature. It does, however, have an aim and is therefore interested. The end aim of empirical aesthetic judgment is subjective: it is the feeling of satisfaction that results from an object's relation to me. Thus, it does not involve necessity and is neither universal nor communicable. Logical judgment lies at the other end of the spectrum. It involves a determinate interplay of the cognitive powers that makes sense of an object in terms of an identifiable concept and thereby commands universality and communicability. The pleasure manifested in logical judgment is the result of rendering nature coherent in terms of concepts, bringing the universal to bear upon the particular.

Pure aesthetic judgment stands between the two. It is subjective but not merely so: "it is required of every judgement that is supposed to prove the taste of the subject that the subject judge for himself, without having to grope about by means of experience among the judgements of others and first inform himself about their satisfaction or dissatisfaction in the same object, and thus that he should pronounce his judgement not as imitation, because a thing really does please universally, but *a priori*."[90] It is objective but not subject to a determinate end: pure aesthetic judgment "relates the representation by which an object is given solely to the subject and does not bring to our attention any property of the object, but only the purposive form in the determination of the powers of representation that are occupied with it."[91]

In short, pure aesthetic judgment is distinguished from both empirical aesthetic judgment and logical judgment in virtue of its reflective disposition, and beauty refers to the disinterested satisfaction that results. In pure aesthetic judgment communication occurs by means of feeling and beauty denotes this. In the light of this it is reasonable to infer that common sense refers to the harmony of the free play of the cognitive

90. Kant, *CJ*, §32, 5:282, 163.

91. Ibid., §15, 5:228, 113; cf. also §31, 5:281, 162; §33, 5:284, 164–65. "Taste makes claim merely to autonomy. To make the judgments of others into the determining ground of one's own would be heteronomy" (ibid., §32, 5:282, 163; §15, 5:228, 112–13).

powers, during which reflection is at its peak. This is confirmed, as we shall now see, by Kant's alliance of pure aesthetic judgment with cognition more broadly.

DISINTERESTED PLEASURE, REFLECTION, AND COGNITION IN GENERAL

The priority of feeling within aesthetic judgment signals its importance within cognition in general. For Kant, reflection lies at the heart of all cognition. Humanity needs to find a universality of principles amidst the multiplicity of the laws of nature:[92] "For it is a command of our power of judgement to proceed in accordance with the principle of the suitability of nature to our faculty of cognition as far as it reaches."[93] Reflection is fundamental to this process, enabling the apparent suitability of nature to be explored in a variety of ways. It is for this reason that Kant defines the power of judgment as the "the faculty for thinking of the particular as contained under the universal."[94] In order for this to be the case, Kant states that reflective judgment assumes that nature is such as to allow empirical concepts to be cognized into a hierarchical system.[95] Kant acknowledges the presence of pleasure within this contingent systematization of nature by the understanding.[96] He affirms, "the discovered unifiability of two or more empirically heterogeneous laws of nature under a principle that comprehends them both is the ground of a very noticeable pleasure, often indeed of admiration, even of one which does not cease though one is familiar with its object."[97]

92. Ibid., Published Introduction, VI, 5:186, 72–3.

93. Ibid., Published Introduction, VI, 5:188, 74.

94. Ibid. The universal may be a rule, a principle, or a law. Ibid., Published Introduction, IV, 5:179, 66–7. Kant defines reflective judgment as a "faculty for reflecting on a given representation . . . for the sake of a concept" (ibid., First Introduction, V, 20:211, 15).

95. Ginsborg states that usually reflective judgment is viewed as the capacity to engage in scientific enquiry by organizing particular empirical concepts and laws into a unified theory of natural phenomena. Cf. Ibid., First Introduction, III, 20:208, 12. However, she notes that the First Introduction, V, suggests an alternative conception of reflective judgment: "here, reflective judgment is not in the first instance a capacity for the higher-level systematization of empirical concepts and laws, but rather a faculty which makes it possible to bring objects under empirical concepts in the first place" ("Reflective Judgement and Taste," 66).

96. Kant, *CJ*, Published Introduction, VI, 5:187, 73.

97. Ibid., Published Introduction, VI, 5:187–88, 74.

The account that Kant gives of pure aesthetic judgment, and the priority therein of feeling, inherently binds it to reflection and thus to general cognition. Disinterested pleasure indicates the satisfaction that results from the harmony of the free play of the cognitive powers and its preoccupation with pure reflection, and this links it to the pleasure involved in the tentative process of reflection upon nature. Kant affirms as much in the connection he makes between pure aesthetic judgment and reflective judgment: "by the aesthetic power of judgement . . . nothing else can be meant than the reflecting power of judgement."[98]

Pure aesthetic judgment and reflective judgment are mutually supportive. On the one hand, it is by virtue of the satisfaction that arises from the very existence of purposiveness that the disinterested satisfaction of aesthetic judgment arises in the first place. Aesthetic judgment does not dwell upon a particular end but enjoys the mere form of purposiveness. On the other hand, Kant states, "It thus requires study to make us attentive to the purposiveness of nature for our understanding in our judging of it."[99] In effect, this is what pure aesthetic judgment accomplishes, for taking pleasure in harmony somehow orients humankind within nature's diversity.[100] In doing so, it returns us to the fundamentals of the cognitive process, its disinterested pleasure drawing attention to the initial and often continued pleasure that results from reflection. In aesthetic judgment the imagination is not tied to the retention or projection of appearance on exact associational lines dictated by a specific concept. Rather, as Paul Crowther notes, it functions "at the level of its definitive being—as a productive capacity which creates possibilities of unity in the manifold."[101]

To illustrate this it is helpful to juxtapose the empirical unity of an object, as Kant sees it, with the aesthetic unity of an object. An example of the former appears in the second analogy of the first *Critique*. Kant takes the example of a house: "My perceptions could begin with the apprehension of the roof and end with the basement, or could begin from

98. Ibid., First Introduction, XII, 20:248–9, 48. Cf. Ginsborg, "Reflective Judgement and Taste," 63–78. For a denial of the basis of aesthetic judgment on the principle of systematicity in nature, see Guyer, *Kant and the Claims of Taste*, 33–67.

99. Kant, *CJ*, Published Introduction, VI, 5:187, 74; cf. Pippin, "Significance of Taste," 566.

100. Cf. ibid., 568. Cf. *CPR*, Appendix to the *Dialectic*.

101. Crowther, "Significance of Kant's Pure Aesthetic Judgement," 114.

below and end above; and I could simply apprehend the manifold of the empirical intuition either from right to left or from left to right."[102] Whichever "arbitrary" succession of perceptions the subject pursues, the objective unity of an object (which comprises the manner in which the manifold of perceptions is connected) remains unaffected.[103] Thus, a house remains a house despite the order of the perceptions. By contrast, the aesthetic unity of an object varies considerably. Herein, the randomness of the judgment partially constitutes the aesthetic unity of an object. Crowther notes, "the *aesthetic unity* of the object is a function of the interplay between phenomenal form and the different *possible* avenues of cognitive exploration and development which it can open up."[104] Through reflection, aesthetic judgment opens up an abundance of possible interpretations.

In a sense, therefore, the beautiful configuration is cognitively unstable since it does not have a definite ground from which it proceeds and to which it returns, as in the case of the perception of a house. Rather than resulting in a loss of intelligibility, however, it thereby takes us to heart of cognition. *It is cognition in the making.* Crowther summarizes this eloquently, "Imagination and understanding rediscover their original and mutual formative power through creating possibilities of conceptualisability. The very fabric and impetus of cognitive life in its more general sense is renewed and replenished."[105]

These considerations establish pure aesthetic judgment as teleological in a subjective sense: "in renewing cognition's structural basis, it can be regarded as teleologically significant in relation to the attainment of knowledge—even though it is not, in itself, a claim to knowledge."[106] Kant notes that although we fail to register pleasure arising from the comprehensibility of nature, including "its division into genera and species,"[107] initially it must have been present. He explains the lack of pleasure as a result of its accommodation within everyday experience, where it goes unnoticed.[108] In such cases, Kant believes that the pleasure

102. Kant, *CPR*, B 237–38.

103. Ibid., B 238–39.

104. Crowther, "Significance of Kant's Pure Aesthetic Judgement," 114.

105. Ibid., 115

106. Ibid.

107. Kant, *CJ*, Published Introduction, VI, 5:187, 74.

108. Ibid.

has become "mixed up with mere cognition."[109] The satisfaction of pure aesthetic judgment therefore serves to return our attention to the innate pleasure within cognition and rekindles our awareness of it.

To re-emphasize, for Kant pure aesthetic judgment is intrinsically pleasurable and is bound to the foundation of cognition. Kant asserts:

> The imagination (as a productive cognitive faculty) is, namely, very powerful in creating, as it were, another nature, out of the material which the real one gives it. We entertain ourselves with it when experience seems too mundane to us; we transform the latter, no doubt always in accordance with analogous laws, but also in accordance with principles that lie higher in reason (and which are every bit as natural to us as those in accordance with which the understanding apprehends empirical nature); in this we feel our freedom from the law of association (which applies to the empirical use of the faculty), in accordance with which material can certainly be lent to us by nature, but the latter can be transformed by us into something entirely different, namely into that which steps beyond nature.[110]

Summary of the First Solution to the Antinomy of Taste

We have seen that pure judgments of taste involve the reflective interplay of the cognitive powers and command universality and communicability in virtue of the satisfaction that arises from attention to their capacity as powers of cognition. The foundation of pure aesthetic judgment in reflection is all-important, involving it with the principle of cognition and with satisfaction and feeling as such. It is this that, for Kant, distinguishes pure aesthetic judgment from logical judgment, for the logical power of judgment subsumes under concepts whereas the pure aesthetic power of judgment subsumes under a relation that is merely a matter of sensation, "that of the imagination and the understanding reciprocally attuned to each other in the represented form of the object."[111]

109. Ibid., Published Introduction, VI, 5:188, 74.

110. Ibid., §49, 5:314, 192.

111. Ibid., §38, Remark, 5:290–91, 171. Kant continues, "Without having any purpose or fundamental principle for a guide, this pleasure accompanies the common apprehension of an object by the imagination, as a faculty of intuition, in relation to the understanding, as a faculty of concepts, by means of a procedure of the power of judgment, which it must also exercise for the sake of the most common experience" (ibid., §39, 5:292, 172).

It is crucial at this point to explicitly outline the dependence of beauty upon the harmony of the free play (the aesthetic subjective process) within the first solution. Beauty is inextricable from reflection: "the pleasure in the beautiful is neither a pleasure of enjoyment, nor of a lawful activity, and not even of a contemplation involving subtle reasoning in accordance with ideas, but of *mere reflection*."[112] It is for this reason that beauty achieves universality. The deduction of the beautiful "asserts only that we are justified in presupposing universally in every human being the same subjective conditions of the power of judgment that we find in ourselves; and then only if we have correctly subsumed the given object under these conditions."[113]

The Second Solution: The "Supersensible Substrate of Appearances"

As we have seen, the paradox contained within the antinomy of taste shapes Kant's pursuit of a solution. To this end, Kant posits the harmony of the free play: it is a priori and indeterminate and, thus, is subsumed by neither empiricist nor rationalist principles. Kant's task is complete. Hence, it comes as a surprise when Kant returns to the antinomy of taste[114] proposing a different solution: the "supersensible substrate of appearances" (*Übersinnliche[s] Substrat der Erscheinungen*).[115]

112. Ibid. My italics.

113. Ibid., §38, Remark, 5:290,170–71. The universality of beauty depends upon the universal possession of the three faculties of the soul and the disposition unique to pure aesthetic judgment, which creates an expectation of necessity and therefore of the possibility of the communication of beauty. It is for this reason that Kant is able to say that it is enough for universal assent to rest on subjective powers: aesthetic judgment deals with cognition *in general*. "In order to be justified in laying claim to universal assent for judgment of the aesthetic power of judgment resting merely on subjective grounds" it is sufficient to admit that "In all human beings, the subjective conditions of this faculty, as far as the relation of the cognitive powers therein set into action to a cognition in general is concerned, are the same, which must be true, since otherwise human beings could not communicate their representations and even cognition itself" (ibid., §38, 5:290 n. 1, 170).

114. In a restatement of the antinomy Kant structures the commonplaces as "thesis" and "antithesis." The thesis reads, "The judgment of taste is not based on concepts, for otherwise it would be possible to dispute about it (decide by means of proofs)"; and the antithesis, "The judgment of taste is based on concepts, for otherwise, despite its variety, it would not even be possible to argue about it (to lay claim to the necessary assent of others to this judgment)" (ibid., §56, 5:338–39, 215).

115. Ibid., §57, 5:341, 216. Guyer suggests some possible reasons for introducing the supersensible, one of which is that Kant intended it as an "ultimate answer" that would

As the harmony of the free play, beauty is fundamentally epistemological. It is concerned with knowing both in the particular sense of pure
aesthetic judgment and in the broader sense that cognition requires.[116]
Our examination has demonstrated this: beauty describes the disinterested pleasure that arises from the principle of free play and underpins
pure aesthetic judgment. It thus secures the uniqueness and importance
of aesthetic judgment and thereby refers to the fundamental pleasure of
all cognition arising from the configuration of the relationship between
the manifold and the universal. The introduction of the supersensible
(*das Übersinnliche*) as the solution potentially implies unnecessary ambiguity since it hints at an ontological rather than an epistemological understanding of beauty, one that anchors beauty in the noumenal world.[117]

In one sense this is true. The supersensible is "the transcendental
concept of reason of the supersensible, which is the basis of all intuition,
and which cannot be further determined theoretically."[118] It is both indeterminate and indeterminable and yet commands universal assent. Kant
says, "by means of this very concept it acquires validity for everyone (in
each case, to be sure, as a singular judgement immediately accompanying the intuition), because its determining ground may lie in the concept of that which can be regarded as the supersensible substratum of
humanity."[119] The supersensible is "the mere pure rational concept of the

---

silence the sceptic once and for all. *Kant and the Claims of Taste*, 336–37, 346. Gotshalk
believes that the introduction of the supersensible may reflect a deeper move in Kant's
thought from "form" to "expression." "Form and Expression in Kant's Aesthetics," 250–60.
For accounts arguing for the supersensible as a means by which the three *Critiques* are
drawn together, cf. Düsing, "Beauty as the Transition," 79–92; Crowther, "Significance of
Kant's Pure Aesthetic Judgement"; Pluhar, "Translator's Introduction," lxxxvi–cix.

116. Guyer notes the clear difference between the free play and the supersensible.
Free play is a concept of the "subjective condition of experience" that is *either* "purely
epistemological," in which case it is a concept of the "conditions" under which manifolds
of intuitions are unified, *or* "psychological," in which case it is a concept of the "mental
state in which unity is felt to obtain" (*Kant and the Claims of Taste*, 340).

117. By contrast with the harmony of the free play, the supersensible is an ontological concept, a "putative explanatory ground of the objects involved in the state just
described" (ibid., 340).

118. Kant, *CJ*, §57, 5:339, 215. For Kant a judgment of taste "is based on a concept (of
a general ground for the subjective purposiveness of nature for the power of judgment),
from which, however, nothing can be cognized and proved with regard to the object,
because it is in itself indeterminable and unfit for cognition" (ibid., §57, 5:340, 216).

119. Ibid.

supersensible, which grounds the object (and also the judging subject) as an object of sense, consequently as an appearance."[120]

As a priori and indeterminate, therefore, the supersensible appears at first sight to undermine the previous solution to the antinomy of taste, the harmony of the free play. However, Kant's definition of both the harmony of the free play and the supersensible substrate as the "subjective principle of the power of judgement"[121] indicates the intimate connection between the two. Just as beauty is a means of discerning the presence of the harmony of the free play of the cognitive powers so, in its free satisfaction, it gestures towards reflective judgment, the foundation of experience itself. It thereby becomes epistemological in a fundamental sense for it grounds all types of judgment and cognition. The appearance of the supersensible substrate in the text thus confirms the link between pure aesthetic judgment, beauty, and that which lies beyond the bounds of human knowledge itself.

This is initially apparent in the contrast between the first and second *Critiques* and the non-accessibility of the supersensible, and the third *Critique*, where the supersensible finds a degree of articulation. In the first and second *Critiques*, the antinomies compel reason to narrow the field of its speculation. Here, reason is allowed to speak only of the realm of appearance (the realm of the supersensible remains beyond comprehension). In the third *Critique*, the range available to reason is not limited in the same way: the supersensible is rendered accessible by means of the harmony of the free play. The use of beauty accentuates this for, as well as referring to disinterested pleasure (the characteristic of the harmony of the free play of the powers), it refers to the exhibition of aesthetic ideas—the expression of the supersensible that arises by means of harmony.[122] The harmony of the free play is the link that draws together both conceptions of beauty and intrinsically binds cognition to the supersensible substrate.

Aesthetic Ideas and Indeterminacy

To summarize, according to the account so far and its emphasis upon the harmony of the free play of the powers, the supersensible substrate (that which lies beneath all experience) remains beyond logical compre-

120. Ibid., §57, 5:339–40, 216.
121. Cf. ibid., §57, 5:341, 217.
122. Ibid., §51, 5:320, 197–98.

hension, as in the first and second *Critiques*, and cannot be expressed directly. With the introduction of the notion of "aesthetic ideas,"[123] however, Kant allows the supersensible a certain mode of articulation, one that is intrinsically indeterminate. In this way, aesthetic ideas serve as the explanatory link between the supersensible substrate and the harmony of the free play.[124] It is vital to note at this point that although Kant introduces indeterminacy as a means of knowing, concepts are not absent: aesthetic ideas act upon the understanding and operate within a *concept-bound* framework. The impact of this will disclose itself fully in Kant's consideration of the fine arts and music.

Aesthetic ideas are intrinsically connected with the harmony of the free play, giving it impetus: the imagination and the understanding reflect upon the representation of an object and explore the possibilities inherent within its cognition. Hence, Kant defines an aesthetic idea as a "counterpart (pendant) of an *idea of reason*."[125] In contrast to reason, wherein a concept absolutely subsumes an intuition, an aesthetic idea is "a concept to which no *intuition* (representation of the imagination) can be adequate."[126] It is "a representation of the imagination that occasions much thinking though without it being possible for any determinate thought, i.e., *concept*, to be adequate to it, which, consequently, no language fully attains or can make intelligible."[127]

Within the Kantian account, therefore, aesthetic ideas are a catalyst for thought. Kant describes how this is so: some presentations of the imagination attempt to exhibit a "concept." Here, the imagination inspires reason to greater thought: a presentation of the imagination belongs to and exhibits a determinate concept but is never fully comprehended by it so that the presentation aesthetically expands the concept itself in an unlimited way. Kant maintains:

> Now if we add to a concept a representation of the imagination
> that belongs to its presentation, but which by itself stimulates so
> much thinking that it can never be grasped in a determinate con-
> cept, hence which aesthetically enlarges the concept itself in an

123. Ibid., §49, 5:314, 192.

124. Hence, Kant later calls the aesthetic idea an "archetype" or "prototype" and calls its expression an "ectype" or "afterimage" (ibid., §51, 5:322, 199).

125. Ibid., §49, 5:314, 192.

126. Ibid.

127. Ibid.

unbounded way. Then in this case the imagination is creative, and sets the faculty of intellectual ideas (reason) into motion, that is, at the instigation of a representation it gives more to think about than can be grasped and made distinct in it (although it does, to be sure, belong to the concept of the object).[128]

Other presentations of the imagination form the "aesthetic attributes" of an object.[129] They express its "context," "implications," and "kinship" with other concepts. Collectively, they yield an aesthetic idea that first, serves the idea of reason "*instead* of logical presentation"[130] and, more importantly, second, animates the mind "by opening up for it the prospect of an immeasurable field of related representation."[131] Kant illustrates with the example of "Jupiter's Eagle, with the lightning in its claws." This is an aesthetic attribute of "the powerful king of heaven." Hence it does not, as a logical attribute might, "represent what lies in our concepts of the sublimity and majesty of creation" but instead "gives the imagination cause to spread itself over a multitude of related representations" that lets one think "more than one can express in a concept determined by words."[132]

Aesthetic ideas promote the free interaction of the imagination and understanding wherein the imagination darts through the seemingly endless set of aesthetic attributes, thereby producing what Kant calls a mutual quickening. In virtue of this fact they constitute the material of free play: "the imagination is free to provide, beyond that concord with the concept, *unsought extensive undeveloped material for the understanding*, of which the latter took no regard in its concept, but which applies, not so much objectively, for cognition, as subjectively, for the animation of the cognitive powers, and thus also indirectly to cognitions."[133] Herein, the mental powers are caught up in a purposive momentum that strives towards "something lying beyond the bounds of experience" and seeks to

128. Ibid., §49, 5:315, 193.

129. Ibid. These are "supplementary" representations.

130. Ibid. My italics.

131. Ibid.

132. Ibid. Andrew Chignell usefully points to the contemporary concept of *free association*, giving a useful insight into the nature of the mental phenomenon at hand: "For while the aesthetic attributes are *of* the object in question in that they are linked to its logical attributes by chains of association, they are also produced freely" (Chignell, "Problem of Particularity in Kant's Aesthetic Theory").

133. Kant, *CJ*, §49, 5:317, 194. My italics.

"approximate a presentation of concepts of reason (of intellectual ideas), which gives them the appearance of an objective reality."[134]

Summary of the Second Solution to the Antinomy of Taste

We have seen that, in contrast to the first solution to the antinomy of taste, the second solution posits the supersensible substrate. Although surprising, the suggestion of a second solution does not necessarily undermine Kant's previous attribution of this position to the harmony of the free play. Rather, the introduction of the supersensible opens up Kant's account beyond the intersubjective validity that the harmony suggests and extends its compass to the noumenal realm. Importantly in this regard, it does so by means of indeterminacy. However, it remains bound by concepts, for although it encourages thoughts that go beyond a single concept it remains conceptually framed.

134. Ibid., §49, 5:314, 192. It is interesting to note Guyer's skepticism with regard to the similarity between the universality of the faculties and their logical association, and the necessary universality of their interaction in aesthetic interplay. Guyer states: the fact that everyone is possessed of faculties which make them capable of "unifying manifolds under empirical concepts" does not "imply that the special case of unifying a manifold without any empirical concept at all must occur in precisely the same circumstance for everyone" (Guyer, *Kant and the Claims of Taste*, 263). In response, Chignell notes that "it is not the content of these thoughts—moral or otherwise—that is of primary importance here, but rather the formal manner in which these thoughts are strung together by the mind into a 'coherent whole' that has the phenomenological 'feel' of being inexhaustible." Thus it is not the case that the precipitation of free play by an object evokes a *particular* set of associations. Rather only *some* set. Chignell, "The Problem of Particularity in Kant's Aesthetic Theory," 4; cf. Kant, *CJ*, First Introduction, 20:199, 6; Published Introduction, 5:183, 70. Chignell maintains that despite the variety of associations that an object evokes we can still trace the associations back to the object that set the "train" in motion and declare it to be beautiful.

6

Creating Beauty

Genius and the Work of Art

BEAUTY AS DESCRIPTION

IT IS NOW THAT we must step aside from Kant's argument, drawing together and making explicit the central aspects of Kant's treatment of beauty that have been identified so far. For this is our main concern insofar as the notion of beauty shapes Kant's understanding of music. In the *Analytic of the Beautiful*, we saw the identification of beauty with certain moments of pure aesthetic judgment. Likewise, in the *Deduction of the Beautiful*, we noted the use of beauty to refer to facets of the harmony of free play.

Kant's treatment of beauty clearly points to its descriptive function: beauty points towards the indeterminate and indeterminable principle that makes pure aesthetic judgment possible and, indeed, unique. In the first solution, Kant suggests that this principle is the harmony of the free play of the cognitive powers, and in the second, he posits the supersensible substrate of appearance. In both instances the implications for beauty remain the same. Beauty is not granted any internal ground and content but derives its meaning from its merely descriptive capacity, whereby it indicates the central aspects of the harmony of the free play of the cognitive powers.

As a result, it is fair to say that Kant understands beauty epistemologically rather than ontologically, as a means of knowing rather than as something to be known in and of and for itself. This is apparent in the equation of beauty with disinterested pleasure: disinterested pleasure is the predominant characteristic of the harmony of the free play of the cognitive powers, acting as confirmation of its presence. Moreover, beauty is a means of discerning whether or not a judgment is aesthetic or not, or indeed authentic, depending on whether or not the subject has correctly related to and considered the object at hand.[1] By virtue of this fact, that beauty draws attention to the form of purposiveness in pure aesthetic judgment, it is aligned with a more profound level of knowing. The purposiveness of nature for our cognition is assumed in order that we cognize at all and the disinterested satisfaction of pure aesthetic judgment confirms this, affirming the satisfaction that obtains when purposive connections are made in general cognition, when an "end" of an object is perceived. Moreover, as the expression of aesthetic ideas, beauty is a means of knowing that which is beyond logical comprehension.[2]

Kant's account is unequivocal: the harmony of the free play is pivotal to the resolution of the antinomy of taste and not beauty. Beauty only indicates aspects of the process of taste. Thus, even if one accepts the legitimacy of the introduction of the supersensible substrate of appearances, the ground of all existence (and thus an ontological concept), which some do not,[3] beauty's relation to it is only indirect, for beauty refers only to the expression of the aesthetic ideas within the harmony of the free play. Without the harmony, beauty does not have any contact

1. The descriptive nature of beauty is indicated in the four "moments" of taste in the *Analytic of the Beautiful*, referred to earlier.

2. An article by Karl Ameriks not only supports my reading, but exacerbates the reduction of beauty to description. He assigns disinterest a functional rather than essential use in the third *Critique*, believing that the notion of *disinterest* is not helpful logically but only epistemologically in distinguishing aesthetic judgments from "sensual" or "moral" judgments. He states: "Logically, there is no way that the mere interest involved in sensual or moral judgements is what makes them distinct from aesthetic judgement; rather they are independent intrinsic distinctions between such judgements [sensual and moral] and aesthetic judgements, and it just happens that sensual and moral judgements share features which Kant thinks allow their being grouped as 'interested'" ("Kant and the Objectivity of Taste," 4). If Ameriks' account is true, beauty stands at one further remove from the principle of the harmony of free play than I suggest: beauty is a description of a description. Ibid., 4.

3. Guyer denies the viability of the introduction of the supersensible substrate and thinks that Kant's argument is "clearly invalid" in presuming that the supersensible is the only option open to him at this particular point in the *Critique*. Cf. *Kant and the Claims of Taste*, 339. Pippin criticizes Guyer's narrow understanding of the subjective principle: "Our focus can become so narrowly concentrated on the aesthetic response, so wary of speculation about the occasion of that response, and the significance of the experience itself, that aesthetic judgement becomes mostly a matter of investigating one's own mental history, as if exclusively a species of psychological self-examination" (Pippin, "Significance of Taste," 554–55).

with that which it potentially expresses, that which lies at the heart of all cognition. It thereby loses any significance. This illustrates the total dependence of beauty upon the notion of the harmony of the free play: the harmony of the free play is the condition of the possibility of beauty's existence, imbuing it with meaning.

Necessity and Universality: The Inter-Subjective Resonance of Beauty

The way in which beauty commands necessity and invokes universality demonstrates the absolute dependence of beauty upon the principle of free play and its harmony. As we have seen in our examination of Boethius, this contrasts with the classical tradition wherein beauty is intrinsic to the fabric of the cosmos. It is an essential feature of its existence and is considered absolutely universal. For Boethius, beauty is both a means of understanding the world and part of that which is to be known. It is simultaneously epistemological and ontological. The contrast with Kant's account is clear: there is nothing inherent within the idea of beauty that requires its necessity and universality. Rather, it depends upon the harmony of the free play of the cognitive powers for its necessity, universality, and communicability.

For this reason, beauty is inter-subjective rather than absolute. Beauty is valid amongst humanity in virtue of their common nature rather than due to any inherent quality that it possesses. As a result, beauty extends only as far as free play allows. As we shall see, this is brought to the fore within Kant's account of the fine arts, where the arts are appraised according to their capacity for the communication of the beautiful. Only those classes of art that betoken free play are considered beautiful. As primarily sensory, music does not engage the cognitive powers in free play and is not classed as beautiful, save in those instances of music where it can be said categorically that free play has been involved. In short, music is mere sensation. It is contentless, intrusive, and distracting.

BEAUTY IN NATURE AND BEAUTY IN ART

Although I have highlighted the reduction of beauty to the harmony of the free play, beauty is present as the content of nature and art to the extent that the harmony is manifested. It is, thus, in Kant's account of nature and art that the coherence of his notion of beauty is brought into focus, for it is here that its implications are worked out. According to Kant's understanding of pure aesthetic judgment, beauty is universal, necessary, and communicable. In his application of beauty to nature and art these claims are put to the test.

For Kant, the notion of beauty is univocal to nature and art: both are disinterested, "whether it is the beauty of nature or of art that is at issue: *that is beautiful which pleases in the mere judging* (neither in sensation nor through a concept)."[4] Moreover, both are a means of supersensible exhibition, "Beauty (whether it be beauty of nature or of art) can in general be called the *expression* of aesthetic ideas."[5] However, natural beauty is classed as superior to artistic beauty. In his introduction, Kant states that the judging of artistic beauty is to be considered as a "mere consequence" of the principles that ground the judgment of natural beauty.[6] This evaluation derives from the aim of the third *Critique* and its exploration of reflective judgment, and corresponds to Kant's account of pure aesthetic judgment, the unique status of beauty, and the absence of determinate concepts. Thus, in the exposition of the third moment of the judgment of taste in the *Critique of Aesthetic Judgment*, Kant infers that beauty "is the form of the *purposiveness* of an object insofar as it is perceived in it *without representation of an end*"[7] and classifies two kinds of beauty, free beauty (*freie Schönheit*) and adherent beauty (*anhängende Schönheit*). Free beauty, or *pulchritudo vaga* in its Latin equivalent, does not presuppose a concept of what the object ought to be and is therefore self-subsisting.[8] Adherent beauty, or *pulchritudo adhaerens*, does presuppose such a concept and is therefore conditioned. It refers to those objects "that stand under the concept of a particular end."[9] In short, free beauty is conceptless and therefore ranks above adherent beauty. It is on these grounds that nature stands above art.

For Kant, art always has concept at its basis: it is a production through freedom arising from a "capacity for choice that grounds its actions in reason." It therefore has an end in mind at all times. To illustrate this, Kant contrasts human art with the artistry attributed to

4. Kant, *CJ*, §45, 5:306, 185.

5. Ibid., §51, 5:320, 197.

6. Ibid., First Introduction, 20:251, 50.

7. Ibid., §17, 5:236, 120.

8. Ibid., §16, 5:229, 114.

9. Ibid., §16, 5:229–30, 114.

nature, in particular, "the product of the bees (the regularly construed honeycombs)"[10] which some regard as a work of art. Kant maintains that this is only true by analogy with human art and that as soon as we recognize that the bees do not ground their work on any rational consideration of their own we regard their work as "a product of their nature (of instinct)" and only as an art when ascribing it "to their creator."[11]

We will begin our examination of Kant's account of beauty by delineating Kant's understanding of free beauty and adherent beauty, the role of concept, and their respective alliance with nature and art. I will then discuss his understanding of fine art and the role of genius, which forms a bridge between art and nature. We will finish by mapping the given distinctions onto music. Throughout the exposition, the ambiguous position of music within the Kantian account will be apparent.

Free Beauty and Nature

According to Kant's account, free beauty is unconstrained by purpose and is therefore more conducive to free play than adherent beauty. Kant says, "In the judging of a free beauty (according to mere form) the judgement of taste is pure. No concept of any end for which the manifold should serve the given object and thus which the latter should represent is presupposed, by which the imagination, which is as it were at play in the observation of the shape, would merely be restricted."[12]

It is in this regard that nature is introduced: nature is paradigmatic of free beauty. Kant says: "Flowers are free natural beauties."[13] He continues, "Hardly anyone other than the botanist knows what sort of thing a flower is supposed to be; and even the botanist, who recognises in it the reproductive organ of the plant, pays no attention to this natural end if he judges the flower by means of taste. Thus this judgement is not grounded on any kind of perfection, any internal purposiveness to which the composition of the manifold is related."[14] Nature is free from concepts and is therefore an example of free beauty: "In order to judge a beauty of nature as such, I do not need first to have a concept of what

10. Ibid., §43, 5:303, 182.
11. Ibid.
12. Ibid., §16, 5:229–30, 114.
13. Ibid., §16, 5:229, 114.
14. Ibid.

sort of thing the object is supposed to be; i.e., it is not necessary for me to know the material purposiveness (its end), but the mere form without knowledge of the end pleases for itself in the judging."[15]

This association is significant: Kant regards natural beauty as exemplary of free beauty and thereby in principle extends the possibility of free beauty to other conceptless objects. Thus Kant proceeds, "designs *à la grecque*, foliage for borders or on wallpaper, etc., signify nothing by themselves: they do not represent anything, no object under a determinate concept, *and are free beauties*."[16] Crucially, Kant classes certain types of music as examples of free beauty: "One can also count as belonging to the same kind what are called in music fantasias (without a theme), indeed all music without a text."[17] Kant places music, in certain instances, on a par with nature, classing it among those examples that exhibit free beauty.

Adherent Beauty and Aesthetic Art[18]

Adherent beauty stands in contrast to natural beauty and is allied with artistic beauty: artistic beauty always implicitly contains some concept or other. Kant says:

> if the object is given as a product of art, and is as such supposed to be declared beautiful, then, since art always presupposes an end in the cause (and its causality), a concept must first be the ground of what the thing is supposed to be, and, since the agreement of the manifold in a thing with its inner determination as an end is the perfection of a thing, in the judging of the beauty of art the perfection of the thing will also have to be taken into account, which is not even a question in the judging of a natural beauty (as such).[19]

This appears again in the discussion "On the Division of the Fine Arts" with regard to free play. Kant notes: "in beautiful art this idea must be occasioned by a concept of the object, but in the case of beautiful nature, the mere reflection on a given intuition, without a concept of what the object ought to be, is sufficient for arousing and communicating the

15. Ibid., §48, 5:311, 190.
16. Ibid., §16, 5:229, 114. My italics.
17. Ibid.
18. Ibid., §44, 5:305, 184.
19. Ibid., §48, 5:311, 190.

idea of which that object is considered as the *expression*."[20] As Allison summarizes the matter, to be aware that something is art is to recognize its "aboutness" or intentionality.[21] Thus, artistic beauty is always at one remove from the communication of true beauty: "A beauty of nature is a *beautiful thing*; the beauty of art is a *beautiful representation* of a thing."[22] However, through the construction of a multi-faceted notion of art (which I suggest parallels the distinction between logical judgment, and pure and empirical aesthetic judgment) Kant connects fine art with nature and allows it to embody free beauty.

Mechanical Art and Agreeable Art

Kant makes a fundamental distinction between "mechanical" art and "aesthetic" art. Mechanical art is grounded in Kant's understanding of logical judgment and the good: it "merely performs the actions requisite to make it actual" adequately to our cognition of that object. By contrast, aesthetic art "has the feeling of pleasure" as its immediate aim[23] and includes agreeable and beautiful (fine) art. Agreeable art is bound up with empirical aesthetic judgment, its pleasure accompanying presentations that are "mere *sensations*." It is therefore merely enjoyable: [24]

> Agreeable arts are those which are aimed merely at enjoyment; of this kind are all those charms that can gratify the company at a table, such as telling entertaining stories, getting the company talking in an open and lively manner, creating by means of jokes and laughter a certain tone of merriment, in which, as is said, much can be chattered about and nobody will be held responsible for what he says, because it is only intended as momentary entertainment, not as some enduring material for later reflection or discussion.[25]

In this regard Kant makes a list of agreeable arts: "the way in which the table is set out for enjoyment, or even, at big parties, *the table-music*—an odd thing, which is supposed to sustain the mood of joyfulness

20. Ibid., §51, 5:320, 197–98.
21. Allison, *Kant's Theory of Taste*, 275.
22. Kant, *CJ*, §48, 5:311, 189.
23. Ibid., §44, 5:305, 184.
24. Ibid.
25. Ibid.

merely *as an agreeable noise*,[26] and to encourage the free conversation of one neighbour with another without anyone paying the least attention to its composition." He also includes here, "all games that involve no interest beyond that of making time pass unnoticed."[27]

The inclusion of music is striking. It is evident even thus far that Kant's account of beauty places music in an ambiguous position. On the one hand, its conceptlessness places it on the same level as natural beauty and thereby associates it with free beauty. On the other hand, music is consigned to mere sensation and rendered only agreeable. This ambiguity will become more explicit within Kant's classification and evaluation of the fine arts.

Fine Art[28]

Fine art (*schöne Kunst*) is connected with pure aesthetic judgment and free play: it is "a kind of representation that is purposive in itself."[29] Its purpose is the pleasure that accompanies representations that are "*kinds of cognition*."[30] In its apparent freedom from constraint, therefore, it appears equivalent to natural beauty. However, Kant maintains that fine art is produced, is therefore to all intents and purposes purposive, and is thus distinct from natural beauty. Kant says: "Now art always has a determinate intention of producing something. If however this were a mere sensation (something merely subjective) that is supposed to be accompanied with pleasure, then this product would please, in the judging, only by means of the feeling of sense. If the intention were aimed at the production of a determinate object, then, if it were achieved through art, the object would not please only through concepts."[31] Kant speaks of the dichotomy thus:

> every art presupposes rules which first lay the foundation by means of which a product that is to be called artistic is first represented as possible. The concept of beautiful art, however, does

26. My italics.

27. Ibid., §44, 5:306, 185.

28. A good introduction to the system of the fine arts in the eighteenth century is presented by Kristeller, "Modern System of the Arts," 496–527.

29. Kant, *CJ*, §44, 5:306, 185.

30. Ibid., §44, 5:305, 184.

31. Ibid., §45, 5:306, 185. Such an object would please as a mechanical art. Ibid. Cf. Ibid., §44, 5:305, 184.

not allow the judgement concerning the beauty of its product to be derived from any sort of rule that has a *concept* for its determining ground, and thus has as its ground a concept of how it is possible. Thus beautiful art cannot itself think up the rule in accordance with which it is to bring its product into being.[32]

To employ a rule that is grounded in concepts would be to forfeit the unique understanding of pure aesthetic judgment and beauty that Kant has constructed. Thus, Kant ratifies the relationship between beauty and fine art, which is apparently confined to adherent beauty, by bringing them into a relationship of imitation. As Henry Allison notes, however, this imitation does not involve art creating a faithful copy or representation of nature, but its appearance as spontaneous and unstudied, or as Kant puts it "unintentional" (*unabsichtlich*).[33] "In a product of art one must be aware that it is art, and not nature; yet the purposiveness in its form must still seem to be free from all constraint by arbitrary rules as if it were a mere product of nature."[34] Even though the purposiveness in a product of fine art is intentional, it must not seem so:

> beautiful art must be *regarded* as nature, although of course one is aware of it as art. A product of art appears as nature, however, if we find it to agree *punctiliously* but not *painstakingly* with rules in accordance with which alone the product can become what it ought to be, that is, without the academic form showing through, i.e., without showing any sign that the rule has hovered before the eyes of the artist and fettered his mental powers.[35]

32. Ibid., §46, 5:307, 186.

33. See Allison, *Kant's Theory of Taste*, 278. This contrasts the imitative function of "art" within Greek thought (*mimēsis*). This mode of musical meaning permeates Boethius' account wherein 'cosmic' harmony is replicated within each instantiation.

34. Kant, *CJ*, §45, 5:306, 185.

35. Ibid., §45, 5:307, 186.

GENIUS[36]

Kant uses the notion of genius (*Genie*) to facilitate this relationship.[37] Genius is "a productive faculty."[38] It is a talent or natural gift that lies in an "inborn predisposition of the mind (*ingenium*)."[39] It produces art through an attunement of its powers. In this way, fine art emerges as a natural capacity endowed with the capacity to give the rule to art.[40] By involving the notion of genius, Kant upholds the indeterminacy of pure aesthetic judgment and beauty: genius produces fine art but does so in an indeterminate way.

Clarifying this, Kant identifies three aspects of genius. First, genius is original: it is "a *talent* for producing that which no determinate rule can be given, not a predisposition or skill for that which be learned in accordance with some rule or other."[41] Second, it is also exemplary, "since there can also be original nonsense, its products must at the same time be models."[42] Third, genius is a natural gift: "it cannot itself describe or indicate scientifically how it brings its product into being." Rather it gives the rule as nature and "hence the author of a product that he owes to his genius does not know himself how the ideas for it come to him, and also does not have it in his power [*Gewalt*] to think up such things

36. Martin Gammon discusses the origin of Kant's understanding of exemplary originality and offers insights that contextualize the paradoxical air of the notion of genius. "Exemplary Originality," 563–92.

37. Allison notes that the whole discussion of fine art and its connection with genius has an "episodic character" about it that makes it difficult to integrate into the overall argument of the third *Critique*. He refers in particular to Zammito, *The Genesis of Kant's Critique of Judgement*. Zammito explains this apparent discrepancy by noting that Kant's fundamental concern is with the nature of *aesthetic judgment* and not *artistic production*; it involves a "reception aesthetic" rather than a "creation aesthetic." Ibid., 131; Allison, *Kant's Theory of Taste*, 271.

38. Kant, *CJ*, §48, 5:313, 191.

39. Ibid., §46, 5:307, 186.

40. Ibid.

41. Ibid.

42. Ibid., §46, 5:308, 187. Rather, "the rule must be abstracted from the deed, i.e., from the product, against which others may test their own talent, letting it serve them as a model, not for *copying* [*Nachmachung*] but for *imitation* [*Nachahmung*]" (ibid., §47, 5:309, 188). Karl Vorländer, editor of the *CJ* in the *Philosophische Bibliothek* edition, notes (v. 39a, 163, n. b) that Kant's manuscript read '*Nachahmung . . . Nachahmung*' ('[not to be] imitated [but to be] imitated'), which was then corrected to the reading found here, but that Kant presumably meant to write '*Nachahmung . . . Nachfolge*' ([not to be] imitated [but to be] followed) in line with what he says elsewhere.

at will or according to plan, and to communicate to others precepts that would put them in a position to produce similar products."[43]

The three aspects are interwoven. Talent is a natural endowment and is thus original, unique, and cannot be taught. Kant says that the artist's skill "cannot be communicated but is apportioned to each immediately from the hand of nature, and thus dies with him, until nature one day similarly endows another, who needs nothing more than an example in order to let the talent of which he is aware operate in a similar way."[44] Its rule cannot be formalized and can only be abstracted from what the artist produces. Thus, pieces of fine art act as exemplary products that allow others to "test their own talent, letting it serve them as their model."[45]

In short, genius offers a rule to fine art that is indeterminate. This is all-important for Kant's account, which does not allow any measure of determinacy. To do so, would allow pure aesthetic judgment and beauty to commingle with logical judgment and the good and would reduce fine art to mechanical art. Kant maintains: "Since the gift of nature must give the rule to art (as beautiful art), what sort of rule is this? It cannot be couched in a formula to serve as a precept, for then the judgement about the beautiful would be determinable in accordance with concepts."[46]

Having said this, Kant notes the fundamental dependence of fine upon mechanical art. He explains, "Although mechanical and beautiful art, the first as a mere art of diligence and learning, the second as that of genius, are very different from each other, still there is no beautiful

43. Ibid., §46, 5:308, 187. Kant also says of Genius: (1) "it is a talent for art, not for science, in which rules that are distinctly cognized must come first and determine the procedure in it;" (2) "as a talent for art, it presupposes a determinate concept of the product, as an end, hence understanding, but also a representation (even if indeterminate) of the material, i.e., of the intuition, for the presentation of this concept, hence a relation of the imagination to the understanding;" (3) "it displays itself not so much in the execution of the proposed end in the presentation of a determinate *concept* as in the exposition or the expression of *aesthetic ideas*, which contain rich material for that aim, hence the imagination, in its freedom from all guidance by rules, is nevertheless represented as purposive for the presentation of the given concept;" (4) "the unsought and unintentional subjective purposiveness in the free correspondence of the imagination to the lawfulness of the understanding presupposes a proportion and disposition of this faculty that cannot be produced by any following of the rules, whether of science or of mechanical imitation, but that only the nature of the subject can produce" (ibid., §49, 5:317–18, 195).

44. Ibid., §47, 5:309, 188.

45. Ibid.

46. Ibid.

art in which something mechanical, which can be grasped and followed according to rules, and thus something academically correct, does not constitute the essential condition of the art."[47] Indeed the rule of fine art—genius—depends upon its mechanical component:

> Now since the originality of his talent constitutes one (but not the only) essential element of the character of the genius, superficial minds believe that they cannot show that they are blossoming geniuses any better than by pronouncing themselves free of the academic constraint of all rules, and they believe that one parades around better on a horse with the staggers than one that is properly trained. Genius can only provide rich *material* for products of art; its elaboration and *form* require *a talent that has been academically trained*, in order to make a use of it that can stand up to the power of judgement.[48]

In short, works of fine art rely upon an indeterminable principle and themselves therefore are "not for *copying* but for *imitation*." They are available only to those who are likewise endowed by nature.[49] Necessity, therefore, results from the subjective powers of cognition and their indeterminate involvement in genius. Thus Kant asserts:

> even if one thinks or writes for himself, and does not merely take up what others have thought, indeed even if he invents a great deal for art and science, this is still not a proper reason for calling such a great *mind* (in contrast to someone who, because he can never do more than merely learn and imitate, is called a *blockhead*) a *genius*, since just this sort of thing *could* also have been learned, and thus still lies on the natural path of inquiry and reflection in accordance with rules, and is not specifically distinct from that which can be acquired with effort by means of imitation.[50]

Thus, according to Kant, Newton is not a genius since "everything that Newton expounded in his immortal work on the principles of natural philosophy" is in principle learnable.[51] This contrasts with "inspired

47. Ibid., §47, 5:310, 188.

48. Ibid., §47, 5:310, 189. My italics.

49. Ibid., §47, 5:309, 188.

50. Ibid., §47, 5:308, 187.

51. "Newton could make all the steps that he had to take, from the first elements of geometry to his great and profound discoveries, entirely intuitive not only to himself but also to everyone else, and thus set them out for posterity quite determinately" (ibid., §47, 5:309, 187).

poetry," which transcends all the rules and models for the art of poetry, however exhaustive.[52] Kant illustrates the same principle in a footnote: "In my region, the common man, when confronted with a problem like that of Columbus and his egg, says *That is not an art, it is just a science.* I.e., if one *knows* it, then one *can* do it; and he says the same thing about all the putative arts of the conjuror. But he would never refuse to call those of the tightrope walker art."[53]

Genius and Taste

Genius is the productive impulse of fine art. However, it requires taste as the faculty that receives and judges it. Successful communication of beauty requires both of them. However, of the two, taste is more important and Kant is clear that where there is a clash of interests in any given product, so that it is required that something is "sacrificed," it must be on the side of genius rather than on the side of taste.[54] This is due to the abiding priority of cognition. Kant explains: "To be rich and original in ideas is not as necessary for the sake of beauty as is the suitability of the imagination in its freedom to the lawfulness of the understanding. For all the richness of the former produces, in its lawless freedom, nothing but nonsense; the power of judgement, however, is the faculty for bringing it in line with the understanding."[55] For Kant, taste is "the discipline (or corrective) of genius, clipping its wings and making it well behaved or polished; but at the same time it gives genius guidance as to where and how far it should extend itself to remain purposive; and by introducing clarity and order into the abundance of thoughts it makes the ideas tenable"[56]

52. Ibid., §47, 5:308–9, 187.

53. Ibid., §43, 5:304 n. 1, 183. This resonates with the theme of disenchantment that will be taken up in chapter seven. For an important factor contributing to it was increasing rationalization and intellectualization.

54. Ibid., §50, 5:319–20, 197. This is due to the fact that without the guidance of taste, genius does not necessarily result in harmony.

55. Ibid., §50, 5:319, 197.

56. Ibid. Zammito maintains that there is an important connection between the free harmony of the faculties, required for the creation of fine art, and that which is required for its proper enjoyment. He suggests that the "architectonic intention" underlying Kant's account of genius "was to read the production of beauty in art as structurally homologous with the appreciation of beauty." *Genesis of Kant's Critique of Judgement*, 143.

Summary: Free Beauty, Adherent Beauty, and the Ambiguity of Music

In summary, the distinction between free beauty and adherent beauty, and the classification of different types of adherent beauty, arise from a translation of the principle by which Kant categorizes the judgments in the *Deduction*. These must rest on a principle that is a priori and indeterminate. It is for this reason that he invokes the notion of genius. As we saw earlier, this subjective principle of taste combines both the harmony of free play and the supersensible substrate, which is thereby revealed.

Free beauty is superior to adherent beauty in virtue of its purposeless purposiveness and, in general terms, free beauty pertains to nature and adherent beauty to art. Kant states, "Beauty (whether it be beauty of nature or of art) can in general be called the *expression* of ideas: only in beautiful art this idea must be occasioned by a concept of the object, but in beautiful nature the mere reflection on a given intuition, without a concept of what ought to be, is sufficient for arousing and communicating the idea of which that object is considered as the expression."[57] Significantly, the importance of conceptlessness permits the inclusion of music that does not have any cohering idea.[58] Thus, in this respect, music seemingly rises above other forms of art (for no others are mentioned) and is aligned with the ideal form of beauty. However, it suffers a change of fortune in Kant's exposition of adherent beauty.

Adherent beauty is understood in the light of free beauty in general and natural beauty in particular. Thus, Kant distinguishes between fine art and agreeable art, its classification depending upon whether or not it imitates the purposeless purposiveness of nature. Within adherent art Kant differentiates between mechanical, fine, and agreeable art, with fine art being closely aligned with nature. Given Kant's previous categorization of music as "conceptless" and free, one might think that music stands unequivocally as a fine art. However, the conceptlessness of music relegates it to mere sensation.

It is evident that, for Kant, the status of music is unclear to say the least: he is uncertain whether music is able to mediate beauty or not.

57. Kant, *CJ*, §51, 5:320, 197–98.

58. This might be instrumental music or "absolute music," as it came to be called after Wagner, who in 1846 announced what he saw to be the death of instrumental music. Cf. Chua, *Absolute Music and the Construction of Meaning*, 224; Dahlhaus, *Idea of Absolute Music*, especially 18–41. Kivy classes it as "music alone." "Fine Art of Repetition," 327–59.

This indicates the problematic nature of Kant's understanding of beauty. Kant's emphasis upon the harmony of the free play introduces ambiguity into his account of beauty, the subjective ground rendering beauty *subjectively universal* and *not absolutely so*. Its universality is paradoxical since it exists between subjects and yet is circumscribed amongst the arts. As we shall see shortly, this circumscription translates to Kant's account of the fine arts which, by employing the model of verbal communication,[59] leads to an imposition of a non-musical standard upon the phenomenon of music. Inconsistent valuation results since the intellectual aspect of music generates a positive evaluation and its sensible aspect produces a negative one.

BEAUTY, THE FINE ARTS AND THE STATUS OF MUSIC

It is thus that we turn our attention to the fine arts, beginning with an examination of the analogy between verbal communication and artistic communication, which Kant uses to guide his reflection. This is important, first, because it demonstrates the use of verbal communication not as an analogy but as a model and, second, because it clearly reveals the imposition of a non-musical framework upon music, one that results in its indefinite status.

The Analogy of Fine Art and Verbal Communication

Kant is clear that his account of the fine arts is exploratory and his theory provisional. "The reader will not judge of this outline for a possible division of the beautiful arts as if it were a deliberate theory. It is only one of the several experiments that still can and should be attempted."[60] Thus, the analogy between verbal communication and artistic communication is tentative: "if we wish to divide the beautiful arts, we can, at least as an experiment, choose no easier principle than the analogy of art with the kind of expression that people use in speaking in order to communicate to each other."[61] Although provisional, tentative, and thus speculative, a methodological precedent for the analogy can be found within the *Critique of Judgment*, specifically, in the *Deduction of the Beautiful*,

59. For clarity, I will use "verbal communication" to refer to the logical mode of expression which Kant sees as analogous to artistic communication.

60. Kant, *CJ*, §51, 5:320 n. 1, 198.

61. Ibid., §51, 5:320, 198.

wherein Kant's understanding of beauty is in large part constructed by means of its contrast with logical judgment and the good. Thus verbal communication, as the outward expression, as it were, of logical judgment, provides a didactic tool.

The use of analogy is at first sight promising, suggesting as it does an emphasis upon the common features of verbal and artistic communication whilst maintaining their difference. Thus, by virtue of the correlation between verbal communication and logical judgment, and artistic communication and pure aesthetic judgment, one presumes that their difference will lie in the reliance of logical judgment upon determinate concepts, and the use of indeterminate concepts within pure aesthetic judgment, and that their similarity will lie in the concern that each type of judgment has with necessity, universality, and communicability.

Indeed, the common concerns of verbal and artistic communication are central to the division of the fine arts. However, the application of the verbal analogy does not proceed as one might expect, for Kant treats verbal communication as a model, providing a framework for understanding artistic communication and impressing a division upon the fine arts, rather than using it to create an analogous partnership offering mutual illumination. Thus, verbal communication becomes a standard by which artistic communication within the fine arts is judged. Importantly, in doing so, Kant undermines the very method that is established in the third *Critique*, wherein beauty is accounted for in its own apparently unique terms.

The Division of the Fine Arts

In his explanation, Kant posits a relationship between the fine arts and the kind of expression that people use in speaking in order to communicate to each other as completely as possible. That is, communicating "not merely in respect of their concepts but in respect of their sensations also."[62] Thus, communication is divided into word, gesture, and tone—that is, articulation, gesticulation and modulation.[63] Kant is clear that it is only in the combination of all three that complete communication is achieved: "For thought, intuition, and sensation are thereby conveyed to

62. Ibid.
63. Ibid.

the other simultaneously and united."[64] This acknowledgement is important for it highlights the continuing role of concepts and, thus, the meaninglessness of sensations apart from concepts.

It is evident that the analysis of verbal communication mirrors the three powers of the soul in cognition. Thus, just as thought, intuition, and sensation are fundamental to cognition in general so word, gesture and tone are made crucial to communication in general. Kant extrapolates from the internal disposition of the mind to verbal communication. He then extends this to a classification of the fine arts, identifying three types of artistic communication: the "art of speech," which is aligned with word and articulation; "pictorial art," which is teamed with gesture and gesticulation; and the "art of the play of sensations," which is identified with tone and modulation. I will explain each parallel in turn. In doing so, we shall see the simplistic and somewhat arbitrary nature of the divisions. This will be especially notable in the case of music, as will the subjectively universal nature of Kant's understanding of beauty. For music is classed as mere tone and thus only hesitantly lays claim to beauty.

THE ART OF SPEECH[65]

The first division includes the arts of speech, those arts that excite representations by means of words. Kant includes both rhetoric and poetry but differentiates between the interplay of the powers that each invokes. Thus, rhetoric is "the art of conducting a business of the understanding as a free play of the imagination."[66] By contrast, poetry is the art of "carrying out a free play of the imagination as a business of the understanding."[67]

This distinction, based on free play, leads Kant, even at this stage, to express a preference for poetry over rhetoric. According to Kant, the proper business of the rhetorician is "the purposive occupation of the understanding."[68] However, instead of this, he offers "an entertaining

---

64. Ibid. Kant notes that the division might also be arranged "as a dichotomy, so that fine art would be divided into that of the expression of thoughts or intuitions, the latter being subdivided according to the distinction between the form and the matter (sensation)" (ibid., §51, 5:321, 198).

65. Ibid.

66. Ibid.

67. Ibid.

68. Ibid., §51, 5:321, 199.

play of the imagination,"[69] providing less than he promises.[70] By contrast, the poet pledges "an entertaining play with ideas" and yet in doing so "as much results for the understanding as if he had merely had the intention of carrying on its business."[71] Thus, according to Kant, the poet provides "nourishment" for the understanding through the interplay it encourages. It gives life to its concepts by means of the imagination and provides more than promised.[72]

PICTORIAL ART[73]

The second division is pictorial art: these arts express ideas in "sensible intuition" and "not through representations of the mere imagination, which are evoked by words."[74] They use "shapes in space" and it is on this basis that Kant justifies their link to gesture in speech: "the spirit of the artist gives a corporeal expression through these shapes to what and how he has thought, and makes the thing itself speak as it were in mime: a very common play of our fantasy, which attributes to lifeless things, in accordance with their form, a spirit that speaks from them."[75]

Kant divides pictorial art into arts of sensible truth and arts of sensible illusion according to the aesthetic idea that is referred to. Thus, if an artwork refers to a "real end" it is classed as sensuous truth; if it refers to the "appearance" of one then it is a sensuous semblance. Underlying this distinction is the distinctiveness of pure aesthetic from logical judgment, the importance of purposeless purposiveness, and the free play of the powers.

Plastic art is an art of sensuous truth. It uses sight and touch and consists of sculpture and architecture. The sole aim of sculpture is "the mere *expression* of aesthetic ideas." By contrast, architecture is concerned

69. Ibid.

70. Ibid.

71. Ibid., §51, 5:321, 198.

72. Ibid. In addition to this comparison of the two, Kant adds, in a later section on the "Comparison of the aesthetic value of the beautiful arts with each other" that, in contrast to rhetoric, poetry "plays with the illusion which it produces at will, yet without thereby being deceitful; for it itself declares its occupation to be mere play, which can nevertheless be purposively employed by the understanding for its own business" (ibid., §53, 5:327, 204).

73. Ibid., §51, 5:322–24, 199–201.

74. Ibid., §51, 5:321–22, 199.

75. Ibid., §51, 5:324, 201.

with "a certain *use* of the artistic object" to which the aesthetic ideas are inevitably subjected.[76] The difference is summed up: "statues of humans, gods, animals, etc., are of the first sort (sculpture); but temples, magnificent buildings for public gatherings, as well as dwellings, triumphal arches, columns, cenotaphs, and the like, erected as memorials, belong to architecture."[77]

Painting is an art of sensuous illusion. It uses sight alone, and can be subdivided into "*painting proper*" ("the beautiful *portrayal of* nature"), and "the beautiful *arrangement* of its *products*" (landscape gardening). For Kant, arts of sensuous illusion are made "strictly for viewing," entertaining the imagination in free play with ideas and engaging the aesthetic judgement independently of any definite end. Painting, therefore, gives only the illusion of bodily extension and the arrangement of nature's products gives only the illusion of "utility and employment for ends other than the play of the imagination in the contemplation of its forms."[78]

THE ART OF THE PLAY OF SENSATIONS[79]

The third division is the art of the beautiful play of sensations. These arts depend upon "sensations that arise from external stimulation." Nevertheless, they permit of universal communication.[80] They are concerned with "the proportion of the different degrees of the disposition (tension) of the sense to which the sensation belongs, i.e., its tone" and are divided into "the artistic play of sensations of hearing and sight," and consequently into "*music* and the *art of colours*."[81]

It is notable that the explanation of the art of the play of sensations immediately plunges Kant into a discussion about the status of such arts. This stems from the abiding importance of the free play of the powers as the channel for aesthetic communication, and the already ambiguous position of music indicated in his analysis of free and adherent beauty. The relation of the art of speech and pictorial art to free play is relatively

76. Ibid., §51, 5:322, 199.

77. Ibid., §51, 5:322, 199–200.

78. Ibid., §51, 5:323, 200. Within painting, Kant also includes all decoration whose sole function is to be looked at.

79. Ibid., §51, 5:324–25, 201–2.

80. Ibid., §51, 5:324, 201.

81. Ibid.

clear. However, the position of the art of the play of sensations is both less defined and less definable. Both hearing and sight "are capable of a special sensation," one that "cannot rightly be made out whether it has as its ground sense or reflection."[82] Thus, Kant maintains that "one cannot say with certainty whether a colour or a tone (sound) is merely agreeable sensations, or is itself already a beautiful play of sensations, which as such involves a satisfaction in the form of aesthetic judging."[83] Kant explains: in the case of the art of color or tone "the rapidity of the vibrations of the light, or in the second case, of the air" in all probability far outstrips our capacity for "judging immediately in perception the proportion of the division of time." Therefore, Kant infers, it is unlikely that it is the "*time-interval* between them" that affects our estimate. Rather, it is the "effect of these vibrations on the elastic parts of our body" which leads to pleasure.[84]

On the one hand, therefore, music and the art of color appear to depend upon sensation: "there is associated only agreeableness, not beauty of their composition."[85] On the other hand, however, as Kant notes, sensation alone does not provide an adequate explanation. In this regard Kant cites two examples. The first is the mathematical character of music, "the proportions of the oscillations in music and of the judging of them, and judges of contrasts among colours." This implies the involvement of reflection.[86] The second is the failure of the senses: there exist "those admittedly rare examples of human beings" who "with the best of sight in the world, cannot distinguish colours and, with the most acute hearing, cannot distinguish tones."[87] With these considerations in mind Kant states, "one may see oneself compelled to regard the sensations of both not as mere sensory impressions, but as the effect of a judging of the form in the play of many sensations."[88]

The status of music, as an art of the play of sensations is unclear: it may be viewed either as dependent upon the sensations it affords and therefore classed as agreeable, or as reflective and thus regarded as

82. Ibid., §51, 5:324, 201–2.
83. Ibid., §51, 5:324, 202.
84. Ibid., §51, 5:324–25, 202.
85. Ibid.
86. Ibid., §51, 5:325, 202.
87. Ibid.
88. Ibid.

beautiful.[89] Although classed among the fine arts, it is clear that Kant is not convinced of music's capacity to engage the understanding: music is therefore precluded from active involvement in the free play of the cognitive powers. This is made explicit at the close of his discussion: music is interpreted either as the "*beautiful* play of sensations (through hearing)" and is thus classed as a fine art, or else comprises "*agreeable* sensations" and is posited "at least in part" as an agreeable art.[90] This echoes Kant's earlier indecision as to whether music belongs to free beauty in virtue of its potential conceptlessness in un-themed and un-worded music, or pertains to adherent beauty in virtue of its sensory aspect.

In short, the division of the arts signals the problematic nature of Kant's understanding both of beauty and music. Beauty is not absolutely universal, for it does not include music, and music itself is considered according to a framework which it clearly does not occupy naturally. Thus, Kant abandons the connection between music and free beauty, granting it only qualified inclusion amongst the fine arts.

The Ranking of the Fine Arts and the Ambiguity of Music

It is evident that the understanding, imagination, and intuition, as paralleled in word, gesture, and tone (within verbal communication) are not used as an analogy for artistic communication within the division. If this were the case, then the "difference" that music presents would surely integrate itself more productively within the discussion. Rather, the parallel acts as a tool whereby the fine arts are classified, the combination of word, gesture, and tone in free play allowing Kant to speculate about the way in which the individual arts communicate and assess their involvement with beauty.

The ranking of the fine arts builds upon this, evaluating each art according to its capacity for free play.[91] Thus, the non-universality of beauty, and the imposition of a non-musical (conceptually biased) framework upon music, is drawn out even more clearly. The ranking of the arts does not adhere strictly to the format set out by the division unfolding thereby in a straightforward manner. Rather, it explores the ambiguity of music embodied within the division (resulting from the imposition of

89. Ibid.
90. Ibid.
91. Kant does not cover all of the individual arts in the section on ranking.

the Kantian understanding of beauty). It therefore includes alternative positions which view the sensory nature of music both positively and negatively.

The ranking of the fine arts appears almost in two parts, with poetry consistently ranking highest. As we shall see, this is due to the continuing emphasis upon free play. Poetry owes its origin "almost entirely to genius." It is "guided least by precept or example" and "expands the mind by setting the imagination free and presenting, within the limits of a given concept and among the unbounded manifold of forms possibly agreeing with it, the one that connects its presentation with a fullness of thought to which no linguistic expression is fully adequate."[92] It thus rises "aesthetically" to ideas. Kant explains: "It strengthens the mind by letting it feel its capacity to consider and judge of nature, as appearance, freely, self-actively, and independently of determination by nature."[93]

Following from this, Kant elaborates upon the separation of poetry and rhetoric proposed in the division of the arts. Rhetoric has recourse to the "machinery of persuasion, which, since it can also be used for glossing over or concealing vice and error, can never entirely eradicate the deep-seated suspicion of artful trickery."[94] By contrast, in poetry "everything proceeds honestly and uprightly. It declares that it will conduct a merely entertaining play with the imagination, and indeed concerning form, in concord with the laws of understanding, and does not demand that the understanding be deceived and embroiled through sensible presentation."[95]

Having established the primacy of poetry, Kant digresses from the expected course and enters upon what might be called the *first part* of the ranking. Herein, he takes "charm and movement of the mind" into account and positively evaluates sensation.[96] It is suggested that music, "the art of tone" (*Tonkunst*), may "very naturally be united" with poetry and hence might be placed higher than any other art of speech. This is paradoxical: music "speaks by means of mere sensations without concepts" and does not offer anything "for reflection" like poetry and yet is placed alongside it. The connection, however, is made by virtue of tone,

92. Ibid., §53, 5:326, 203–4.
93. Ibid., §53, 5:326, 204.
94. Ibid., §53, 5:327, 204.
95. Ibid., §53, 5:327, 204–5.
96. Ibid., §53, 5:328, 205.

which is evocative in language and substantive in music. In language every expression has "an associated tone suited to its sense." Kant explains: "This tone more or less designates an affect of the speaker and conversely also produces one in the hearer, which then in turn arouses in the latter the idea that is expressed in the language by means of such a tone."[97] Thus, in music the modulation involved in verbal communication is isolated from language per se but maintained by mechanical association.[98] In short, this brief digression, upholding the significance of the sensory aspect of music, does so only by virtue of the meaning that is thereby given through the harmony of the free play and its association with language. Music without words, it seems, is a shadow of language, bearing meaning only through the imitation of language in tone.

Kant's diversion is brief, and he returns, in what might be called the *second part* of the ranking, to the framework of the division. Herein, the sensory nature of music leads to its devaluation. Kant considers the fine arts according to the "culture" they supply to the mind and judges them according to "the enlargement of the faculties that must join together in the power of judgement for the sake of cognition."[99] In this respect, he maintains, music is "far surpassed" by the pictorial arts.[100] Kant juxtaposes music with the pictorial arts, compiling a series of contrasts that side against music. Hence, the two types of art pursue "completely different paths." The pictorial arts advance from definite ideas to sensations. They leave a lasting impression so that the imagination can recall its sensations, and "agreeably entertain" itself with them. Music proceeds

97. Ibid.

98. As I noted earlier (chapter four), the idea of a doctrine of affects prefigures and grounds Kant's position on music. The idea of 'affect' permeates many treatises of the period. Classic in this regard is the treatise by J. J. Quantz: affects may "be discerned by whether the intervals between the notes are great or small, and whether the notes themselves ought to be slurred or articulated. Flattery, melancholy and tenderness are expressed by slurred and close intervals, gaiety and boldness by brief articulated notes" (*On Playing the Flute*, 125–26). There is an excellent article by Anthony Rowland-Jones discussing the use of "affect" in music-making of the Baroque period, with regard to the recorder in particular. He advises using "a series of appropriate adjectives or descriptive phrases" to ascribe a "mood or character" when studying the recorder sonatas of G. F. Handel, noting that Handel himself sometimes did so: "Walsh's edition marks the third movement of the D minor sonata "Presto," but Handel's autograph states "Furioso," and it uses the language of the operatic aria with its torrent of semi-quavers between the bass and treble parts" ("Baroque Recorder Sonata," 58).

99. Kant, *CJ*, §53, 5:329, 206.

100. Ibid.

from sensations to indefinite ideas, its sensations vanishing entirely or, if "involuntarily recalled" by the imagination, proving more "burdensome" than agreeable.[101]

In contrast to music, the pictorial arts promote the "urbanity" of the powers of cognition. The pictorial arts both encourage free play while carrying on a serious business in which "they bring about a product that serves the concepts of the understanding as an enduring and self-recommending vehicle for its unification with sensibility."[102] Conversely, there is a lack of urbanity in music owing chiefly to "the character of its instruments" by means of which "it extends its influence further (into the neighbourhood) than is required, and so as it were imposes itself, thus interfering with the freedom of others, outside of the musical circle."[103] Its difference from those arts that "speak to the eyes" is clear. Therein, "if one would not admit their impressions" one need only "turn one's eyes away."[104] This is not possible in the case of music, which Kant compares to "the case of the delight from a widely pervasive smell."[105] Here, "Someone who pulls his perfumed handkerchief out of his pocket treats everyone in the vicinity to it against their will, and forces them, if they wish to breathe, to enjoy it at the same time."[106] One has no choice but to engage with sound.

101. Ibid., §53, 5:330, 206–7.

102. Ibid., §53, 5:329, 206. Among the pictorial arts, Kant ranks painting the highest: "partly because it is the art of design and, as such, the groundwork of all the other pictorial arts; partly because it can penetrate much further into the region of ideas, and in conformity with them give a greater extension to the field of intuition than it is open to the others to do" (ibid., §53, 5:330, 207).

103. Ibid.

104. Ibid.

105. Ibid.

106. Ibid. This attitude is exemplified in the opening quote of my exposition of Kant. Herein music, specifically (in this case) singing, imposes itself upon those in the vicinity and intrudes upon the business of thought. It is also echoed more widely than the third *Critique*. In July 1784, not long having moved into private accommodation, Kant writes to Hippel on account of nearby prisoners' singing, "You were so good to promise to act upon the complaint of the residents of the street at *Schloßgarten* in regard to the loud prayers of the hypocrites in the prison. I do not believe that they have reason to complain about the presumed danger to the salvation of their souls, if their voices were lowered so that they could hear themselves even by closed windows . . . and without screaming with all their might then . . . They could still receive the favourable judgement of the warden that they are god-fearing people. This seems to be their real concern anyway. One word to the warden . . . will be enough to curb this abuse and will

In the event, then, Kant focuses upon the sensory aspect of music and alienates it from the power of understanding and concepts. The term beautiful is attributed by Kant to an object that encourages the harmony of the free play of the powers of imagination and understanding. It is grounded primarily in concepts. Since music is not bound to concepts in the same way as arts of word and pictorial arts it is thought to be *mere* sensation. Hence, in the worst instance for Kant, music is noise.

CONCLUSIONS

The Adequacy of Beauty

We have seen that Kant's account of beauty is constructed in response to the antinomy of taste, and the priority of the third *Critique* is its solution. Kant achieves this: he succeeds in suggesting grounds for aesthetic delight that are a priori, either through the harmony of the free play or the supersensible substrate, or a combination of both, and yet in such a way that precludes the determinative involvement of concept. He thus mediates between the rationalist and empiricist concern with taste and the objective and subjective accounts of beauty that they offer respectively.

However, in the end, beauty plays a subsidiary role, characterizing, indicating, and authenticating pure judgments of taste not by means of any inherent quality it possesses but through those qualities imputed to it by the necessity that Kant's account demands. In one sense it seems that beauty is the content of aesthetic judgment. At a primary level it is the exhibition of aesthetic ideas, which in some measure sets forth the supersensible substrate of appearances, and at a secondary level it is its accompanying pleasure. This is misleading. Rather, as I have shown, the converse is true: the content of beauty is the harmony of the free play. Beauty is that which makes sense of the free interplay of the cognitive powers, differentiating it from other forms of judgment. Beauty describes the process of free play in which neither concept nor intu-

---

help the person whose quiet state you have many times tried to help so graciously." A biographer, Ludwig Ernst Borowski, notes that nothing more is heard from Kant about the unruly singing of hymns after this complaint, but that it appears that he never really obtained the peace and quiet that he sought for his work. Borowski reports that all that was achieved was that the windows were closed. The "nonsense" outside continued. Borowski, *Leben*, 76; Malter, *Kant in Rede und Gespräch*, 255, cited in Kuehn, *Kant*, 269–70. Borowski was one of three people who had known Kant well during different periods of his life, and who were to give accounts of Kant's life as they knew it. The other two were Reinhold Bernhard Jachmann and Ehregott Christian.

ition is sufficient to the other and expresses the pleasure which results from this overabundance. In short, beauty indicates the relentless and self-fulfilling need of the human mind to synthesize and comprehend nature, to which it seems fitted.

Thus in the Kantian account, beauty is not something inherently meaningful that is mediated through nature and art, but refers solely to the subjective process of aesthetic appreciation. This challenges the classical aesthetic tradition, which we met in Boethius, wherein beauty is itself necessary and universal and not as Kant implies, dependent and conditional. This is of course evident in Kant's evaluation of the fine arts, wherein beauty is delimited to those instances in which free play is patent. It is reinforced in Kant's application of the notion of beauty to the fine arts via the model of verbal communication, wherein only the full co-operation of thought, intuition, and sensation in word, gesture, and tone, ensures successful communication.

Kant's exposition of the fine arts demonstrates the circumscription of beauty: beauty is not granted absolute extension and thus sensation is considered as mere. Music is a case in point: Kant regards it as primarily sensory and, as a result, maintains that it communicates beauty only conditionally. He thus ultimately neglects its formal basis and views its unique properties entirely negatively, such as its physicality and indeterminacy. As a result, music is consigned to the border between fine and agreeable art and is exiled to the no-man's land between the beautiful and the agreeable.

The Ambiguity of Music

Although eschewing determinacy, concepts retain a level of importance due to the subjective locus of meaning within the harmony of the free play. It is for this reason that the two-fold aspect of music, which is both intellectual and sensible, proves problematic. Kant considers these two aspects separately and thus music resists classification. Eventually however, he favors an understanding of music that regards it as primarily sensory. Kant thus devalues it, rendering it meaningless.

To summarize: in the division of the arts, Kant is unable to identify the ground of music and decide whether the sensation that it evokes is anchored in sense or reflection. Kant cannot decide whether music is a series of "merely agreeable sensations" or a "beautiful play of sensations," in which case it would involve aesthetic satisfaction.[107] This uncertainty is insoluble and, as we have seen, Kant ends by countering his own argument.[108] As a result of Kant's hesitancy, music is evaluated differently at points in the third *Critique*. At times Kant seemingly holds an elevated understanding of music, for example in the section that considers the distinction between free beauty (which "presupposes no concept of what the object ought to be") and adherent beauty (which "does presuppose such a concept and the perfection of the object in accordance with it").[109] Herein, the conceptlessness of music leads to its classification as free beauty and guarantees its place alongside nature: both a particular sort of music (music without a theme or accompanying text) and nature are free from concepts and therefore enable a pure judgment of taste to be made, wherein one judges according to mere form. Thus, both nature and music are thought superior to adherent beauty. More often and, ultimately, in conclusion, understanding music as sensation influences Kant's overall evaluation of music, which he considers as the "art of tone." Thus, more often than not, the indeterminacy of music is viewed through its sensory rather than formal aspect: music proceeds to indeterminate ideas but does so by means of sensation. Kant thus dissociates music from the harmony of the free play of the cognitive powers, the foundation of beauty, stating that music is more at home amongst the agreeable arts, in fact finding itself quite highly placed therein:

> If, on the contrary, one estimates the value of the beautiful arts in terms of culture that they provide for the mind and takes as one's standard the enlargement of the faculties that must join together in the power of judgement for the sake of cognition, then to that extent music occupies the lowest place among the beautiful arts (just as it occupies perhaps the highest place among those that

---

107. Kant, *CJ*, §51, 5:325, 202. In the elucidation of aesthetic judgment, Kant acknowledges the *ambiguous status* of colour and music: if one assumes with Euler first, that "the colours are vibrations of the air immediately following one another, just as tones are vibrations of the air disturbed by sound" and second, "that the mind does not merely perceive, by sense, their effect on the animation of the organ, but also, through reflection," then colours and tones would not be mere sensations, but would already be a formal determination of the unity of a manifold of them, and in that case could also be counted as beauties in themselves" (ibid., §14, 5:225, 110).

108. Ibid., §51, 5:325, 202.

109. Ibid., §16, 5:229, 114.

are estimated according to their agreeableness), because it merely plays with sensations.[110]

As an agreeable art, music does not partake in cognition and is devoid of content, neither involving disinterested pleasure nor conveying aesthetic ideas, and thus leaving behind a "transitory" rather than a "lasting" impression.[111]

In terms of communication therefore, music is either an embellishment upon content, color, and timbre, making drawing and composition "more precisely, more determinately, and more completely intuitable." (It also enlivens the representation through its charm, "thereby awakening and sustaining attention to the object itself").[112] If it is to comprise a channel of communication in itself, music finds a medium of expression that accords with its sensible nature, since according to Kant music cannot inherently communicate aesthetic ideas.[113] Thus, as we have seen, Kant suggests that the art of tone is the "language of affects," communicating mechanically via the "law of association" through the "dominant affect" of a piece and thereby conveying aesthetic ideas.[114] As we have seen, speech has an accompanying tone by means of which the affect of the speaker is communicated. In the absence of speech, music continues to communicate affects, although in an indeterminate way.

Thus, the capacity of music derives from the effect it has upon the body: "All changing free play of sensations (which is not grounded in any intention) gratifies, because it promotes the feeling of health, whether or not we take satisfaction in the rational judging of its object and even in this gratification."[115] It is on this basis that music is placed alongside "material for laughter":

> Music and material for laughter are two kinds of play with aesthetic ideas or even representations of the understanding by

110. Ibid., §53, 5:329, 206.

111. Ibid., §53, 5:330, 207. For this reason, as mere enjoyment, music needs to be changed frequently. However, nor can it bear "frequent repetition without inducing antipathy" (ibid.).

112. Ibid., §14, 5:225–26, 110.

113. Kant is clear that of "that which pleases merely in the *judging*" and "that which gratifies (pleases in the sensation)" only the former can be required of everyone. Ibid., §53, Remark, 5:330–31, 207.

114. Ibid., §53, 5:328, 205.

115. Ibid., §53, Remark, 5:331, 208.

which in the end nothing is thought, and which can gratify merely through their change, and nevertheless do so in a lively fashion; by which they make it fairly evident that the animation in both cases is merely corporeal, although it is aroused by ideas of the mind, and that the feeling of health resulting from a movement of the viscera corresponding to that play constitutes the whole gratification in a lively party, which is extolled as so refined and spirited.[116]

Neither music nor laughter involves reflection. Rather, they are concerned with "the promotion of the business of life in the body, the affect which moves the viscera and the diaphragm." This is "the feeling of health (which otherwise cannot be felt without such a stimulus), which constitutes the gratification in which one discovers that one can get at the body through the soul and use the latter as the doctor for the former."[117]

The Adequacy of Kant's Treatment of Music

The Kantian account of music is obviously problematic and clearly does not do it justice, at a fundamental level precluding the beauty of music, except in a formal way. This counter-intuitive claim undoubtedly derives from Kant's emphasis upon reason. However, it may also arise from Kant's unfamiliarity with the phenomenon of music. I would like to suggest some possible indications to this effect.

First, in his account of music Kant seems to use terms inconsistently. Thus, within his discussion of the purposiveness of a judgment of taste, the third moment of four, Kant elucidates his point "by means of examples."[118] He distinguishes between pure and empirical judgments of taste and in doing so referring to both "mere colour" and "tone (*in distinction* from sound and noise)."[119] He considers both within the same class of art.[120] Kant says that those who claim the beauty of the green of a lawn and the tone of a violin are mistaken: "it cannot be easily assumed that the agreeableness of one colour in preference to another or of the

116. Ibid., §53, Remark, 5:332, 208.

117. Ibid., §53, 5:332, 209. Note the implicit reversal of the Boethian account wherein the soul was in some measure "healed" by means of the body through music.

118. This is the title given to *CJ*, §14, 5:223, 108.

119. Ibid., §14, 5:224, 108. My italics.

120. Jean Jacques Rousseau argues against the equation of color and sound, calling it a "false analogy," cf. excerpt from "Essays on the Origin of Languages, which Treats of Melody and Musical Imitation" (c. 1760) 951–53. However, for ideas about how music "paints," cf. Engel, "On Painting in Music" (1780) 954–65.

tone of one musical instrument in preference to another will be judged in the same way by everyone."[121] Later, in the division of the arts,[122] Kant maintains the association of music and the art of color but casts it in different terms: previously, the elucidation of the purposiveness of the judgment of taste defines tone as timbre. By contrast, the division of the arts uses tone to refer to sound, speaking as he does of music's oscillations.[123] There is nothing wrong as such with this differentiation since tone can refer to both of these. Yet concern arises from the parallel of each definition with color without any corresponding differentiation.[124]

Second, at a general level, the division of the arts only deals with the broad class of music. For although Kant refers in particular to music without a theme or set of words in his examination of free beauty, he does not make any distinction between types of music in the division of the arts, by means of which he would perhaps be able to construct a more nuanced account.[125] It is for this reason that Kant fails to acknowledge music's association with concepts, a consideration that might involve music within free play. To clarify: a guiding concept can be involved in the composition and reception of a piece of music, as in the case of 'program' music (for example, where the music is composed with a definite impression or series of impressions in mind that takes the composer, performer, and listener on a journey of thought).[126] Moreover, the mere suggestion of a title can precipitate free play: it can set a stream of thoughts emerging from those evoked by a piece into motion. Thus, contra Kant, music can have an effect on both the body *and the mind*. This is true even beyond explicitly conceptual pieces: music has the capacity to stimulate the mind to a manifold movement through association, memory, and

121. Kant, *CJ*, §14, 5:224, 108.

122. Ibid., §51, 5:320–25, 197–202.

123. Ibid., §51, 5:325, 202.

124. Moreover, it is interesting to note that Kant does not speak of the art of *tone*, as the natural parallel to the art of colors, tone being the 'stuff' of which music consists, as color is of pictorial art, but of the art of music.

125. However, this criticism is not unique to music and can be leveled at Kant's treatment of all of the arts that he considers: they are considered in block categories and do not reflect the subtleties of the individual arts.

126. Liszt introduced the term 'program' music, defining it as a "preface added to a piece of instrumental music, by means of which the composer intends to guard the listener against a wrong poetical interpretation, and to direct his attention to the poetical idea of the whole or to a particular part of it" (Scruton, "Programme Music").

feeling. Third (although not acknowledged by Kant), the fact that music exists as the organization of tones means that it is never mere sound if one is actively listening to it: the mind is always engaged at some level. Implicitly this means, in contrast to Kant, that music has the capacity to leave behind a lasting mental impression.

However, the recognition that the mind is engaged in music as well as the body should not mitigate the role of the senses, in which the uniqueness of music undoubtedly consists, at least in part. The physicality of music is undeniably challenging for Kant, who sees no value in sense apart from active cognition. However, it must be addressed if one is to offer an account of the meaning of music. This is something that is undeniably challenging for Kant, who sees no value in sense apart from active cognition. This is problematic and must be addressed if one is to offer an account of the meaning of music. This leads us to note something especially counter-intuitive in Kant's evaluation of music, resulting from his account of beauty. Although Kant grants that pure aesthetic cognition and beauty are a way of entering into a relationship with the world, a way of rendering it intelligible and allowing the subject a sense of feeling at home by orienting it within the world (as Boethius had done) he prohibits music's ability to facilitate this. The suggestion that music has this capacity for orientation will be taken up in chapter seven of this book.

Responding to the Kantian Account of Music

The problems inherent within Kant's evaluation of music are clear: he has an overly rational understanding (conceptually speaking) of the aesthetic response and beauty and, consequently, is unable to validate music as sound. Responses to Kant are therefore various: his account is criticized and re-conceived. However, in many cases no attempt is made to eschew Kant's conceptual bias. I will summarize two such accounts. The first, presented by Peter Kivy, accepts Kant's conclusion that music is merely sensory pleasure (exempt from what might be called beauty) and proceeds on this basis to elaborate an account of musical meaning. The second, suggested by Jeanette Bicknell, involves a re-examination of the third *Critique*. She attempts to find a loophole within Kant's own principles that permits a more positive evaluation of music. Bicknell thus offers an account of the semantic meaning of music in the light of Kant's thought on aesthetic ideas and aesthetic attributes.

AN ACCEPTANCE?

Kant's evaluation of music is not a historical anomaly. On the contrary, the train of thought re-emerges in contemporary philosophy of music in various guises. Kivy accepts the Kantian account as it stands and does not re-imagine or manipulate what is stated there. Kivy thus works authentically within Kant's remit by criticizing those elements that might have been better if developed differently. In this way, he extends Kant's conclusions.

According to Kivy, music does not have cognitive content: he is skeptical of the idea, prevalent in Romanticism, that music expresses thoughts that are indescribable in words. On the contrary, he believes that our inability to paraphrase or gloss music is not due to any kind of ineffability but is evidence for its lack of content.[127] He thus concludes that the "unspeakable wealth of thought" of which Kant speaks is not only a romantic cliché but a dangerous pretension.[128] Denying any conceptual basis Kivy recognizes that, for Kant, music is mere pleasure. He thus grasps the essence of Kant's account. More generally in his work on music, he goes further than this simple recognition and eradicates any residual ambiguity about the status of music. He maintains that an understanding of music as mere pleasure is enough to justify it as meaningful. Kivy is unequivocal: music does not have content.

Emphatic about this, Kivy believes that Kant's main achievement is his indication of how and in what way music means. Importantly, for Kivy, by considering music as the "language of affect," Kant provides an insight into the "logic" or "syntax" of music,[129] which acts upon the passions and communicates emotions. According to Kivy, Kant's emphasis upon the emotional evocation of music is a positive step that potentially grants Kant the opportunity to offer something new to what was the commonplace view of music throughout the eighteenth century, the arousal theory, wherein "music arouses the *emotions* through its representation of the passionate accents of the human speaking voice."[130] Kivy is disappointed in this regard, however, observing a discrepancy between the actual answer that Kant gives and the ideal one that Kivy wishes

127. Kivy, "Kant and the 'Affektenlehre'," 254.

128. Ibid.

129. Ibid., 255

130. Ibid., 257. My italics.

he had given. For Kant elucidates the emotional affect of music, not by means of the central and unique notion of the third *Critique*, aesthetic ideas, but by espousing arousal theory. Kant thus adheres to the arousal theory of the eighteenth century. Ideally, Kivy believes, Kant should have suggested that satisfaction issues from the free play of the cognitive powers rather than from a physiological satisfaction.[131]

Kivy's disappointment is not quite a criticism, and in fact it merely articulates the majority wish that Kant's account demonstrate the exhibition of the supersensible substrate of appearances in music. However, it seems to me that Kivy's wish is for the impossible: understanding beauty as the harmony of the free play precludes music's participation. Kant is clear that music is sensation and nothing more. It is therefore inconceivable that Kant would allow music to exhibit aesthetic ideas in the same way as the other fine arts. Kivy concedes this:

> Kant must have connected the ability of the aesthetic ideas in poetry to engage the free play of the cognitive faculties with the nature of their source, namely, a cognitive content; and, by parity of reasoning, he must have connected the inability of the aesthetic ideas in music to engage the free play of the cognitive faculties with the nature of its source, which was by contrast, completely devoid of stable cognitive content. What was left for the aesthetic ideas in music to engage were merely the pleasurable sensations of the body, which did, after all, coincide with general opinion in the eighteenth century, as with Kant's rather low opinion of music's intellectual pretensions.[132]

In the light of this acknowledgement, it is interesting that Kivy expresses disappointment in Kant's inability to move beyond arousal theory and that he suggests an alternative at all. All the more so in the light of his own project which attempts to create an account of music which understands it as meaningful in virtue of its status as mere pleasure.[133] It is thus that elsewhere Kivy defines absolute (instrumental)

---

131. The arousal theory is controversial within contemporary aesthetics: a recent proponent of it is Matravers, *Art and Emotion*.

132. Kivy, "Kant and the 'Affektenlehre'," 262.

133. Kivy suggests that "philosophical thinkers about music until the end of the eighteenth century had things exactly right, and that the nineteenth century began to get them exactly wrong. Since the end of the sixteenth century there have been *two* arts of music: the fine art of musical text setting, which is basically the art of representing human expression in musical tones, and the decorative art of absolute music" ("Is Music an Art?" 371).

music as a "decorative art" in which we are content to trace its patterns.[134] In all fairness to Kant, it seems most likely that the attempted alliance of music with aesthetic ideas results from Kant's concession to its inclusion amongst the fine arts.

A revision?

Bicknell provides a contrasting approach to Kivy, modifying a specific element of Kant's own account in order to extend it so that it might embrace music, giving it what appears to be a more reasonable basis of inclusion amongst the fine arts. Interestingly in the light of Kivy's criticism of Kant's account, she does so by means of aesthetic ideas.

Bicknell calls upon Bach's D Minor Chaconne for solo violin in the light of Roger Scruton's suggestion that it provides an effect of "titanic strain, as of a giant Atlas, bearing the burden of *the world's greatest sadness*."[135] Proceeding according to Kant's account of aesthetic ideas and assuming that "Scruton's description does in fact capture some of the music's structural and expressive properties," Bicknell suggests that "the world's sadness" is a rational idea that is not given in experience and that, therefore, a competent performance of Bach's Chaconne will inspire much thought in a listener, some of which will not be adequately expressed by any concept. It is by means of these thoughts that music expresses aesthetic ideas. Bicknell states:

> The particular aesthetic ideas that the Chaconne expresses, while not adequately conveyed in language, might include the inevitability of suffering, the contingency of human life, and the psychic strain brought about by acknowledging these. The aesthetical attributes by which these ideas are evoked are the form of the Chaconne—a series of rhythmic pitches as perceived by the listener. A difference in aesthetic form (the series of rhythmic pitches that underlie another musical work, or even different patterns of emphasis in a different performance of the Chaconne) would inspire different aesthetic ideas.[136]

This approach is fruitful in terms of making sense of the interaction that takes place within the listener's musical experience, since music can and does involve concepts. It is not merely sensation since it is under-

134. Kivy, "Fine Art of Repetition."

135. Scruton, *Aesthetics of Music*, 452. My italics.

136. Bicknell, "Can Music Convey Semantic Content?" 253–61.

stood to have a form of some sort, it is an intentional structure, and does evoke different types of concept such as emotion and representation, albeit in an indeterminate way. Thus it does involve some form of cognitive content. Moreover, the pleasure evoked through music does not simply arise from its physical impact on the body. Often it emerges from a sense of engagement with a form or concept (or set of indeterminate concepts) that occurs with, in, and through a piece.

However, in the light of Kant's account the approach is questionable. The third *Critique* clearly classifies music as mere sensation and concludes that music is not beautiful and has no aesthetic meaning to convey. Bicknell recognizes that the use of Kant's application of aesthetic ideas to the case of music is unorthodox in terms of the *Critique of Judgment* and notes in particular Peter Kivy's rejection of the notion that Kant sought to ascribe content to music in his doctrine of aesthetic ideas.[137] However, this does not caution her against the use of Kant's account as it stands. Bicknell says: "The fact that Kant was unlikely to have thought that music possessed semantic content need not stop us from using his doctrine of aesthetic ideas to make sense of some listeners' propensity to *hear* music as meaning-bearing."

Bicknell's account does not challenge the Kantian framework of beauty and the meaning that is given to music as a result. Rather, she takes up the concept of aesthetic ideas and applies them to music as the exhibition of rational ideas, something explicitly in opposition to Kant's account, without offering any explanation of the grounds on which she does so other than "it is useful." Thus the linguistic model of meaning that Kant uses in his account of the fine arts remains unchallenged and unmodified, and Bicknell forces music to fit the same framework. Moreover, Bicknell does not suggest how on her account music is able to convey aesthetic ideas.

The effectiveness of Bicknell's approach is limited: she works from the Kantian account but without attending sufficiently to its framework. Hence, she makes an unconvincing case for the ability of Kant's account (in particular the notion of aesthetic ideas) to explain musical meaning. Bicknell's approach refrains from acknowledging that Kant's account may be potentially wrong or at least misguided, trying instead to redeem it by seizing upon what she judges to be its most adaptable aspect. In effect, Bicknell refuses the Kantian distinction between beautiful art and

137. Kivy, "Kant and the 'Affektenlehre,'" 254–55.

agreeable art, and yet accepts the linguistic paradigm which determines this distinction. She thus transforms music, as Peter Kivy maintains more generally, "into one kind or another of crypto-representation."[138]

A PREOCCUPATION WITH FORM

In addition to those approaches that accept the conceptual bias of Kant's account, there are others who attempt to proceed from Kant's preoccupation with form. The importance of form for Kant is indisputable (indeed, he is maintained by some to be the founder of musical "formalism").[139] Thus, there are many who, responding to the Kantian account of music, concentrate upon its formal element both in diagnosing its weaknesses and in suggesting alternatives. Thus, even within those examples that we have considered, Bicknell's account suggests that aesthetic ideas are exhibited through the structural properties of music and Kivy, in his disappointment with Kant's account of music, suggests that Kant's failure to exploit the possibility of aesthetic ideas stems from his inadequate grasp of musical form.[140]

138. Kivy, "Is Music an Art?" 372. Kivy continues: this rests on the "all too frequently unexpressed premise that only as representation can it really be taken seriously, which, manifestly, it is" (ibid.).

139. Cf. Neubauer, "Kant and the Origins of Formalism," 182–92. "Formalism" is explained by musicologist Leo Treitler: "Reduced to its simplest terms the attitude of formalism is that the contents of music are nothing other than notes—either sounded or written—and their patterns, and that understanding music, i.e., apprehending its meaning, is understanding those elements and patterns" (Treitler, "Language and the Interpretation of Music," 25). Peter Kivy makes a case for "enhanced formalism," a term suggested by Philip Alperson. He suggests that *contra* Hanslick, emotive properties are compatible with "formalism" in the same way that "a billiard ball possesses roundness and redness as seen properties." Thus music "does not mean 'melancholy' or represent 'melancholy.' It just *is* melancholy" (*Introduction to a Philosophy of Music*, 89–90).

140. Kivy notes: "If Kant, for example, had been conversant with the structural principles of sonata form—the most important musical form of the classical period—he would have seen that although such musical works as were cast in sonata form had no stable cognitive content, they were far from haphazard plays of emotion, but followed, rather, a statable sequence of musical elements with a palpable sense of logic and syntax. And their affective properties were part of that logical and syntactical progression" (Kivy, "Kant and the 'Affektenlehre,'" 263). In the same article, Kivy states that Kant is ignorant of music "as an art," showing "absolutely no evidence whatever that its author had the slightest acquaintance with anything that a musician or music lover would recognize as musical form: that is to say, sonata form, song form, rondo, theme-and-variations, and so forth, which would be, along with the elements that make them up, such as melodic structure and harmonic and contrapuntal syntax, the bearers of expressive properties as I conceive of them" (ibid., 257).

The same emphasis appears elsewhere in interpretations of Kant. Form is focused upon in the work of musicologist Carl Dahlhaus, who names musical contingency as the real problem. Observing Kant's classification of instrumental music as "merely agreeable art" and as "more pleasure than culture," Dahlhaus notes that this is due either to the view that music lacks form, or from the idea that its forms are weak and unsatisfactory.[141] Dahlhaus draws attention to the fact that, as we have seen, the musical form Kant bears in mind is the 'mathematical form' of tone-relations,[142] and that he could thus have substantiated music's claim amongst the fine arts, but does not because of music's "transitory aspect."[143] Hence at the same time as criticizing Kant, Dahlhaus posits a way out, suggesting that one might mitigate the transitory nature of music by recognizing "that events in time can also be fixed in forms (*Gestalten*)."[144]

Form is also emphasized by Philip Bowman in his work on Kant. Echoing the issues implicit within my examination,[145] and proceeding in a similar manner to Dahlhaus, Bowman recognizes the conceptlessness and indeterminacy of music, noting that although it "should have been a

141. Dahlhaus, *Esthetics of Music*, 31–38.

142. Dahlhaus summarizes, "upon this mathematical form alone—mathematical though not represented by definite concepts—depends the satisfaction that connects mere reflecting on such a crowd of feelings, simultaneous or consecutive, with their play, as a universally valid condition of its beauty" (Kant, *CJ*, §53; in Dahlhaus, *Esthetics of Music*, 32).

143. Kant says, "Surely mathematics has no part whatsoever in the charm and the agitation of the heart produced by music, but it is rather only an indispensable condition" (*CJ*, §53; in Dahlhaus, *Esthetics of Music*, 33). Dahlhaus notes the similarity between Kant's thought and that of Francis Hutcheson's in *An inquiry into the origin of our ideas of beauty and virtue* (1726): "Both Kant and Hutcheson define musical beauty formally, as a harmony of representation of tones; both sharply divided the emotional effect of music from esthetic judgement, although they do not deny emotion but even emphasise it" (Dahlhaus, *Esthetics of Music*, 33).

144. Ibid., 34.

145. Bowman seems to misunderstand what Kant says about beauty and the expression of aesthetic ideas. He says of music: "Musical value extends beyond Kant's pure aesthetic judgement, and music's forms are vital forms vivified by the human imagination . . . They are not empty abstractions, but rich, concrete, temporally unfolding realities. A 'pure' aesthetic response, as defined by Kant names a musical impossibility" (Bowman, *Philosophical Perspectives on Music*, 91). However, in reply, Kantian aesthetic judgment is not an empty abstraction and "pure" formality in the sense in which Bowman seems to suggest. It contains a "wealth" of thought that derives from the activity of the imagination.

virtue" it is in fact for Kant "an artistic defect since its forms are so sensual and fleeting."[146] He asks whether these conclusions are "inescapably implicated" by Kant's critique or whether they are "the indiscretions of a musically naïve intellectual."[147] He suggests that musical meaning might be redeemed, as it were, by valuing and classing music as an art of time rather than an art of tone.[148]

Summary of Part Two

I have shown how the antinomy of taste embodies central Enlightenment concerns and how it shapes Kant's understanding of beauty. In order to resolve the antinomy and negotiate the boundary between subject and object, Kant requires a principle that is both a priori and indeterminate. This leads him to locate meaning in the subject, albeit in a universal way. As a result, beauty is used to signal key features of the subjective process of aesthetic appreciation: the form of beauty is located within the powers of the subject rather than featuring as an aspect of the object itself. Thus, subject and object are wrenched apart, for the intellectual is emphasized to the detriment of the physical. It is for this reason that the sensibility of music is rendered ambiguous within Kant's account of the fine arts and, crucially, it is for this reason that sounded music is implicitly abstracted from in favor of its formal basis. Although beauty is indeterminate, concepts remain necessary and, thus, sensation *as such* is meaningless: it is mere *non*-sense, distracting from the pursuit of reason.

Although replies to the Kantian account demonstrate the legitimacy of a discussion of musical form, it seems that there is a recalcitrant unwillingness to delve deeper, to speak about musical meaning at a core level. That is, there is a reluctance to submerge oneself in the structure

---

146. Ibid., 86.

147. Ibid.

148. Bowman refers both to the *CPR*, where Kant establishes time as part of the *a priori* frame of experience, and to Dahlhaus' comments on Kant's conception of time in his *Esthetics of Music*. "There is little reason to doubt that music was, for him [Kant], fleeting and sensuous. Certainly, music's tones—conceived as material sense data—are quite transient. But tones perceived musically are no longer sense data, bearing as they do on the imprint of the mind. Music does not reside in the realm of pure materiality and sensation. Indeed, for those fluent in particular musical universes of discourse, music consists of processive patterns and configurations that are stable and secure. It is comprised not of evanescent tones, but of dynamic, temporal *gestalten* that deeply engage the mind" (Bowman, *Philosophical Perspectives on Music*, 88–89).

in and through which music lays hold of us and imparts its manifold of meaning, for it is evident that one can account for musical meaning through its connection with form, emotion, pleasure, and (even for Kant in his positive moments) indeterminate concepts. Moreover, one may well experience what one would declare to be beautiful on this basis. However, if we follow Boethius and Kant in understanding beauty epistemologically, as referring to those moments of experience within which there is a certain interrelationship between subject and object, self and world, whereby a certain fittingness between the two is felt to be the case (a sensation that is characteristically pre-reflective), it may be that we can begin to do justice to music whilst also contributing to an understanding of beauty. It is to this that we now turn.

7

Musical Beauty

An Enchanted Mode of Attention

Oᴜʀ ᴇxᴘʟᴏʀᴀᴛɪᴏɴ ᴏꜰ Bᴏᴇᴛʜɪᴜs and Kant has led us to see that, historically, the relationship between subject and object has been formative for the concept of beauty. Beauty has served as a cipher for epistemological concerns as well as a space within which these are worked out. We have also seen how the epistemological relationship is underpinned by understandings about the nature of the world, its physicality in particular, and the type of knowledge that it yields. Hence, even though within both the Boethian and Kantian accounts beauty serves to articulate the form of the relationship between the self and the world, it is ultimately biased towards *either* the object *or* the subject, in each case abstracting from the physical towards a ground of meaning which in each instance is in some way conceptual, offering "certainty" and thereby stability. It is this ground of meaning that acts as an end towards which all else is directed as a means. Music is one such means and the result is that its ontology is determined by, and valued through, non-musical frameworks. Hence the physical is of no importance in and of itself. Rather, it is significant only in so far as it propels one towards a meaning that is located in and generated by a ground beyond the physical.

Given this particular history of the concept of beauty and its intrinsic relation to epistemological concerns, the aim is to see, programmatically, how music *in and through its physicality* might elucidate and develop the relationship between subject and object, self and world, and perhaps impact upon an understanding of beauty, epistemologically understood. In doing so, I shall suggest that the physical character of musical experience discloses a first-order mode of being, one that involves a suspension of the distinction between subject and object (promoting instead their mutuality) or, rather, a retrieval of the pre-reflective moment before this distinction asserts itself. Furthermore, I shall suggest that, thereby, it encourages a subtler model of beauty than offered by either Boethius or Kant. This model does not call for transcendence of the physical, for music is inherently indeterminate and cannot articulate any one particular avenue of meaning. Nor does it consign the physical to the merely subjective. As we shall see this is to miss the point. Rather, to speak about musical beauty is to speak about the occurrence of a certain stance towards the world wherein one focuses outwards and experiences an abundance of meaning that is not self-generated but is presented from without whilst resonating within. Experienced as a sense of richness or fullness, music can thus be said to encourage what might be called an "enchanted" mode of attention.

Before exploring this further, it is important to note that attending to music's physicality does not lead inevitably to its absolutization as some kind of channel through which transcendence flows, for this is beyond the scope of the physical which can only point towards an immanent transcendence.[1] Nor will music be considered as a completely autonomous and free-floating entity.[2] In short, no form of neutrality is presumed. On the contrary, the inextricability of music from practice is intrinsic to the methodology that structures what follows. The objective is to illuminate those aspects of the musical experience that facilitate the diversity of its meaning and practice. In doing so, we are led to favor a

---

1. Jeremy Begbie warns against certain methodologies that arise within theology of music and, amongst these, "theological aestheticism." Within such approaches music is to be understood in its own terms with an "open and value-free mind" such that, in some instances, music becomes a "new theological master" giving us "supreme access to God or perhaps to some (again undefined) 'spiritual realm'" (Begbie, *Resounding Truth*, 22).

2. On the autonomy of music, see Clarke, "Musical Autonomy Revisited," 159–70. On the idea of the musical 'work' see Goehr, *Imaginary Museum of Musical Works*; Strohm and Blackburn, *Music as concept and practice in the late Middle Ages*; Carl Dahlhaus, *Nineteenth Century Music*. In his phenomenology of musical ontology, Benson draws out the 'messiness' of music as practice, the bleeding of composition into performance and vice versa. For this reason he favors talk of pieces rather than works: "the 'structures' that we call pieces of music are 'composed' of the activity of music making itself, rather than music making 'plus some other thing' (that we would call a 'work')" (*The Improvisation of Musical Dialogue*, 161).

phenomenological approach. That is to say, we are led to an approach that attempts to attend to the given phenomenon as it presents itself and not as viewed through and colored by prior presuppositions or frameworks. It is thus that Merleau-Ponty endorses the "phenomenological reduction" for this allows one to become aware of and postpone our normal interaction with the world, one by means of which we in some sense pre-judge, shape, and dominate it. Within such an approach, it is instances and not universals that matter. Merleau-Ponty says:

> It is because we are through and through compounded of relationships with the world that for us the only way to become aware of the fact is to suspend the resultant activity, to refuse it our complicity . . . or yet again, to put it "out of play." Not because we reject the certainties of common sense and a natural attitude to things—they are, on the contrary, the constant theme of philosophy—but because, being the presupposed basis of any thought, they are taken for granted, and go unnoticed, and because in order to arouse them and bring them into view, we have to suspend for a moment our recognition of them.[3]

To adopt a phenomenological stance is necessarily to delimit the scope of questioning since it aims only ever to deal with what is given through experience: it eschews definitive explanations and, instead, explores the potentiality of what is given. The results of this approach are necessarily indeterminate and this, rather than being a defect, indicates the richness of experience and perception. This is particularly so in the case of music for musical meaning is splendidly manifold: it can mean through the internal relations that constitute its form; it can also represent, evoke, and express a variety of things through extra-musical allusions. Importantly, however, our examination will not rest on these forms of meaning for these are consequent upon music's first-order mode of being. It is this, the first-order, with which we shall remain: music's capacity to suspend the distinction between subject and object, as revealed within its physicality. Thus, we will examine music *qua* music, that is, music *as sound*, for this is its basis. This will involve attention to a variety of its physical aspects. We will explore music as *produced* sound before moving on to an examination of music as *received*. Although these are distinguishable in principle, their interweaving will be evident, for music

3. Merleau-Ponty, *Phenomenology of Perception*, xv.

is an embodied art-form and practice that requires participation and engagement through simultaneous action and reception.[4]

The terms *impact, absorption,* and *ekstasis* will serve to encapsulate key aspects of the musical experience as well as indicating moments of the relationship between self and world, specifically, the pre-reflective mode of attention of the subject. The notion of *impact* will allow us to explore the physical basis that lies at the heart of music. The idea of *absorption* will allow us to examine the ways in which the subject is absorbed by the musical experience and the term *ekstasis*, a transliteration of the Greek term ἔκστασις (literally meaning "standing outside oneself") will allow us to express this absorption in terms of the outward-facing relationship that results. In fact, these terms map onto the Boethian and Kantian accounts for, despite their ultimate reservation about the physicality of music, they yield positive intimations about it.

As we have seen, for Boethius the ears are a conduit through which sound travels and impacts upon the body. It is by virtue of this that music speaks directly to the human person. The *Consolation of Philosophy* demonstrates this clearly. Lady Philosophy treats Boethius through music: the song of Philosophy impresses upon and absorbs Boethius and he is courted by the pleasure and satisfaction that it creates. It is thus that music encourages ekstasis: Boethius turns his gaze away from himself and his concerns and focuses on what is presented to him by means of music. Significantly, this engagement is pre-reflective, for Boethius is unable to reason to the truth of things, his rational capacity is impaired. Thus, it is the physicality of the musical experience that encourages a mode of attention which sets him on the road to recovery.

For Kant, as we have seen, music is wholly physical in its effect. In a similar vein to Boethius the ears provide an open channel. However, Kant adopts a more negative stance since music assails us, impacting upon the body and interrupting thought. It is the action of music upon sense which ultimately prevents Kant from classing music as a fine art. In his positive moments, however, certain forms of music are ranked as beautiful for they are aligned with natural beauty and are thereby el-

4. To suggest treatment of these two characteristics of music is to be attentive to the nature of its operation. Acknowledging music as practice circumvents central issues of contention within the history of music's treatment. Thus, the division of action and contemplation presented by the "Grand Modern Narrative of the Arts" set forth by Nicholas Wolterstorff is lessened. Wolterstorff, "Beyond Beauty and the Aesthetic," 121. See also Begbie, *Resounding Truth*, 38; Cook and Everist, *Rethinking Music*, idem.

evated in status. It is at these points, when music is thought to encourage pure aesthetic judgment, that an absorbed engagement results, one bearing satisfaction and a feeling of pleasure with no further end in mind. It is thus that ekstasis occurs: the normal working of the everyday powers of understanding is suspended and, instead, one is called to dwell in the abundance of meaning presented through experience. Crucially for Kant the experience is pre-reflective: pure aesthetic judgment not only anticipates but in fact engenders rational thought and logical judgment.

Fundamentally, in both accounts music creates a certain mode of attention that is pre-reflective. Through this attention the world presents itself to the subject in an indeterminate and yet significant way. Importantly, music impacts, absorbs, and engages the subject through its physical character. These moments will now be explored in terms of music, first, through music performance, and second, by means of music reception.

MUSIC PERFORMANCE

The performance of music is an embodied event, comprising a succession of physical actions. At a fundamental level it involves the manipulation of wave vibrations: the lengths of channels of air and pieces of string are altered through the impression of the human body. This manipulation runs reciprocally for the sound yielded in turn has an impact on the player, who responds to it. In short, what might be called an "attunement" takes place between player, instrument, sound, and music. Here, the physical body becomes one with the instrument and with the sound produced.[5] Importantly, attunement is not an isolated moment but a process, one identifiable within different levels of playing and accompanying modes of attention. At all levels, the notions of impact, absorption, and ekstasis are present and interconnecting, sketching a

---

5. Richard Sennett observes a similar kind of melding of subject and object within the relationship between a craftswoman and molten glass: "The viscous glass will sag unless the pipe is constantly turned. In order to get a straight bead, the hands have to do something akin to twirling a teaspoon into a pot of honey. All the body is involved in this handwork. To avoid strain when twirling the pipe, the glassblower's back must incline forward from the lower rather than upper torso, like a rower reaching for the beginning of a stroke. This posture also steadies the craftsman in drawing back molten glass out of the furnace. But critically important is the relation of hand and eye" (Sennett, *Craftsman*, 173).

movement away from an *enclosed* sense of self towards an awareness of self in relation, an *open* self.

The process of attunement, and associated levels of attention, begins when the musician picks up an instrument, its impact as a physical item experienced by the body. Initially, one becomes accustomed to its weight and feel, accommodating one's posture. In this way, one is quite literally absorbed in the instrument since it becomes an extension of the body. Thus, Johann Joachim Quantz says:

> The structure of the flute resembles that of the windpipe, and the formation of the tone in the flute resembles the formation of the tone in the human windpipe. The human voice is produced by the exhalation of air from the lungs, and by the motion of the larynx. The diverse attitudes of the various parts of the mouth such as the palate, the uvula, the cheeks, the teeth, the lips, and of the nose as well, cause the tone to be produced in diverse ways, either well or poorly.[6]

To this end, wind players check their embouchure and hold of the instrument. String players ensure that the hairs of the bow have enough rosin in order to produce friction when contact with the strings is made and monitor their bow hold and its location on the instrument. The musician then tunes-up: keeping a "fixed pitch" in mind she plays a note, listens to whether it accords or whether it is sharp or flat, making physical adjustments to the instrument if necessary. In some way, therefore, the attention paid is "mechanical" for the musician amends variables in order to feel sufficient connection with the instrument. However, simultaneously, by means of this physical attunement the musician focuses beyond, to the sound that will surface. This is the ultimate aim, for in the case of a stringed instrument, for example, whether the bow is placed near the bridge or the fingerboard is decisive to the character and strength of the sound. The musician concentrates upon sound production from the very beginning.

Having established a connection with the instrument, the musician's mode of attention develops within the practice session. The kind of attention elicited is not homogenous since it intrinsically depends on the stage of practice. Within the initial stages there is a close attention to the "nuts and bolts" of the physical process. In general terms, the concerns of a wind player will include breath pressure and control, in addition

6. Quantz, *On Playing the Flute*, Chap IV. §1, 48.

to embouchure, as well as a concentration upon the co-ordination of tongue and finger movement. The tongue interrupts the air flow in order to articulate notes; the fingers produce different note pitches through their movement by means of which they cover holes or press keys. The string player will focus on bow and finger co-ordination, on whether one should play near the tip of the bow or towards the frog, on the pressure of the bow upon the string. All are adjustable and adjusted according to what is being played and how one wants to play it. Here, working on passages in detail in order to master co-ordination and sound production, patterns and phrases are repeated over and again. Upon each repeat micro-adjustments are made if change is necessary or avoided if consistency of execution is desired. In each instance the attention to physical action is bound up with the production of sound.

With the "nuts and bolts" set in place the musician's attention broadens, shifting from the more "mechanical" mode involved in the production of specific note patterns towards one that is more "musical." For with the physical foundation in place, one is free to consider more explicitly and deeply the sound as music: one is able to explore its shape and internal movement. Thus, details are situated within phrases which are then placed within the musical whole, understood as pointing both forwards and backwards "intentionally" within the larger musical structure. They stand as announcements, iterations, and developments. One becomes completely absorbed in the sound *as music*.

Repetition and variation structure and sustain both the "mechanical" and "musical" modes of attention. It is thus that the musician is seemingly entranced: one is entwined with the instrument through the physical actions involved in playing and is thereby united with the sound, since the sound evolves as the movements adjust and become more attuned. It is this mapping of action onto sound and their coterminous evolution that drives the process forward. Through repetition the physical impact upon the instrument molds the sound that is produced and this sound feeds back to the physical process, shaping the repeated physical action and, thereby, the subsequent sound. Thus, one is caught up in both the physical pattern and its sonic corollary. One is immersed simultaneously in the pattern as it *has been* and as it *will be*. Repetition, however, is satisfying not simply when viewed directionally, through the improvement of the physical action, but intrinsically, because of the sound itself. It is for this reason that the musician is engrossed in the apparently mundane motions of practice, wholly present in and through the physical action. Richard Sennett encapsulates this: "When I am deep practicing the cello, I want to do a physical gesture again and again to make it better but also do it better so that I can do it again."[7]

The story of Clive Wearing illustrates the interlacing of the "mechanical" and the "musical" modes of attention, as well as the absorption that obtains between the musician and music. Previously an eminent musician and musicologist, Clive retains his capacity to make music despite a devastating amnesia that has virtually obliterated his entire past and reduced his memory span to a few seconds. In making music Clive seemingly transcends his condition, regaining something of his former self, a self that continues beyond a few ephemeral moments, a self sustained through the course of a piece's duration. Although in some sense this capacity is due to a bedding-in of actions during years of practice (that which Oliver Sacks refers to as "procedural memory") it is not simply a consequence of this. Rather, it arises through Clive's absorption in the music. For engaging with music, its "present" becomes Clive's "present" and his "present" becomes its "present." He is absorbed by the music and is carried along by it. His wife Deborah remarks: "The momentum of the music carried Clive from bar to bar. Within the structure of the piece, he was held, as if the staves were tramlines and there was only one way to go. He knew exactly where he was because in every phrase there is context implied, by rhythm, key, melody. It was marvelous to be free. When the music stopped Clive fell through to the lost place. But for those moments he was playing he seemed normal."[8]

The musician and the music unite. The musician attends to the instrument, the sound, and music. She is absorbed by music, cohering with

7. Sennett, *Craftsman*, 176. Sight-reading provides a special case, requiring not only the simultaneous and immediate involvement of the mechanical and musical (one must attempt "nuts and bolts" at the same time as grasping musical intention) but highlighting the concurrence of past, present, and future within music. For, indeed, one may be more acutely aware that one is anticipating what is on the musical horizon. However, each note is caught up with the last and with that which follows. In fact, the skill of sight-reading consists not simply in anticipating but in engaging in a coherent musical communication which itself requires a concurrent forward and retroactive perception.

8. Sacks, *Musicophilia*, 209. The musical "history" anchors Clive: "Clive's performance self seems, to those who know him, just as vivid and complete as it was before his illness. This mode of being, this self, is seemingly untouched by his amnesia, even though his autobiographical self, the self that depends on explicit, episodic memories, is virtually lost" (ibid., 209–10).

its "present," its direction, and its flow, becoming an embodiment of it.[9] The self is thus ekstatic, its attention wholly outward facing. The outward focus, however, does not only extend between musician, instrument, and sound, but obtains between musicians, other practical participants. Describing this interaction John Potter notes:

> An audience listening to Cipriano de Rore's "O Morte, eterno fin," for example, will probably only be aware that the piece has started when they hear the C major triad that begins the madrigal. By the time the listener hears the first chord, the performers will have been engaged with each other for at least a beat, having agreed a tempo in what the audience will perceive as the silence out of which the piece emerges. This silence is not as quiet as it may seem: the singers' breath acts like an upbeat.[10]

Potter signals the implicit attunement that occurs between musicians. Here the singers observe the collective drawing of breath by means of which sound will express itself. It is in this silence that the music begins and from which it weaves its course. It is thus also, through the outward focus instilled by music, that the attention of a group of individuals with Tourette's syndrome becomes absorbed in and by rhythm and, thereby, with others in the group. The participants of a drum circle focus beyond themselves. Their ticcing subsides and the individuals form a collective. The beat provides not only an aural focus but a focus for their entire being and attention.

> Music here had a double power: first, to reconfigure brain activity, and bring calm and focus to people who were sometimes distracted or preoccupied by incessant tics and impulses; and second, to promote a musical and social bonding with others, so that what began as a miscellany of isolated, often distressed

9. Perceptively, Merleau-Ponty notes: "The performer is no longer producing or reproducing the sonata: he feels himself, and the others feel him, to be at the service of the sonata; the sonata sings through him or cries out so suddenly that he must 'dash his bow' to follow it" (Merleau-Ponty, *Intertwining*, 177). It is this embodiment of the performer by the music that distinguishes a good performance. Thus, Quantz says, "If you contradict the passions that should be expressed, or in general execute everything without sentiment, and without being moved yourself . . . The listener who hears the piece thus poorly rendered is more apt to overcome with drowsiness than sustained and diverted, and will be glad when it is over" (Quantz, *On Playing the Flute*, XI, §21, 128).

10. Potter, "Communicative Rest," 164.

or self-conscious individuals almost instantly became a cohesive group with a single aim . . .[11]

To summarize: music practice is grounded in the physical. Through the impact both of the musician on the instrument and thereby on sound, and of the sound thereby on the musician and the instrument, the focus of the musician is directed beyond itself. It is through this interrelationship that the musician and music become entwined, mutually absorbed. The musician is facing that which is without but also to that which she is simultaneously intimately connected, acting and being acted upon.

MUSIC RECEPTION

The reception of music is as physical an act as that of its production. Music impacts not only upon the ears but impresses directly upon the body. John Shepherd and Peter Wicke explain: "the human experience of sound involves, in addition to the sympathetic vibration of the eardrums, the sympathetic vibration of the resonators of the body. Sound, shaped and resonating with the properties of the internal and external configurations, textures and movements of the objects of the external world, can thus be felt in addition to being heard."[12] In short, the body is open to music: music doesn't simply enter through the ear but infuses the body through its vibration. It causes it to "resonate." It is this that initiates an attunement between the recipient and the music. For through its physical impact music signals its presence and invites the subject's attention and engagement.

It is the immediacy of the physicality of sound that discloses a permeability of the boundary between the two. Indeed, the aural space is singular in nature. For the distance between the subject and the object is eliminable. It is thus that the aural experience is contrasted with the visual. Jeremy Begbie explains:

> In the world I see, an entity cannot be in two places at the same time, and two things cannot occupy the same place at the same time. Visual experience and discrete location become inseparable—seeing this lamp "here" means I cannot see it "over there." But in aural experience, although a sound may have a discrete

11. Sacks, *Musicophilia*, 229.

12. Shepherd and Wicke, *Music and Cultural Theory*, 127. See also, DeNora, *After Adorno*, 101.

material source whose discrete location I can identify ("the
trumpet is on the left, not on the right"), the sound I hear is not
dependent on attention to that "place." It surrounds me, it fills my
whole aural "space."[13]

The distinction between the visual and aural is central to many
understandings of music. Thus Igor Stravinsky characterizes music as
a "chronologic" art, placing it against painting which is a "spatial" art.[14]
It is on this basis also that Roger Scruton describes music as "pure
event." He maintains that within a piece of music the source of sound
becomes secondary to the sound itself. Thus, the "something heard" is
not the intentional object of hearing but simply the "cause of what I
hear." His example is the use of off-stage trumpets in Mahler's first and
second Symphonies. These evoke a sense of distance which, according to
Scruton, is metaphorical since the trumpets "are present in the musical
structure as the other sounds with which they coincide."[15]

13. Begbie, *Theology, Music and Time*, 24. The potential to locate physical objects is
obviously more central within the visual realm. However, even here experience of the
visual fluctuates. Hence, Merleau-Ponty's rankle with the introduction of perspective
within visual art: "Before, I had the experience of a world of teeming, exclusive things
which could be taken in only be means of a temporal cycle in which each gain was at the
same time a loss. Now the inexhaustible being crystallizes into an ordered perspective
within which backgrounds resign themselves to being only backgrounds (inaccessible
and vague as is proper), and objects in the foreground abandon something of their
aggressiveness, order their inner lines according to the common law of the spectacle,
and already prepare themselves to become backgrounds as soon as it is necessary. A
perspective, in short, within which nothing holds my gaze and takes the shape of a present. The whole scene is in the mode of the over and done with or of eternity" (Merleau-
Ponty, "Indirect Language," 251).

14. Stravinsky, *Poetics of Music*, 28. Jean-Jacques Rousseau notes a similar distinction between music and painting. Rousseau, "Essay on the Origin of Languages," 952.

15. Scruton, *Aesthetics of Music*, 12. For a more detailed working out of this see
Scruton, *Understanding Music*, 20–32. Scruton is correct on the detachment of sounds
from their source, positing an acousmatic theory of music. For more details on the
acousmatic experience of sound (including objections to it) see Hamilton, *Aesthetics
of Music*, 96–111. Proceeding along the same lines of thought, Edward A. Lippman distinguishes between two opposed modes of hearing: "In the first, hearing is perceptually
oriented; the sources of sound are objects of interest; and since precision of location
and the identity of the sound producer are of primary importance, hearing cooperates
with vision and is subjected to it, as the sense of superior clarity and perceptual ability."
In the second, "Romantic hearing," "sound is not taken in its usual practical importance
as an index of the location and identity of objects of the external world, but more in
its own terms, in its peculiar sensational qualities, and in their meaning as a revelation
of emotion and being—of the inner nature of life and the natural world" (Lippman,
Philosophy and Aesthetics of Music, 131).

In some sense, Scruton is right: it is the detachment of sound from its source that enables it to fill our aural space. It is this physical assertiveness that grounds music's capacity to capture our attention and create ekstasis. Thereby it elicits engagement. Importantly, however, not all modes of attention permit the musical experience to be fully involving and not all involve attunement. To this extent, the music is dependent upon the listener. For a number of listening strategies are evident, particularly within modern society where music more or less pervades our every waking moment:[16] one can give sole attention to the music getting caught up in its internal movement. One can accept its function as "background," attending to music in so far as it structures the progress of the day or involves personal mood.[17] One can also arrange specific activity through music by means of "latching" on to key aspects of it, such as rhythm (as we shall see shortly). Furthermore, one can of course "tune out" altogether, an exercise that comes easier to some than to others. However, even here, music has the capacity to "snap" us out of this mode so that we engage with it, even if just momentarily, before "switching off" again. It is through active and full engagement and attunement that absorption and ekstasis emerge most completely since it is thereby that the subject enters into the proximity of music, and it is *through time*, the fundamental structure of music, that experience is constituted and reconfigured. For at a basic level the musical process arises from the *temporal* organization of a series of tones that sound and fade, each yielding to each other. Begbie, summarizing Victor Zuckerkandl, says:

> The tone must give way to the next tone in order to be completed, it does not simply add the next tone to itself, it ceases to sound. Yet the tone is not thereby gone forever, for the second tone is precisely the completion of the first, internally connected to the first. The same applies to its future orientation. The present . . . is charged with its future.[18]

16. Simon Frith discusses the pervasiveness of sound, evolving modes of attention and the power of music to command attention and thereby cross boundaries, personal and social. *Music and Everyday Life*, 2003.

17. See DeNora, *Music in the Everyday*; Johnson, *Who Needs Classical Music?* 34.

18. Begbie, *Theology, Music and Time*, 62. This observation is echoed by composer Arnold Schoenberg: "Every tone which is added to a beginning tone makes the meaning of that tone doubtful . . . The addition of other tones may or may not clarify this problem. In this manner there is produced a state of unrest, or imbalance which grows throughout most of the piece. . . The method by which balance is restored seems to me the real *idea* of the composition" (Schoenberg, *Style and Idea*, 123).

In short, the succession of tones is internally related. It is from this fundamental relation of tones (each of which comes in and out of existence but which is multi-directional in its "intention") that higher levels of relation, or schemes, emerge. Schemes create and structure a horizon of expectation against which the musical unfolding is placed and through which it is sustained by means of repetition and anticipation, and their corollary, suspension.[19] It is through convention that such schemes of organization arise. The schemes germinate in an individual during their time in the womb and develop thereafter, with some level of formation by the age of five. Thereafter, schemes develop and expand in and through each and every musical experience.[20] It is by means of these schemes (and familiarity with certain conventions) that the attunement of the recipient is encouraged. Through convention the recipient is secured to a musical experience. More specifically, whether or not one is familiar with the particular scheme that a piece embodies has the capacity to encourage or deter one from engaging with the music, becoming attuned to it. In addition, it is the horizon of expectation created by means of a particular scheme that shapes music's contours, for it is thus that expectations are confirmed, postponed, and altogether subverted.[21]

One such scheme, or level of relation, is tonality. This is foundational to many forms of music but is predominant in Western music. Here, structure arises through the relation of a series of keys. Within this scheme, one key features predominantly generating a sense of "home" or "centre." It is from this and in relation to it that the rest of the music evolves. The home key exerts almost a gravitational pull which shapes musical movement. Thus, having established a tonal centre the music

19. "Music communicates to us emotionally through systematic violations of expectations. These violations can occur in any domain—the domain of pitch, timbre, contour, rhythm, tempo, and so on—but occur they must. Music is organized sound, but the organization has to involve some element of the unexpected or it is emotionally flat and robotic" (Levitin, *This is Your Brain on Music*, 172–73).

20. Ibid., 116–17. Daniel Levitin outlines the neurobiological bases of musical structure and experience in the fourth chapter, "Anticipation," ibid., 111–31.

21. DeNora brings this out in her summary of Adorno's juxtaposition of Schoenberg and Stravinsky (Adorno favors Schoenberg): "Adorno emphasised Schoenberg's antipathy to affirmation, his disdain of musical formulas . . . Schoenberg's music was unfamiliar and did not attempt at tone-painting (making itself subservient to external images or ideas . . .) Because of this strangeness, Schoenberg's music did not afford stock responses, did not 'remind' listeners of existing phenomena but rather challenged listeners to attend to the world in new ways . . ." (*After Adorno*, 74).

moves away, stretching harmonic boundaries as well as exploring melodic trajectories. It then very often returns home and closes the piece. In this way, tonality organizes the musical experience, providing a context in and through which process can be felt and understood.[22] For motifs move through and develop by means of, in part, keys. Hence, within a piece, the eventual return to home is expected. This sense of anticipation is fulfilled by moving, for example, from the dominant key to the tonic, the home key, thereby creating a perfect cadence and a feeling of rest. Conversely, the drive towards the home key can be displaced and suspended, by travelling, for example, to the subdominant rather than the tonic when it is the latter that is expected. This creates an interrupted cadence and a moment of surprise. In some instances, resolution is avoided altogether: the home key is conspicuous by its absence.

There are of course other means of structuring larger-scale relations aside from tonality, and yet it is repetition that structures the musical experience. Schoenberg, for instance, did not work within conventional Western harmonic structures, eventually coming to rely upon the interrelationship of certain groupings of notes within the twelve-tone system.[23] However, he still recognized the centrality of repetition. To summarize briefly: the foundation of composition was, for Schoenberg, the musical Idea[24] (the "theme, melody, phrase, or motive" of a composition, or in his own case the *totality* of the piece).[25] The musical Idea is the content of music and the foundation of musical composition: it is that which is communicated to the audience.[26] Schoenberg states, "There is no great work of art that does not convey a new message to humanity; there is no great artist who fails in this respect. This is the code of honour of all the great in art, and consequently in all great art works of the great we will find that newness which never perishes whether it be of Josquin de

22. Cf. Carpenter, "Aspects of Musical Space," 341–73.

23. For an overview of Schoenberg's compositional development, see Stearns, *Unity, God and Music*.

24. The Idea is that which "its creator" wants to present. Schoenberg, "New Music," 123.

25. Ibid.

26. "A composer does not, of course add bit by bit, as a child does in building with wooden blocks. He conceives an entire composition as a spontaneous vision. Then he proceeds, like Michelangelo who chiselled his *Moses* out of marble without sketches, complete in every detail, thus directly *forming* his material" (Schoenberg, *Fundamentals of Musical Composition*, 2).

Préz, or Bach, or Haydn, or any other great master."[27] Thus, composition has two functions: first, it attends to the musical Idea, outworking each successive tone into a balanced whole and thereby orienting the Idea internally.[28] Second, it acts as a vehicle by which the musical Idea is conveyed more generally. Style is operative within both of these aspects of composition and, as the means by which the musical idea is presented and comprehended, is completely at its service: "One thinks only for the sake of one's idea. And thus art can only be created for its own sake. An idea is born; it must be moulded, formulated, developed, elaborated, carried through and pursued to its very end."[29] Repetition is an aspect of style and is an aid to the communication of the musical Idea. Schoenberg writes: "The first phrase is not repeated immediately, but united with more remote (contrasting) motive-forms, to constitute the first half of the period, the *antecedent*. After this contrast *repetition cannot be longer postponed without endangering comprehensibility*.[30] Thus, the second half, the *consequent*, is constructed as a kind of repetition of the antecedent."[31] In short, anticipation and repetition are vital to musical communication and comprehensibility. The sense of anticipation is perhaps not felt as keenly within twelve-tone music, for example, as within music created through the interrelationship of keys, perhaps in part due to the lack of convention and sense of expectation and anticipation.[32] Nevertheless it plays an important role.

27. Schoenberg, "New Music," 123.

28. Schoenberg states: "Every tone which is added to a beginning tone makes the meaning of that tone doubtful. If for instance, G follows after C, the ear may not be sure whether this expresses C major or G major, or even F major or E minor; and the addition of other tones may or may not clarify this problem" (ibid.).

29. Ibid., 124. Also: "Creation to an artist should be as natural and inescapable as the growth of apples to an apple tree. Even if I tried to produce apples in response to the demands of a fashion or of the market, I could not. Thus artists who want to 'go back to a period', who try to obey laws of the obsolete aesthetic or of a novel one, who enjoy themselves in eclecticism or in the imitation of a style, alienate themselves from nature. The product shows it—no such product survives time" (Schoenberg, "Criteria for the Evaluation of Music," 134).

30. My italics.

31. Schoenberg, *Fundamentals of Music Composition*, 21.

32. "Such anticipation, such singing along, is possible because one has knowledge, largely implicit, of musical 'rules' (how a cadence must resolve, for instance) and a familiarity with particular musical conventions (the form of a sonata, or the repetition of a theme). But anticipation is not possible with music from a very different culture or tradition—or if musical conventions are deliberately shattered" (Sacks, *Musicophilia*, 211). See also Levitin, *This is Your Brain on Music*, chapter 4.

Other schemes include rhythm, melody, and also timbre and style. Thus, in Nigel Kennedy's recording of the second movement of Mozart's fourth violin concerto we are for the most part immersed in the suspensions of harmonic and melodic expectations that arise from Mozart's writing.[33] The expressively lyrical line of the violin explores the timbre of the instrument by moving fluidly, but not expectedly, from the velvety depths of its lower range to the clarity of its higher register. The real surprise, however, arrives in the cadenza, one of Kennedy's own improvisation. The lyricism of the melody is transformed: it becomes wholly expansive. It is infused with a different sense of time from that which has preceded it and to which it eventually returns: the strings hold a series of sustained atmospheric notes and the violin, which is now electric rather than acoustic, sits high. The entire quality of sound is altered. It is resonant in an ethereal way as it winds its way almost directionless. The only sense of activity emerges from the double bass, but even this energy is diffuse, the beats are not regular but free-form. This cadenza shatters expectations on many levels; it is for this reason that it enraptures and moves the listener.

The multi-directionality of music through time is shaped not only through the interrelationship of sound but also by means of silence, "framing" and "punctuating" musical structure. Jenny Doctor notes, with particular reference to music from the classical era, that silences provide audiences with "welcome signposts to make their musical journeys more comfortable and comprehensible." In this way, musical details are highlighted and "higher-order" structural features are signaled.[34] Thus, in movements based on sonata-form written by Mozart, according to which broadly speaking a theme is articulated, developed, and recapitulated, Doctor draws attention to the "dramatic pause" that often surfaces at the end of the development section. This, she says, marks the moment "when the recapitulation becomes inevitable."[35] Direction is present within each silence: "silence, in these cases lacks sound, but not motion, the moment of no-sound carrying forward and raising urgent expecta-

33. Kennedy, *Mozart: Violin Concerto No. 4.*

34. "Within the well-defined conventions of these frameworks, classically built from regular, periodic blocks, silence is of course often present in the form of structural articulations, rests providing momentary spaces between the usual two or four-bar phrases, or rhythmic pauses defining the ends of structural sections" (Doctor, "Texture of Silence," 18–19).

35. Ibid.

tions of what is to come . . . Silence is thus recognizable as a vital entity within the fabric of this music's soundscape."[36]

We have seen, then, that the musical horizon is created by means of time, whichever type of tonal inter-relationship forms its structure. It is this that contributes to the singularity of the experience, for ordinary time and musical time are synchronized such that the "real" time of the subject is caught up in and absorbed by "musical" time. However, the correlation is not a straightforward one since both senses of time impact upon one another. Their attunement is mutual. Hence, the interpenetration of subjective and musical time leads to a distinction between the time that music *takes* and the time it *evokes*.[37] Stravinsky says:

> Everyone knows that time passes at a rate which varies accord-
> ing to the inner dispositions of the subject and to the events that
> come to affect his consciousness. Expectation, boredom, anguish,
> pleasure and pain, contemplation—all of these thus come to ap-
> pear as different categories in the midst of which our life unfolds,
> and each of these determines a special psychological process, a
> particular tempo. These variations in psychological time are per-
> ceptible only as they are related to the primary sensation whether
> conscious or unconscious—of real time, ontological time.[38]

Tia DeNora exemplifies this with a personal example: the usually frustrating experience of waiting for a slow computer connection
is altered by the intervention of the Habanera tune (made famous by
Bizet's opera *Carmen*). Its distinctive rhythm shapes the tapping of the
computer keys which she engages in while she waits for email access

---

36. Ibid. Julie Sutton states: "It is not possible to discuss musical silence without brief reference to musical time, for silences in music appear to alter time. At the very least, they interrupt our perception of the ongoing flow of musical sounds, ranging from the spaces between individual notes through music's pauses to the overall arching structure of silence framing the beginning and ending of a musical work" (Sutton, "Air Between Two Hands," 173).

37. Begbie makes this distinction. *Theology, Music and Time*, 34. Nicholas Wolterstorff talks about the "temporality and historicity" of worlds of works of art: although it is in the context of literary fiction and drama, the ideas about temporality apply to music: "Time enters in various ways, into the structures of the worlds of works of art; and those worlds themselves are in various ways tied down to the history of our actual world." He thus notes the temporality internal and external to a work: "temporal duration" and "temporal succession" are internal to the structure of art; however, art can also be an-chored in certain events in history and set within a certain stretch. Wolterstorff, *Works and Worlds of Art*, 185–89.

38. Stravinksy, *Poetics of Music*, 30–31.

and transforms her experience of the passing of time such that "Defined in relation to the interrupted musical phrase, the email was then re-experienced as arriving 'too soon.'"[39]

The relationship between "real" time and "musical" time, and the sense of its passing, also works conversely. For not all music is explicitly directional. At times, in fact, direction can seem absent altogether.[40] Minimalist music is interesting in this regard since goal-orientated directionality is set aside so that music becomes almost without intention, the perceptual changes are slight. This arises from the aesthetic of minimalism, encapsulated by Steve Reich: "I want to be able to hear the processes happening throughout the sounding music. To facilitate closely detailed listening, a musical process should happen extremely gradually . . . so slowly that listening to it resembles watching the minute hand on a watch—you can perceive it moving after you stay with it a little while."[41] Thus, movement and direction inhere in all music, even if at a subtle level. For music is the relation of tones selected and placed within a sequence. The relations may not be immediately obvious yet they are still present, structuring the musical experience of the recipient.

At a fundamental level, then, we are caught up by music within a certain mode of attention. Our orientation is turned outwards. This orientation then finds structure through time. Importantly, here, our own time is not negated. Rather, "real" time is infused with and transformed by a different time, a "musical" one. Here, time passes quickly, or slowly, with energy or diffusely. More than this, the musical time experienced is fundamentally integrated with real time since it is by means of embodied experience that musical experience is shaped: our conceptualization of musical time arises from physical experience (we have a sense of music

39. DeNora, *Music in Everyday Life*, 8.

40. Lippmann notes this also: "Temporal progression or temporal process is hardly evident, for example, in the first movement of Webern's Symphony opus 21, where we seem to perceive a pattern of tonal interrelationships for which a presentation in time is almost incidental. And again, is not the revery of Debussy's *Nuages* or the lassitude of parts of the second act of *Tristan* without any conspicuous property of forward progress?" Lippman even considers "still more extreme types of music" which renounce tone in favor of sounds which are ill-defined in pitch or "impulsive sounds." He admits that a series or succession of audible events is of course found but that often there is little feeling of temporal progress or flow. *The Philosophy and Aesthetics of Music*, 40.

41. Reich, "Music as a Gradual Process." Cf. Schwarz, *Minimalists*, 11.

as moving,[42] of points on a musical landscape,[43] and of music as a moving force).[44] In addition, more fundamentally, our indwelling of music is molded in and through experience. For entering into the motion of music, we experience pre-reflectively "all the ways it moves, swells, hops, rushes, floats, trips along, drags, soars, and falls" since we have a sense of types of movement arising from our own movement, our own embodied experience.[45]

Within the musical experience, the music's "present" is the listener's "present" and vice versa. Musical "latches" serve to impact upon, focus, and sustain attention. These musical invariants or "affordances" (such as the structural specificities of tone, rhythm, cadence, and gesture) resonate with the recipient within its environment, context, and specific occasion. Thus, "music affords dancing, worship, co-ordinated working, persuasion, emotional catharsis . . . and marching."[46] Latches, or affordances, evoke physical responses such as head-nodding, foot-tapping, swaying, singing, and humming and, in some cases, it is primarily the physical response that acts as a platform for absorption and ekstasis. Hence, the initial chance use by DeNora of the Habanera rhythm upon the keys of her computer and her continued employment of it. With "latches" standing as a common focus, the listener is not only oriented towards the music but to others. Night clubs provide one such example: the dance floor is saturated by and is buzzing with music with regular and driving beats. They act as a "latch" and a common focus, both mental and physical (overseen and controlled by the DJ): one moves, synchronizes with

42. In using this metaphor we mean that "our experience of a bit of music shares something with our experience of seeing objects move in physical space" such as a path and manner of motion. Johnson, *Meaning of the Body*, 249.

43. Within this metaphor, we refer to musical events as locations on a musical landscape: "what has already been heard is conceptualized as points in the landscape that are behind the listener-traveler, while parts of the music not yet heard are future points on the path that one will encounter later . . . This explains expressions like the following: 'We're *coming to* the coda . . .' At measure 4, the horns *enter*'" (ibid., 250).

44. Within this metaphor music is a causal force that moves the hearer "from one location (state) to another (different state)" (ibid., 254).

45. Ibid., 239. See also, Cox, "Hearing, Feeling, Grasping Gestures," 45–60.

46. Clarke notes: "To a person, a wooden chair affords sitting, while to a termite it affords eating. Equally, the same chair affords self-defence to a person under attack" (Clarke, *Ways of Listening*, 37). The same is true of music: the same music affords different things to various people within distinct contexts.

the beat and thereby with other dancers. Each becomes aware of each other; each is perceptible in and through the music.[47]

This outward orientation implicit in the more physically responsive musical engagement is powerfully demonstrated within music therapy which employs "a range of musical and psychological applied theory" in order for the therapist to respond appropriately to the client and thereby develop a relationship.[48] Music is used to create a space within which communication is opened up, a space in which the patient can express themselves through their sometimes seemingly wayward gestures. In this way absorption and ekstasis occur, therapist and client facing onto each other, music providing the means of interaction. DeNora recounts the words of a therapist who says, commenting on a video she has made of a session:

> I don't have any way of communicating with Mandy at all, so what she is giving me is basically nothing. She has got this—she grinds her teeth which is awful and there is *no way* I am going to reflect that back! And she has got this vocal sound she makes and she is doing this with her head all the time. So what I am trying to do in this video is I am singing a greeting song to her, which is the way I always start the session so that she knows that we have begun, and then I am following the rhythm of her head and the idea that she gets the impression that she is in control of something that when her head stops the music stops and when she starts moving her head again it starts so I am giving her some control in the hope that at some stage she will start to interact.[49]

In summary: through musical time, the physicality of the musical experience incorporates the subject and thereby transforms the "ordinariness" of the present moment or more specifically series of moments. They become translucent to the musical. In this way the movement and process contained within the musical experience overflows into everyday experience, changing the subject's relationship to its own movement through time. Ultimately, therefore, the subject focuses beyond itself, attending to the musical experience as well as to others of whom one is made aware, including those whose physical actions and musicianship bring the music about in performance and those who share through

47. See Gilbert and Pearson, *Discographies*, 1–37.

48. Sutton, "Air Between Two Hands," 170.

49. DeNora, *Music in the Everyday*, 71.

various modes of listening. There are also grounds for maintaining that, through the musical experience, the musical recipient attunes in some measure with the composer (as other), music acting as a window between them. By extension, this openness extends to those within the tradition implicitly constituting the piece and their own experience of the piece.[50] It is this opening outwards (through participation in) that the significance of the musical experience is grounded. For through its physical impact and engagement music has the capacity to absorb one's attention and, thereby, to take one beyond oneself. It is thereby also that the impact of different levels of philosophical, sociological, and theological meaning is grounded. Such meanings acquire presence and immediacy that are traced through time and move the listener.

MUSIC AS ENCHANTMENT

In short, the beauty of music, epistemologically speaking, is its capacity to instill a certain mode of attention. One that is ekstatic and non-reductive. For music *impacts* upon the human body, *absorbs* the perceiving subject, and thereby creates *ekstasis*. To explain: it turns the subject outwards and in doing so creates a focus on that which is irreducibly other, sustaining the interest of the subject and thereby encouraging it to dwell in this encounter. Importantly, this encounter is non-reductive since it is mutual and indeterminate. The subject becomes receptive to the object and the object likewise to the subject. It is this interaction which is paramount. It grounds the epistemological strength of music, since within this pre-reflective moment the boundary between subject and object is postponed. Music thus reveals a deep connection, what might be called a "fittingness," between the subject and the object. This sense of music's

---

50. Elaborating three main kinds of reading of Proust, Richard Kearney says of the third kind, which involves "the very process of writing and reading, of configuring and refiguring," that here "we encounter an opening of the world of the text towards the post-textual world of the reader, and backwards (by way of implied regress from character to narrator to author) to the pre-textual world of the writer" (Kearney, "Sacramental Aesthetics," 353). The significance of this statement is the recognition of the embedded character of the text. The same holds true for music, even extending further. At every level music is rooted in practice, it emerges within a particular tradition and is practiced and received within specific contexts. For we (and thereby music) are formed by communities and traditions. Benson brings this out well in his *Improvisation of Musical Dialogue*.

engagement is reflected in both the Boethian and Kantian accounts, positively understood.

Appreciated in this way, music stands in particular relation to certain forms of rationalization. Specifically, it bears upon the world's disenchantment. This is an issue that re-emerges in recent discussion by virtue of its role in secularization, because rationalization is involved with the decline of belief within society (particularly with respect to religion). To elucidate: it is possible, historically speaking, to trace elements from the sixteenth century onwards that feed into the process of disenchantment, including the impetus to Reform as well as scientific and technological developments.[51] The term itself, *Entzauberung der Welt*, was brought to prominence by Max Weber.[52] Importantly, although it is often rendered as "disenchantment of the world" it is better translated as "the elimination of magic from the world" in order to better represent Weber's sense, since Weber used the term to identify what one might describe as a foreclosure of the transcendent, a dimming of the world's luminosity. Thus, within the domain of religion Weber highlights the movement away from ecclesial sacraments (through which one is assisted in one's progression towards salvation) towards rationalized ethical action (through which one attests to one's own pre-destination).[53] He says:

> This absolute disappearance of all aids to salvation through the church and the *sacraments* constituted an absolutely decisive contrast to Catholicism ... That overarching process in the history of religion—the *elimination of magic* from the world's occurrences (*Entzauberung der Welt*)—found here, with the doctrine of predestination, its final stage. This development, which began with the prophecy of ancient Judaism in the Old Testament, rejected,

51. Sherry, "Disenchantment, Re-enchantment, and Enchantment," 370. See also, Gauchet, *Disenchantment of the World*. The relationship between the Reformation and "Disenchantment" is not undisputed and is by no means clear-cut, see Walsham, "Reformation and 'The Disenchantment of the World' Reassessed."

52. The term does not originate with Weber, for it is mentioned earlier by Wieland and Schiller. Sherry, "Disenchantment, Re-enchantment, and Enchantment," 369.

53. As Alexandra Walsham notes, "these ideas were developed independently in a more nuanced form by Weber's contemporary, the Heidelberg theologian Ernst Troeltsch, who likewise heralded the Reformation as an agent (albeit an indirect and accidental one) of modernization" ("Reformation and 'The Disenchantment of the World' Reassessed," 497).

in conjunction with Greek scientific thought, all *magical* means
for the salvation quest as superstition and sacrilege.[54]

More generally, within society, Weber points to increasing rationalization and intellectualization, for what was previously attributable
to the supernatural becomes explicable by more mundane means, ones
uncovered through rational and scientific enquiry. In brief, this means
"the knowledge or belief that if one but wished one *could learn it at any
time* . . . it means that principally there are no mysterious incalculable
forces that come into play, but rather that one can, in principle, master
all things by calculation."[55]

For Weber, it is the world that becomes demystified and disenchanted, its luster tarnished, since what was once attributable to transcendent
forces is brought within the compass of the human whose idea of knowledge becomes increasingly centered upon conceptual, propositional (and
verifiable) content. Clearly, however, it is the subject's perception that is
central. For the subject's delight diminishes: the world is now reduced
and quantified. It seems therefore that the world's disenchantment goes
hand in hand with the subject's disenchantment. The disenchantment of
the world involves a flattening-out of the epistemic stance of the subject,
a collapsing of the vertical, such that meaning is no longer something
objectively present in the world but is situated within the subject, either
intrinsically or through its rational operation. In a sense, therefore, the
subject retreats within, understanding itself self-sufficiently rather than
receptively. It thus implements a division between subject and object,

---

54. Weber, *Protestant Ethic*, 26. Elsewhere, Weber says that "the demand is placed
upon the believer that he 'testify' to his status as being called by God—namely, as among
the saved—through the ethical quality of his action in the world's spheres—and *only*
in this manner. This implies that the virtuous must actually testify to his salvation to
himself." Also, "The state of grace, and of being among the chosen, experienced by
the religiously qualified, was testified to precisely in everyday life—not, to be sure, in
everyday life as given, but in methodical-*rationalized* daily activity in service to the
Lord" (Weber, "Main concepts," 249). Later, Adorno and Horkheimer ally disenchantment with the program of the Enlightenment since it entails "the dissolution of myths
and the substitution of knowledge for fancy" (Horkheimer and Adorno, *Dialectic of
Enlightenment*, 3).

55. Weber, "Science as Vocation," 139. Brown observes the close connection of the
two senses: "enchantment can easily suggest spells and magic; Weber's linking of the rise
of rationality with the decline in focus on sacraments is no doubt not accidental" (*God
and Enchantment of Place*, 17).

self and world.[56] In its extreme form the scope and certainty provided by conceptual knowledge leads to a dismissal (or privatization) of anything that is non-propositional and non-verifiable in a logical sense. The world becomes wholly immanent since there is no reason why any type of transcendentally oriented cosmic vision should be kept in view.[57] Intimations of this shift have appeared within our own narrative: Boethius upholds a realm of meaning that is beyond human reason (whilst simultaneously underpinning it). Thus beauty is present throughout the cosmos, and the subject finds meaning that is already present outside itself. In contrast, Kant prizes knowledge which can be achieved through reason. Meaning is situated in the subject, as is beauty, and it is the subject who is the source of meaning.

The shift from reception to self-sufficiency is envisioned by Charles Taylor through the opposition of the "porous" self and the "buffered" self. Specifically, Taylor speaks of a "boundary" separating the subject from the world and its objects. In the enchanted world, Taylor suggests, meaning is received from outside of the self by virtue of the fact that the world has significance aside from and prior to any interaction with it. Consequently, meaning is something that enters us.[58] Thus, the boundary between the self and the world is in some sense "porous." Taylor explains: "Once meanings are not exclusively in the mind, once we can fall under the spell, enter the zone of exogenous meaning, then we think of this meaning as including us, or perhaps penetrating us."[59] By contrast, the self of the disenchanted world, one thought particularly characteris-

56. "The story of the modern epoch, at least on the level of mind, is one of progressive disenchantment. From the sixteenth century on mind has been progressively expunged from the phenomenal world. At least in theory, the reference points for all scientific explanation are matter and motion." This results, according to Morris Berman, in a dominant mode of thinking that is best described as "disenchantment" and "nonparticipation" since "it insists on a rigid distinction between observer and observed . . . there is no ecstatic merger with nature, but rather total separation from it" (Berman, *Reenchantment of the World*, 16–17).

57. Weber notes: "Every increase of rationalism in empirical science increasingly pushes religion from the rational into the irrational realm" (Weber, "The intellectual sphere," 351). Manifestations of this immanent tendency emerge within some circles of contemporary thought, especially within the recent forms of rational fundamentalism, including "scientism." A major figure of the rationally reductive approach can be found in Dawkins' *God Delusion*. For a response to Dawkins see McGrath and McGrath, *Dawkins Delusion*.

58. Taylor, *Secular Age*, 34.

59. Ibid., 35.

tic of modernity, cultivates a boundary that keeps it "buffered" from the outside world. As a result it is able to distance and disengage from things outside the mind as well as generate its own purpose and meaning.[60]

It is clear, then, that it is the subject who needs to be addressed in any attempt to re-enchant. It is on this basis that Patrick Sherry questions the disenchantment of the world suggesting instead that "the world may still be enchanted, for those who have eyes to see, and who have kept fresh the responses of wonder, reverence, and delight."[61] This being the case, a reinvigoration of perception is crucial. To this end, logically speaking, what must be aimed for is a shift from the "buffered" self to the "porous" self or, using my own terms, a shift from the *enclosed* self to the *open* self, the self in relation (to the other which appears as more than simply an object of consciousness). Here, the subject will not be required to dominate the object but will be receptive to its meaning(s). With this in mind, experiences that encourage this shift may be significant. As we have implicitly suggested through our exploration of music performance and reception, and as we shall see explicitly in a moment, music is pre-eminently such an experience.

Taylor recognizes the importance of experiences which convey what he calls a "sense of fullness." For, he observes, they shape and sustain conditions of belief which then facilitate people's everyday functioning. Characterizing such experiences he says, "Somewhere, in some activity, or condition lies a fullness, a richness, that is, in that place (activity or condition), life is fuller, richer, deeper, more worthwhile, more admirable, more what it should be."[62] Such experiences manifest in different ways and to different degrees but at their most striking they may appear as "limit" experiences. As such they shatter "our ordinary sense of being in the world, with its familiar objects, activities and points of reference."[63] In each instance, the subject is provided with "a kind of orientation."[64]

---

60. Ibid., 38. It is a world in which "the only locus of thoughts, feelings, spiritual élan, is what we call minds; the only minds in the cosmos are those of humans... and minds are bounded, so that these thoughts, feelings, etc., are situated 'within' them" (ibid., 30).

61. Sherry, "Disenchantment, Re-enchantment, and Enchantment," 369.

62. Taylor, *Secular Age*, 5.

63. Ibid.

64. He says that experiences may be felt to be "the presence of God, or the voice of nature, or the force which flows through everything, or the alignment in us of desire and the drive to form" (ibid., 6).

It is this last point that is most important: some experiences have the capacity to orient us, something we noted in Boethius and Kant. Taylor, however, makes a distinction between the experiences of "fullness" encountered by both believers and non-believers. He suggests that authentic reception, that is, reception from outside, occurs only for the believer, for in the case of the unbeliever the ground of the "sense of fullness" is generated from within. Taylor uses Kant's categorical imperative as a case in point. The categorical imperative is that which gets Kant's morality underway. The human subject is necessarily free and autonomous and needs to legislate for himself in matters of morality, since laws cannot be externally imposed. The categorical imperative generates a sense of "ought" whilst remaining anchored within the subject. Taylor says: "We have a feeling of receptivity, when with our full sense of our own fragility and pathos as desiring beings, we look up to the power of law-giving with admiration and awe. But this doesn't in the end mean that there is any reception from outside, the power is within; and the more we realize this power, the more we become aware that it is within, that morality must be autonomous and not heteronomous."[65] According to Taylor the experiences of the unbeliever only achieve a semblance of the enchanted world for ultimately they are produced by the subject.

One must, however, be careful to maintain a distinction between the enchanted *world* and what might be called the enchanted *self*, that is, the delighted self. For it is surely mistaken to think that experiences imparting a "sense of fullness" can lead to anything like a re-enchantment of the world. To do so they would need an accompanying framework by means of which they are to be understood. This is manifestly beyond the scope of experience *qua* experience. That said, to consider moments that disclose a "sense of fullness" as encouraging an enchanted mode of attention is certainly quite conceivable. For such experiences can permeate the boundary surrounding the subject rendering the subject open to meaning derived, at least in part, from outside, thereby enabling re-enchantment or rather an enchanted mode of attention.

The distinction between enchanted world and enchanted mode of attention is gestured towards by Sherry. Sherry underlines the role of beauty with reference to David Brown's attempt at enchantment: Brown makes occasional appeal to beauty but says relatively little about it. Brown suggests that enchantment arises "from perceiving particular

65. Ibid., 8.

ways of God relating to human beings and their world."[66] He therefore
wants to extend the idea of "sacrament" beyond its ecclesial conception
in order to consider the ways in which God can be said to relate to the
world, thereby establishing a kind of natural religion.[67] It is arguably for
this reason that the role of beauty is taken as a given since, as Sherry
notes, the category of beauty has long stood as a mode of divine presence
in the world as well as a means of (limited) knowledge.[68] Sherry, however, observes quite rightly that one can experience beauty "as a source
of enchantment without explicitly appealing to any religious belief." He
explains, "For behind our responses to beauty there are, I believe, the
wider and more fundamental reactions of wonder and perhaps reverence . . . and also delight."[69] One cannot, we may conclude, position
wonder in relation to any particular framework since it is an immanent
phenomenon. Rather it encapsulates an attitude towards the world, one

66. Brown, *God and Enchantment of Place*, 24.

67. His aim is to "engage the reader in a form of perception that has largely been lost
in our utilitarian age, experiencing the natural world and human imitations of it not
just as a means to some further end but as themselves the vehicle that makes possible
an encounter with God discovering an enchantment, an absorption that like worship
requires no further justification" (ibid., 36).

68. See Sherry, *Spirit and Beauty*, 40–45.

69. Sherry, "Disenchantment, Re-enchantment, and Enchantment," 379. Elsewhere,
Sherry maintains that whilst natural beauty is interpreted by some as a religious and
mystical experience in which the presence of God is felt, "It is unlikely, I think, that such
an experience would, just by itself, convert someone to a religious belief. But it is often
interpreted in terms of an already existing belief and may help to confirm it" (*Spirit and
Beauty*, 56). Hepburn notes, similarly, "I am unconvinced that the beauty and rational
interests of the world are sufficient grounds for postulating God; but this puts no em-
bargo upon responding to these features with wonder—or indeed to any other features
of the world which theism has taken to be the signatures of God" (*Wonder and Other
Essays*, 141). For a broader address of the scope and limits of phenomenology in terms
of metaphysics (specifically addressing the work of Richard Kearney) see Masterson,
who questions whether it "is really satisfactory to seek to legitimize an experiential
affirmation of divine transcendence within a phenomenological frame of reference"
(Masterson, *Sense of Creation*, 129). This is in keeping with what Johnson calls "horizontal transcendence." Johnson conceives two forms of transcendence, a vertical one
and a horizontal one. The vertical one is the "alleged capacity to rise above and shed
our finite human form and to 'plug into' the infinite." The horizontal "recognizes the
inescapability of human finitude and is compatible with the embodiment of meaning,
mind, and personal identity. From this human perspective, transcendence consists in
our happy ability to sometimes 'go beyond' our present situation in transformative acts
that change both our world and ourselves" (Johnson, *Meaning of the Body*, 281).

within which, as we shall see, subject and object intertwine and meaning becomes abundant.

BEAUTY AND WONDER

Since its inception wonder has been contrasted with reason whose reach dispels it by uncovering explanations. Reason is the day burning off the mist. Hence, Plato tells us by means of Socrates in the *Theaetetus* that "wonder is the feeling of a philosopher, and philosophy *begins* with wonder."[70] Moreover, in the *Metaphysics*, Aristotle states that "It is through wonder that men now *begin* and originally *began* to philosophize."[71] Wonder is prior to the rational. It is this interaction that gives impetus to philosophy and the systematization of the world through cognition, that which Kant calls logical judgment. Herein, the object is analyzed and made intelligible by the subject, by the intellect. Thus, if wonder stands in contrast to this kind of reflection, and if everyday cognition operates in some sense through the domination of the object by means of the subject, then wonder must indicate a distinct interaction between subject and object, self and world, one that is necessarily pre-reflective and thus more fluid.

To maintain this is to cohere with the phenomenological approach to which I have appealed implicitly in my own treatment of music, since wonder is central to phenomenological philosophy. In the introduction to the *Phenomenology of Perception*, Merleau-Ponty outlines the role of the "phenomenological reduction" which, as we mentioned earlier, aids one's capacity to attend to experience *qua* experience. In doing so, it seeks to suspend the usual, more "scientific" (or "logical" in Kantian terms), mode of engagement with the world. In this way the world presents itself as it is rather than as we shape it to be by means of our concepts and schemes. It is for this reason that Merleau-Ponty attributes the best formulation of the phenomenological reduction to Eugen Fink, Husserl's assistant. Fink speaks of "'wonder' in the face of the world."[72] For the reduction "slackens the intentional threads . . . it alone is consciousness of the world because it reveals that world as strange and paradoxical."[73]

70. Plato *Theaetetus* 155d. My italics.
71. Aristotle *Metaphysics* 982b11–12. My italics.
72. Merleau-Ponty, *Phenomenology of Perception*, xv.
73. Ibid. This slackening is expressed elsewhere: "To return to the things in themselves is to return to that world which precedes knowledge, of which knowledge always

In practical terms, wonder can be summarized in language which resonates with that already employed in our treatment of music: wonder arises within physical *encounters* that arrest our attention. These encounters *immerse* and sustain the subject, thereby supplying an abundance of meaning since no one particular meaning emerges of its own accord; in doing so, they cause *the subject to face outwards* onto the physical. Wonder arises from the intrinsic connection between subject and object, self and world. Thus, Jeff Malpas remarks: "The experience of the wondrous is an experience in which we find ourselves already moved, already affected, already opened up to what is before us."[74] In short, wonder can be said to pertain to those experiences that reveal the intimate connection between subject and object, those experiences wherein attunement obtains, where (pre-reflectively) we already open out onto the world through our bodies. This is manifested through the impact of the physical encounter, the subject's immersion in it, and the non-reductive relationship which results. As Ronald Hepburn states: "Wonder does not see its objects possessively: they remain 'other' and un-mastered."[75]

Defined in this way, such wonder-full experiences may well be allied with those which Taylor designates as imparting a sense of fullness. Thus, the connection between beauty and epistemology arises once more. It is the sense of wonder (and beauty understood in terms of wonder) which re-enchants the subject, suggesting a particular interaction between subject and object and a certain mode of attention. In terms of music, therefore, to suggest that music encourages an enchanted mode of attention is to make a two-fold claim. First, it is to claim that music signals a particular mode of attention which involves a different way of being in the world. This way of being indicates a shift from an enclosed self to an open self. Here, meaning is generated from outside and yet is intimately connected. Second, it is to claim as a consequence that music alters our everyday interaction with the world, which is dictated by certain conceptual modes, such that we engage with reality in a pre-reflective way. The meaning presented is neither entirely self-generated nor able to be mastered. Rather, meaning presents itself indeterminately

---

speaks, and in relation to which scientific schematization is an abstract and derivative sign-language, as is geography in relation to the countryside in which we have learnt beforehand what a forest, a prairie, or a river is" (ibid., x–xi).

74. Malpas, "Beginning in Wonder," 287.

75. Hepburn, *Wonder and Other Essays*, 134.

and the percipient relishes its complexity and richness. Such a mode of engagement can be characterized by the notion of wonder.

In relation to the first part of the claim, that music encourages a shift from the enclosed to the open self, we have observed the permeability of the boundary between subject and object through music's physicality. The subject is overcome by an experience that is external to it and yet to which it is intimately attuned. Its attention focuses beyond itself as it is immersed in the fittingness of the physical experience. Thus, as Eric Matthews notes in relation to Merleau-Ponty, "the perceiving subject is not some 'inner' entity, but something which by its very nature 'opens out on to' the world . . . Perceiving cannot be just an ordinary causal relation between objects in the world, any more than it can be a relation between a subject outside the world and objects inside. It must involve both subject and object, but the subject must be in some sense 'inside' the world."[76] The same holds true of the musical experience, the subject opens out onto the world and is part of the world it encounters. The subject is fitted to the world since the subject is part of the fabric of the world: it is both subject and object. Thus, it can act upon as well as be acted upon. The performer impacts upon music through the manipulation of sound and modifies her action as a result of the sonic feedback. The recipient structures the musical experience through prior embodied knowledge and attends to the music (or not) and is moved by it (or not). We have seen how this sense of presence and absorption extends from the physical action of making music with instruments to that of participating within the musical experience. Here, although the sense of physical presence infuses the self it does not annihilate it, for ultimately each remains distinct.

In relation to the second part of the claim, following from the first, the relationship between music and wonder is grounded in music's capacity to "slacken" the normal ties binding one to the world. For through music the conceptual mode of attention to the world is deferred and a pre-reflective connection is instantiated, one wherein the physical burgeons with significance. Within music, the self and the world are fitted together in a pre-reflective way that is self-sustaining and inherently satisfying. This is due to the impact and effect of the music and the non-determinate array of meanings that are potentially conveyed. For in the first instance, the physical impact of music and the focus it generates is

76. Eric Matthews, *Guide for the Perplexed*, 47.

one that is all-encompassing. It is primarily a physical experience and it is this that is paramount *rather than reflection upon it*. Thus, even though one can talk about musical experience, there is for example a wealth of written material guiding the listener through particular pieces, such paraphrase is only ever a shadow of that which is experienced by means of music. Moreover, it is only one way in which a given piece "means." It is thus that talk "about" musical experience is at best analogous to the musical experience itself, for there is no sense in which it can completely encapsulate it. If this were the case the musical experience would be dispensable and this is clearly not the situation. Thus, in talking about the uniqueness of music Gordon Graham says, in the light of an appeal to T. S. Eliot's poetry to explicate Beethoven's late quartets: "It is hard to see how one work could be said to correspond exactly to another, but if ever such an explanation were successful, the music would in a sense be redundant; we could read the poem instead."[77]

In the second instance, meaning is not presented "definitively" within the musical experience. Musical meanings are abundant. This is not simply true of music's indeterminacy understood as expression and evocation but obtains also for its first-order mode of being. The otherness encountered is varied for it includes the otherness of the music, the otherness of those who are also held captivated, and the otherness of those comprising the tradition in which music is embedded. (For some, it may even reveal the otherness of a transcendent being, although this assumption is to abstract from the immanence of the physical and import external presuppositions). In sum, the exact "otherness" of the other eschews absolute definition and resists determination. It thus always and ever remains more than the subject can perceive and "know" in a conceptual sense. The wealth of musical meaning is also due to the implicit non-homogenization of consciousness: it is not assumed that all ought to undergo the same experience (a presumption held by Kant in virtue of the fact that all of humanity shares the same rational powers). On the contrary, no single experience can be authorized since music is experienced variously by each individual and differently by the same person at given points in time. In this way the physical constantly presents itself afresh: it impacts upon the human person and forms the means and sustenance of connection. Moreover, since it has no particular end in mind the experience becomes inherently satisfying and sustaining. In

77. Graham, *Philosophy of the Arts*, 82.

short, music encourages a pre-reflective and "wonder-full" mode of attention, since it does not bind us with the cognitive ties that operate in everyday and scientific judgment. Rather it encourages an in-dwelling of experience.

MUSICAL BEAUTY: NEGOTIATING THE BOUNDARY BETWEEN SUBJECT AND OBJECT

In so far as our narrative has shown us that, historically, the notion of beauty has had an epistemological inflection it remains for us to summarize music's contribution in physical terms. Attention to the musical experience, in particular its performance and reception, has shown that key aspects of music's ontology render it epistemologically significant. Music's physicality arrests and sustains our attention. It encourages a focus on that which is other than ourselves and thereby promotes an interweaving of subject and object, an attunement between the two (in fact an already existing mutuality). It thus establishes an interaction that is pre-reflective in character, since the relationship eschews the domination exerted by any conceptual mode. For this reason, the forms of otherness presented by and through music remain indeterminate.

It is by means of indeterminacy that the musical experience is intrinsically connected to wonder, since wonder indicates something of the pre-reflective interaction between subject and object, in which the usual ties to the world are relaxed. It is thereby also, that wonder is connected to beauty. Such a connection has a significant history. As we have seen, it is implicit within the Boethian and Kantian treatments of beauty. However, it goes back to Ancient Greece. For Plato, Beauty is the visible form of the Good, the latter being the source that structures and shapes all reality. As such, Beauty is an unsurpassed channel of "otherness" experienced within and through the physical. However, the knowledge that it imparts is intrinsically indeterminate and, ultimately, unfathomable. It can thus be characterized by the notion of wonder, for it encourages a "slackening" of the normal ties binding us to the world as well as indicating the presence of indeterminate significance.

Beauty, understood by means of wonder, gains a transformative power. The slackening of ties leads to exposure to that which is uncategorized and uncategorizable, that which is not already part of our framework of experience and thus has the capacity to strike us and surprise us.

It is thus a means of making the familiar unfamiliar,[78] a means through which one becomes exposed to "otherness." It provides a moment within which one is exposed to "the arrival of the unanticipated in the midst of the ordinary."[79] It is in this way that experiences are shaped and re-shaped. The arrival of the unanticipated is integral to music. For as we have seen, expectation, anticipation, and suspension (or as Levitin terms it "violation") comprise the fibers of its being. Importantly in this regard, beauty does not only embody that which is pleasant and gratifying but can be terrifying in that which it reveals.[80] The unexpected is thus knitted into the fabric of music in an essential way granting it the capacity to de-familiarize the familiar and shape experience. It is thus that music is a means of transformation.

Musical beauty, then, can be said to concern moments that are wonder-full, moments within which a sense of fullness is felt. Here, a mutuality of subject and object obtains as well as an abundance of meaning within an ekstatic mode of attention. It is this mode of attention, indicated by beauty and wonder, which is the source of enchantment. Herein, the subject is taken out of itself and exposed to that which is other in an immediate way. It is thus that the subject becomes open to meanings not generated by it, open to encounters beyond its control. Music is produced and yet is something that does not derive solely from within the subject: its meaning arises externally to the subject, is never entirely comprehended, and yet resonates with it. In some sense, therefore, beauty underpins all other aesthetic concepts; it is pre-eminent amongst them since it is that which gets the others off the ground. It is the kind of attention that emerges when one participates in a certain way with particular types of music. Herein, the boundary between subject and object is postponed and the intimate connection between the two is disclosed.

78. Hepburn, *Wonder and Other Essays*, 148.

79. Rubenstein, "Certain Disavowal," 17.

80. For a discussion of the connection between wonder and that which is terrifying, see ibid., 12–13.

Conclusion

Not only does music offer the possibility of transcending daily life; it offers, in as many forms as there are musics, a reshaping of those categories. It doesn't obliterate them in some narcotic emptiness but reworks them and thus offers us new models of experience. And this has a real power, because as we participate in this process of enactment, we experience new ways for ourselves. When we leave ... and return to daily life, we have tasted a different way of being, a different perception of the world. Potentially, this leaves us marked by the experience. It subsequently produces an altered perception of the world.

—Julian Johnson, *Who Needs Classical Music?* 129.

T HE NARRATIVE TRACED IN this book reveals the epistemological frameworks underlying the concept of beauty. Herein, a certain disjunction between subject and object, self and world, is presumed and beauty becomes a way in which both Boethius and Kant configure the relationship between them. Thus, for Boethius, the source of everything is God and meaning is objective. The subject forms part of a cosmic (divinely instantiated) whole and beauty (understood as harmony) is a conduit of both physical and intellectual knowledge. In the course of things, physical knowledge gives way to the determinacy of intellectual knowledge and physical beauty submits to intellectual beauty. Beauty is a means of absolute knowledge originating from a transcendent source. For Kant, one cannot talk about knowledge of the world as it is in itself. One cannot postulate an absolute source and guarantor and, hence, the world-in-itself remains opaque. Due to this opacity, knowledge is conceived primarily as a conceptually (albeit indeterminately) structured enterprise. For the stable ground from which knowledge arises is located within the subject itself, specifically within the mind's own powers to structure appearance. Beauty, therefore, is not objective but subjective, obtaining only *inter*-subjectively due to the commonality of the powers of the understanding. Theoretically, all subjects are able to experience the aesthetic satisfaction yielded through the harmonious interaction of the cognitive powers.

These radically distinct understandings of the world, and the differing emphases upon object and subject, are manifest in the Boethian and Kantian accounts of music. Boethius values the physicality of music. Indeed, within his scheme, sounded music is crucial to human identity and well-being. However, its action is limited as it prepares the ground for, and gives way to, conceptual assertions. Kant finds the physicality of music profoundly problematic, leading him to view it ambiguously and, ultimately, negatively. At a certain point, Kant suggests that music's lack of explicit conceptual content elevates its status. He implicitly aligns music with ideas imparted through indeterminacy (knowledge of the supersensible). Elsewhere, however, Kant asserts that music is a distraction to thought since it acts more on the senses than on the rational powers of the subject: it is an agreeable art devoid of conceptual content.

The Boethian and Kantian accounts provide vital clues to music ontology. For as a result of approaching music through non-musical and conceptually biased frameworks (ones that over-emphasize either the object or the subject) they are compelled to take issue with two features that are in fact central to music's ontology: its *physicality* and its *indeterminacy*. For as physical, *as sound*, music is necessarily indeterminate in its meaning. Exploring these features as they are manifest in both music practice and reception (by means of the notions of *impact, absorption*, and *ekstasis*) we have seen that the polarity of object and subject assumed by Boethius and Kant dissipates within the musical experience. Meaning is not located in either party absolutely but emerges within their mutuality, for both impact upon and integrate the other. Within the musical experience, the subject is incorporated and sustained physically within and through the music. This, as I have suggested, gives rise to an "enchanted" mode of attention, that is, a *non-reductive* and *receptive* stance within which the subject does not attempt to master what is presented to it but dwells in the musical experience. Consequently, music stands not only as a point of orientation but as a means of transformation. For music impacts upon the subject and is responded to and interpreted in a variety of ways: music thus carries an abundance of meaning that leads one to experience it as a sense of fullness or richness. However, because one engages with the music in an embodied manner (and one not explicitly conceptual) it becomes a means of transformation since the musical experience opens one up to meanings not already contained within the intellectual purview. One becomes receptive to the uncategorized and uncategorizable.

Grounds for the aporetic nature of beauty are thus uncovered, since it resides between subject and object. Beauty designates those experiences within which the distinction between the two is postponed, those experiences where an abundance of meaning obtains rather than its restriction through rational categories. Beauty thus indicates a retrieval of a pre-reflective being-with and -in the world and reveals a fittingness between the two: the subject already opens onto the world and the world likewise onto the subject. Thus, the paradoxical nature of beauty announces itself only when one attempts to think conceptually about such experiences (experiences imparting a sense of fullness or richness). For these experiences are necessarily subjective and objective at one and the same time since there are certain invariants that one can point to and yet which each individual experiences, responds to, and reflects upon in a distinct manner. For each subject is embedded within a particular context, culture, and set of experiences, and responds uniquely to musical invariants (although to a certain extent particular conventions and situations may dictate responses). Each subject is already with and in the world in a distinct way.[1]

It is the ontology of music, understood by means of its physicality and indeterminacy, that grounds the many layers of musical meaning (including sociological, philosophical, and theological) as well as its variety of accompanying functions (individual and communal). For music has the capacity to take the human subject beyond itself and place it in relation to that which is other, thereby orienting it and transforming it, doing so in an immediate and dynamic way. It is this mode of attention that yields an intimation of beauty, epistemologically understood, for within the wonder-full ekstatic stance elicited by music the veil between subject and object is at its most transparent.

---

1. Conceiving beauty as indicative of such a mode of attention, encouraged by the physicality of the musical medium, wherein the distinction between the subject and object is negotiated (and deferred), opens up lines of inquiry along which other art forms may be explored. What is unique to the ontology of each art form, and impacts upon, absorbs, and creates ekstasis? This is beyond the immediate scope of this book.

Bibliography

Adorno, Theodor. W. "Music and Language: A Fragment." Translated by Rodney Livingstone. In *Quasi una Fantasia: Essays on Modern Music*, 1–6. London: Verso, 1992.

———. "On the Fetish Character in Music and the Regression of Listening." In *The Culture Industry*, edited by J. M. Bernstein, 29–60. Routledge, 2001.

Adorno, Theodor W., and Max Horheimer. *Dialectic of Enlightenment*. Translated by John Cumming. London: Allen Lane, 1973.

Allison, Henry. *Kant's Theory of Taste: A Reading of the Critique of Aesthetic Judgement*. Cambridge: Cambridge University Press, 2001.

Almén, Byron, and Edward Pearsall. *Approaches to Meaning in Music*. Indianapolis: Indiana University Press, 2006.

Ameriks, Karl. *Interpreting Kant's Critiques*. Oxford: Oxford University Press, 2003.

———. "Kant and the Objectivity of Taste." *British Journal of Aesthetics* 23 (1983) 3–17.

Anderson, M. S. *Europe in the Eighteenth Century: 1713–1789*. Harlow: Pearson, 2000.

Annas, Julia. *A Very Short Introduction to Ancient Philosophy*. Oxford: Oxford University Press, 2000.

Aran Murphy, Francesca. *Christ the Form of Beauty: A Study in Theology and Literature*. Edinburgh: T. & T. Clark, 1995.

Aristotle. *De caelo (On the Heavens)*. Translated by J. L. Stocks. Oxford: Clarendon, 1922.

———. *Metaphysics*. Translated by Hugh Lawson-Tancred. London: Penguin, 1998.

Augustine. *Confessions*. Translated by Henry Chadwick. Oxford: Oxford University Press, 1992.

———. *De Musica (On Music)*. Translated by Robert Catesby Taliaferro. The Fathers of the Church: A New Translation 4: 153–379. New York: CIMA, 1947.

Backus, John. *The Acoustical Foundations of Music*. New York: Norton, 1977.

Beardsley, Monroe C. *Aesthetics from Classical Greece to The Present: A Short History*. Birmingham: University of Alabama Press, 1975.

Begbie, Jeremy. *Resounding Truth: Christian Wisdom in the World of Music*. London: SPCK, 2008.

———. *Theology, Music and Time*. Cambridge: Cambridge University Press, 2000.

Benson, Bruce Ellis. *The Improvisation of Musical Dialogue: A Phenomenology of Music*. Cambridge: Cambridge University Press, 2003.

Berman, Morris. *The Reenchantment of the World*. Ithaca, NY: Cornell University Press, 1981.

Bicknell, Jeanette. "Can Music Convey Semantic Content? A Kantian Approach." *Journal of Aesthetics and Art Criticism* 60:3 (2002) 253–61.

Blackwell, Albert L. *The Sacred in Music*. Louisville: Westminster John Knox, 1999.

Boethius, Anicius Manlius Severinus. *Boethian Number Theory: A Translation of the* De Institutione Arithmetica. Translated by Michael Masi. Amsterdam: Rodopi, 1983.

———. *The Consolation of Philosophy*. Translated by Victor Watts. London: Penguin, 1999.

———. *De Institutione Musica* (*Fundamentals of Music*). Translated by Calvin M. Bower. Edited by Claude V. Palisca. New Haven: Yale University Press, 1989.

———. *De Institutione Musica, liber I. Thesaurus Musicarum Latinarum*. Checked by Luminita Aluas and Penelope Mathiesen; approved by Thomas J. Mathiesen. Online: http://www.music.indiana.edu/tml/6th-8th/BOEMUS1_TEXT.html.

———. *The Theological Tractates; With the Consolation of Philosophy*. Translated by H. F. Stewart, E. K. Rand, and S. J. Tester. Loeb Classical Library 74. London: Heinemann, 1973.

Bohlman, Philip V. "Ontologies of Music." In *Rethinking Music*, edited by Nicholas Cook and Mark Everist, 17–34. Oxford: Oxford University Press, 1999.

Bower, Calvin. M. "Boethius and Nichomachus: An Essay Concerning the Sources of *De Institutione Musica*." *Vivarium* 16 (1978) 1–45.

———. "The Role of Boethius' *De Institutione Musica* in the Speculative Tradition of Western Musical Thought." In *Boethius and the Liberal Arts: A Collection of Essays*, edited by Michael Masi, 157–74. Bern: Lang, 1981.

———. "The Transmission of Ancient Theory into the Middle Ages." In *The Cambridge History of Western Music Theory*, edited by Thomas Christensen, 136–67. Cambridge: Cambridge University Press, 2002.

Bowie, Andrew, *Aesthetics and Subjectivity: From Kant to Nietzsche*. Manchester: Manchester University Press, 2003.

———. *Music, Philosophy, and Modernity*. Cambridge: Cambridge University Press, 2007.

Bowman, Wayne D. *Philosophical Perspectives on Music*. Oxford: Oxford University Press, 1998.

Brown, David. *God and Enchantment of Place: Reclaiming Human Experience*. Oxford: Oxford University Press, 2004.

Brown, David, and Anne Loades. *The Sense of the Sacramental: Movement and Measure in Art and Music, Place and Time*. London: SPCK, 1995.

Brown, Peter. *Religion and Society in the Age of Augustine*. London: Faber & Faber, 1972.

Bruyne, Edgar de. *The Esthetics of the Middle Ages*. Translated by Eileen B. Hennessy. New York: Ungar, 1969.

Budd, Malcolm. *Music and the Emotions: The Philosophical Theories*. London: Routledge, 1985.

Bukofzer, Manfred F. "Speculative Thinking in Mediaeval Music." *Speculum* 17:2 (1942) 165–80.

Burnham, Douglas. *An Introduction to Kant's Critique of Judgement*. Edinburgh: Edinburgh University Press, 2000.

Bychkov, Oleg V., and James Fodor. *Theological Aesthetics after Von Baltasar*. Aldershot, UK: Ashgate, 2008.

Cahn, Steven M., and Aaron Meskin. *Aesthetics: A Comprehensive Anthology*. Oxford: Blackwell, 2008.

Caldwell, John. "The *De Institutione Arithmetica* and the *De Institutione Musica*." In *Boethius: His Life, Thought and Influence*, edited by Margaret Gibson, 135–54. Oxford: Blackwell, 1981.

Candler, Peter M., Jr., and Conor Cunningham. *Transcendence and Phenomenology.* Veritas. London: SCM, 2007.

Cantrick, Robert. "Kant's Confusion of Expression with Communication." *The Journal of Aesthetics and Art Criticism* 53 (1995) 193–94.

Capella, Martianus. *De Nuptiis Philogiae et Mercurii (The Marriage of Philology and Mercury).* Translated by William Harris Stahl, Richard Johnson, and Evan Laurie Burge. New York: Columbia University Press, 1977.

Carpenter, Patricia. "Aspects of Musical Space." In *Explorations in Music, The Arts, and Ideas: Essays in Honour of Leonard B. Meyer*, edited by Eugene Narmour and Ruth A. Solie, 341–73. Festschrift Series 7. Stuyvesant: Pendragon, 1988.

Carroll, Noël. "Formalism." In *The Routledge Companion to Aesthetics*, edited by Berys Gaut and Dominic McIver Lopes, 87–96. London: Routledge, 2001.

———. *Philosophy of Art: A Contemporary Introduction.* London: Routledge, 2000.

Cassiodorus. *Institutiones.* Translated by Helen Dill Goode and Gertrude C. Drake. Colorado Springs: Colorado College Music Press, 1980.

Cassirer, Ernst. *The Philosophy of the Enlightenment.* Translated by Fritz C. A. Koelln and James P. Pettegrove. Princeton: Princeton University, 1951.

Cavell, Stanley. *Must we Mean What we Say? A Book of Essays.* New York: Scribners, 1969.

Caygill, Howard. *A Kant Dictionary.* Oxford: Blackwell, 2003.

Cazeaux, Clive. *The Continental Aesthetics Reader.* London: Routledge, 2000.

Chadwick, Henry. *Boethius: The Consolations of Music, Logic, Theology and Philosophy.* Oxford: Oxford University Press, 1981.

———. "Philosophical Tradition and the Self." In *Interpreting Late Antiquity: Essays on the Postclassical World*, edited by G. W. Bowersock, Peter Brown, and Oleg Grabar, 60–81. Cambridge: Harvard University Press, 2001,

Chamberlain, D. S. "Philosophy of Music in the *Consolatio* of Boethius." *Speculum* 45 (1970) 80–97.

Chignell, Andrew. "The Problem of Particularity in Kant's Aesthetic Theory." *ΠΑΙΔΕΙΑ: Aesthetics and Philosophy of the Arts.* Online: http://www.bu.edu/wcp/Papers/Aest/AestChig.html.

Chua, Daniel K. L. *Absolute Music and the Construction of Meaning.* Cambridge: Cambridge University Press, 1999.

Cicero, Marcus Tullius. *De re publica (On the Commonwealth).* Translated by Clinton Walker Keyes. Cambridge: Harvard University Press, 1977.

———. *Tusculanae disputations (Tusculan disputations).* Translated by J. E. King. Cambridge: Harvard University Press.

Clark, Suzannah, and Alexander Rehding. *Music Theory and Natural Order from the Renaissance to the Early Twentieth Century.* Cambridge: Cambridge University Press, 2001.

Clarke, David. "Musical Autonomy Revisited." In *The Cultural Study of Music: A Critical Introduction*, edited by Martin Clayton, Trevor Herbert, and Richard Middleton, 159–70. New York: London: Routledge, 2003.

Clarke, Eric. *Ways of Listening: An Ecological Approach to the Perception of Musical Meaning.* Oxford: Oxford University Press, 2005.

Clayton, Martin, et al. *The Cultural Study of Music: A Critical Introduction.* New York: London: Routledge, 2003.

Cohen, Ted. "Why Beauty is a Symbol of Morality." In *Essays in Kant's Aesthetics*, edited by Ted Cohen and Paul Guyer, 221–36. Chicago: University of Chicago Press, 1982.

Cook, Nicholas. "Epistemologies of Music." In *The Cambridge History of Western Music Theory*, edited by Thomas Christensen, 78–105. Cambridge: Cambridge University Press, 2002.

———. *Music: A Very Short Introduction*. Oxford: Oxford University Press, 2000.

Cook, Nicholas, and Mark Everist. *Rethinking Music*. Oxford: Oxford University Press, 1999.

Cooke, Deryck. *The Language of Music*. Oxford: Clarendon, 1959.

Copleston, Frederick. *A History of Philosophy: Volume One, Greece and Rome*. Kent, UK: Burns & Oates, 1999.

Covey-Crump, Rogers. "Pythagoras at the forge: tuning in early music." In *Companion to Medieval and Renaissance Music*, edited by Tess Knighton and David Fallows, 317–26. Oxford: Oxford University Press, 2003.

Cox, Arnie. "Hearing, Feeling, Grasping Gestures." In *Music and Gesture*, edited by Anthony Gritten and Elaine King, 45–60. Aldershot, UK: Ashgate, 2006.

Crabbe, Anna. "Literary Design in De Consolatione." In *Boethius: His Life, Thought and Influence*, edited by Margaret Gibson, 238–41. Oxford: Blackwell, 1981.

Crawford, Donald W. "Kant." In *The Routledge Companion to Aesthetics*, edited by Berys Gaut and Dominic McIver Lopes, 51–64. London: Routledge, 2001.

———. *Kant's Aesthetic Theory*. Wisconsin: University of Wisconsin Press, 1974.

Crowther, Paul. "The Significance of Kant's Pure Aesthetic Judgement." *The British Journal of Aesthetics* 36:2 (1996) 109–20.

Dahlhaus, Carl. *Esthetics of Music*. Translated by William Austin. Cambridge: Cambridge University Press, 1995.

———. *The Idea of Absolute Music*. Translated by Roger Lustig. Chicago: University of Chicago Press, 1991.

———. "Music—or Musics?" (1985). In *Source Readings in Music History*, edited by Oliver Strunk, 1509–14. New York: Norton, 1998.

———. *Nineteenth Century Music*. Translated by J. Bradford Robinson. Berkeley: University of California Press, 1989.

Davidson, Scott C. "The Ambiguous Meaning of Musical Enchantment in Kant's Third Critique." In *The Aesthetics of Enchantment in the Fine Arts*, edited by Marlies Kronegger and Anna-Teresa Tymieniecka, 115–20. Boston: Kluwer Academic, 2000.

Davies, Stephen. "Music." In *The Oxford Handbook of Aesthetics*, edited by Jerrold Levinson, 489–515. Oxford: Oxford University Press, 2003.

———. "Ontology of Art." In *The Oxford Handbook of Aesthetics*, edited by Jerrold Levinson, 155–80. Oxford: Oxford University Press, 2003.

———. *Philosophical Perspectives on Art*. Oxford: Oxford University Press, 2007.

Dawkins, Richard. *The God Delusion*. London: Bantam, 2006.

DeNora, Tia. *After Adorno: Rethinking Music Sociology*. Cambridge: Cambridge University Press, 2003.

———. *Music in Everyday Life*. Cambridge: Cambridge University Press, 2000.

Dickie, George. *Introduction to Aesthetics: An Analytic Approach*. New York: Oxford University Press, 1997.

Doctor, Jenny. "The Texture of Silence." In *Silence, Music, Silent Music*, edited by Nicky Losseff and Jenny Doctor, 15–36. Aldershot, UK: Ashgate, 2007.

Düsing, Klaus. "Beauty as the Transition from Nature to Freedom in Kant's Critique of Judgement." *Noûs* 24 (1990) 79–92.

Engel, Johann Jakob. "On Painting in Music" (1780). In *Source Readings in Music History*, edited by Oliver Strunk, 954–65. New York: Norton, 1998.

Faas, Ekbert. *The Genealogy of Aesthetics*. Cambridge: Cambridge University Press, 2002.

Farley, Edward. *Faith and Beauty: A Theological Aesthetic*. Aldershot, UK: Ashgate, 2001.

Fricke, Christel. "Explaining the Inexplicable. The Hypothesis of the Faculty of Reflective Judgement in Kant's Third Critique." *Noûs* 24 (1990) 45–62.

Frisch, Walter. *Schoenberg and his World*. Princeton: Princeton University Press, 1999.

Frith, Simon. "Music and Everyday Life." In *The Cultural Study of Music: A Critical Introduction*, edited by Martin Clayton et al., 92–101. New York: Routledge, 2003.

Galbraith, Elizabeth. "Was Kant a Closet Theologian?" *Theology* 95 (1992) 245–54.

Gammon, Martin. "'Exemplary Originality': Kant on Genius and Imitation." *Journal of the History of Philosophy* 35 (1997) 563–92.

Garcia-Rivera, Alejandro. "On a New List of Aesthetic Categories." In *Theological Aesthetics After Von Baltasar*, edited by Oleg V. Bychkov and James Fodor, 169–83. Aldershot, UK: Ashgate, 2008.

Gardner, Sebastian. *Kant and the Critique of Pure Reason*. London: Routledge, 1999.

Gauchet, Marcel. *The Disenchantment of the World*. Translated by Oscar Burge. Princeton: Princeton University Press, 1997.

Genetter, Gérard. *The Work of Art: Immanence and Transcendence*. Translated by G. M. Goshgarian. Ithaca, NY: Cornell University Press, 1997.

Gibson, Margaret. "The Opuscula Sacra in the Middle Ages." In *Boethius: His Life, Thought and Influence*, edited by Margaret Gibson, 214–34. Oxford: Blackwell, 1981.

Gilbert, Jeremy, and Ewan Pearson. *Discographies: Dance Music, Culture and the Politics of Sound*. New York: Routledge, 1999.

Ginsborg, Hannah. "Reflective Judgement and Taste." *Noûs* 24 (1990) 63–78.

Godwin, Joscelyn. *The Harmony of the Spheres: A Sourcebook of the Pythagorean Tradition in Music*. Rochester, VT: Inner Traditions, 1993.

————. "The Revival of Speculative Music." *The Musical Quarterly* 68 (1982) 373–89.

Goehr, Lydia. *The Imaginary Museum of Musical Works: An Essay in the Philosophy of Music*. Oxford: Clarendon, 1997.

Goldman, Alan. "The Aesthetic." In *The Routledge Companion to Aesthetics*, edited by Berys Gaut and Dominic McIver Lopes, 181–92. London: Routledge, 2001.

Goodman, Nelson. *Languages of Art: An Approach to a Theory of Symbols*. London: Oxford University Press, 1969.

Gotshalk, D. W. "Form and Expression in Kant's Aesthetics." *British Journal of Aesthetics* 3 (1967) 250–60.

Graham, Gordon. "Art as a Vehicle for Religious Truth." *British Journal of Aesthetics* 23:2 (1983) 124–37.

————. *The Philosophy of the Arts: An Introduction to Aesthetics*. London: Routledge, 2000.

————. *The Re-enchantment of the World: Art versus Religion*. Oxford: Oxford University Press, 2007.

Gritten, Anthony, and Elaine King. *Music and Gesture*. Aldershot, UK: Ashgate, 2006.

Grube, G. M. A. *Plato's Thought*. London: Methuen, 1958.

Guthrie, W. K. C. *A History of Greek Philosophy, Volume I, The Earlier Presocratics and the Pythagoreans.* Cambridge: Cambridge University Press, 1962.

Guyer, Paul. *Kant and the Claims of Taste.* Cambridge: Harvard University Press, 1979.

———. *Kant and the Experience of Freedom.* Cambridge: Cambridge University Press, 1993.

———. "Kant's Conception of Fine Art." *The Journal of Aesthetics and Art Criticism* 52 (1994) 275–85.

———. *Values of Beauty: Historical Essays in Aesthetics.* Cambridge: Cambridge University Press, 2005.

Haldane, John. "De Consolatione Philosophiae." In *Faithful Reason: Essays Catholic and Philosophical,* 266–79. London: Routledge, 2004.

Hamilton, Andy. *Aesthetics and Music.* London: Continuum, 2007.

Hammermeister, Kai. *The German Aesthetic Tradition.* Cambridge: Cambridge University Press, 2002.

Hanslick, Eduard. *On the Musically Beautiful.* Translated by Geoffrey Payzant. Indianapolis: Hackett, 1986.

Harries, Richard. *Art and the Beauty of God: A Christian Understanding.* London: Mowbray, 1993.

Harrison, Carol. *Beauty and Revelation in the thought of Saint Augustine.* Oxford: Clarendon, 1992.

Hart, David Bentley. *The Beauty of the Infinite: The Aesthetics of Christian Truth.* Grand Rapids: Eerdmans, 2003.

Hepburn, R. W. *Wonder and Other Essays.* Edinburgh: Edinburgh University Press, 1984.

Herlinger, Jan. "Medieval Canonics." In *The Cambridge History of Western Music Theory,* edited by Thomas Christensen, 168–92. Cambridge: Cambridge University Press, 2002.

Hindemith, Paul. "Methods of Music Theory." *Musical Quarterly* 30 (1944) 20–28.

Hume, David. *Selected Essays.* Edited by Stephen Copley and Andrew Edgar. Oxford: Oxford University Press, 1993.

Hyer, Brian. "Tonality." In *The Cambridge History of Western Music Theory,* edited by Thomas Christensen, 726–52. Cambridge: Cambridge University Press, 2002.

Ingarden, Roman. *The Work of Music and the Problem of its Identity.* Translated by A. Czerniawski. Berkeley: University of California Press, 1986.

Isacoff, Stuart. *Temperament: How Music Became a Battleground for the Great Minds of Western Civilisation.* London: Faber & Faber, 2002.

Jaki, Stanley L. *The Cosmos and Creator.* Edinburgh: Scottish Academic, 1980.

James, Jamie. *The Music of the Spheres: Music, Science and the Order of the Universe.* London: Abacus, 1993.

Janaway, Christopher. "Plato." In *The Routledge Companion to Aesthetics,* edited by Berys Gaut and Dominic McIver Lopes, 1–13. London: Routledge, 2001.

Johnson, Julian. *Who Needs Classical Music?* Oxford: Oxford University Press, 2002.

Johnson, Mark. *The Meaning of the Body: Aesthetics of Human Understanding.* Chicago: University of Chicago Press, 2007

Kant, Immanuel. *Anthropology from a Pragmatic Point of View.* Translated by Victor Lyle Dowdell. Carbondale: Southern Illinois Press, 1978.

———. *The Critique of Judgement.* Translated by Paul Guyer and Eric Matthews. Cambridge: Cambridge University Press, 2000.

———. *Critique of Judgement*. Translated by Werner S. Pluhar. Indianapolis: Hackett, 1987.

———. *The Critique of Pure Reason*. Translated by Norman Kemp-Smith. London: MacMillan, 1973.

———. *Prolegomena to Any Future Metaphysics*. Translated by Peter G. Lucas. Manchester: Manchester University Press, 1959.

———. "What Is Orientation in Thinking?" In *Critique of Practical Reason and Other Writings*, translated by Lewis White Beck, 293–305. Chicago: University of Chicago Press, 1949.

Kearney, Richard. "Sacramental Aesthetic: Between Word and Flesh." In *Transcendence and Phenomenology*, edited by Peter M. Candler Jr. and Conor Cunningham, Veritas, 334–69. London: SCM, 2007.

Kemal, Salim. *Kant's Aesthetic Theory: An Introduction*. London: Macmillan, 1997.

———. "The Importance of Artistic Beauty." *Kant-Studien* 71 (1980) 488–507.

Kennedy, Nigel, and the Polish Chamber Orchestra. *Beethoven: Violin Concerto/Mozart: Violin Fourth Concerto No. 4/Horace Silver: Creepin' In*. EMI Records. 2008.

Kirkby, Helen. "The Scholar and His Public." In *Boethius: His Life, Thought and Influence*, edited by Margaret Gibson, 44–69. Oxford: Blackwell, 1981.

Kirwan, James. *Beauty*. Manchester: Manchester University Press, 1999.

Kivy, Peter. "The Fine Art of Repetition." In *The Fine Art of Repetition: Essays in the Philosophy of Music*, 327–59. Cambridge: Cambridge University Press, 1993.

———. *Introduction to a Philosophy of Music*. Oxford: Clarendon, 2002.

———. "Is Music an Art?" In *The Fine Art of Repetition: Essays in the Philosophy of Music*, 360–73. Cambridge: Cambridge University Press, 1993.

———. "Kant and the 'Affektenlehre': What He Said, and What I Wish He Had Said." In *The Fine Art of Repetition: Essays in the Philosophy of Music*, 250–64. Cambridge: Cambridge University Press, 1993.

———. "Platonism in Music: A Kind of Defense." In *The Fine Art of Repetition: Essays in the Philosophy of Music*, 35–58. Cambridge: Cambridge University Press, 1993.

Knighton, Tess, and David Fallows. *Companion to Medieval and Renaissance Music*. Oxford: Oxford University Press, 1997.

Kristeller, Paul O. "The Modern System of the Arts." *Journal of Historical Ideas* 12 (1951) 496–527.

Kuehn, Manfred. *Kant: A Biography*. Cambridge: Cambridge University Press, 2002.

Kuntz, Marion Leathers, and Paul Grimley Kuntz. *Jacob's Ladder and the Tree of Life: Concepts of Hierarchy and the Great Chain of Being*. New York: Lang, 1987.

Lackoff, George, and Mark Johnson. *Metaphors We Live By*. Chicago: University of Chicago Press, 2003.

Leibniz, Gottfried Wilhelm. *Discourse on Metaphysics and Other Essays*. Edited and translated by R. N. D. Martin and Stuart Brown. Manchester: Manchester University Press, 1988.

———. *New Essays on Human Understanding*. Edited and translated by Peter Remnant and Jonathan Bennett. Cambridge: Cambridge University Press, 1981.

———. *The Philosophical Works of Leibniz*. Translated by George Martin Duncan. New Haven: Yale University Press, 1908.

———. *Philosophical Writings*. Translated by Mary Morris. London: Dent, 1934.

Lerer, Seth. *Boethius and Dialogue: Literary Method in The Consolation of Philosophy*. Princeton: Princeton University Press, 1985.

Levinson, Jerrold. *Music, Art, and Metaphysics: Essays in Philosophical Aesthetics*. Ithaca, NY: Cornell University Press, 1990.

Levitin, Daniel. *This is Your Brain on Music*. London: Atlantic, 2006.

Lippman, Edward A. *The Philosophy and Aesthetics of Music*. Lincoln: University of Nebraska Press, 1999.

Lovejoy, Arthur O. *The Great Chain of Being: A Study of the History of an Idea*. Cambridge: Harvard University Press, 1950.

Macrobius. *Commentari in Somnium Scipionis (Commentary on the Dream of Scipio)*. Translated by William Harris Stahl. New York: Columbia University Press, 1952.

Mair, John. "The Text of the Opuscula Sacra." In *Boethius: His Life, Thought and Influence*, edited by Margaret Gibson, 206–13. Oxford: Blackwell, 1981.

Malpas, Jeff. "Beginning in Wonder: Placing the Origin of Thinking." In *Philosophical Romanticism*, edited by Nikolas Kompridis, 282–98. New York: Routledge, 2006.

Marenbon, John. *Boethius*. Oxford: Oxford University Press, 2003.

Margolis, Joseph. "Medieval Aesthetics." In *The Routledge Companion to Aesthetics*, edited by Berys Gaut and Dominic McIver Lopes, 27–36. London: Routledge, 2001.

Masterson, Patrick. *Sense of Creation: Experience and the God Beyond*. Aldershot, UK: Ashgate, 2008.

Matravers, Derek. *Art and Emotion*. Oxford: Oxford University Press, 2001.

Mattheson, Johannes. "Der vollkommene Capellmeister" (The Complete Music Director) (1739). In *Source Readings in Music History*, edited by Oliver Strunk, 696–703. New York: Norton, 1998.

Matthews, Eric. *Merleau-Ponty: A Guide for the Perplexed*. London: Continuum, 2006.

Matthews, John. "Anicius Manlius Severinus Boethius." In *Boethius: His Life, Thought and Influence*, edited by Margaret Gibson, 15–43. Oxford: Blackwell, 1981.

McGrath, Alister, and Joanna Collicutt McGrath. *The Dawkins Delusion? Atheist Fundamentalism and the Denial of the Divine*. London: SPCK, 2007.

McKinnon, James. *Antiquity and the Middle Ages: From Ancient Greece to the 15th Century*. London: Macmillan, 1990.

———. *Music in Early Christian Literature*. Cambridge: Cambridge University Press, 1993.

McMahon, Jennifer Anne. "Beauty." In *The Routledge Companion to Aesthetics*, edited by Berys Gaut and Dominic McIver Lopes, 227–38. London: Routledge, 2001.

Merleau-Ponty, Maurice. "Cezanne's Doubt." In *The Merleau-Ponty Reader*, edited by Ted Toadvine and Leonard Lawlor, 69–84. Evanston, IL: Northwestern University Press, 2007.

———. "Eye and Mind." In *The Merleau-Ponty Reader*, edited by Ted Toadvine and Leonard Lawlor, 351–78. Evanston, IL: Northwestern University Press, 2007.

———. "Indirect Language and the Voices of Silence." In *The Merleau-Ponty Reader* edited by Ted Toadvine and Leonard Lawlor, 241–82. Evanston, IL: Northwestern University Press, 2007.

———. "The Intertwining—The Chiasm." In *The Continental Aesthetics Reader*, edited by Clive Cazeaux, 164–80. London: Routledge, 2000.

———. *The Phenomenology of Perception*. Translated by Colin Smith. London: Routledge, 1962.

Middleton, Richard. *Studying Popular Music*. Philadelphia: Open University Press, 1990.

Morrison, Charles. "Musical Listening and the Fine Art of Engagement." *British Journal of Aesthetics* 47 (2007) 401–15.

Mothersill, Mary. *Beauty Restored*. Oxford: Clarendon, 1984.

Neubauer, John. *The Emancipation of Music from Language*. New Haven: Yale University Press, 1986.

Nichols, Aidan. *Redeeming Beauty: Soundings in Sacral Aesthetics*. Aldershot, UK: Ashgate, 2007.

Nicomachus of Gerasa. *Enchiridion (The Manual of Harmonics)*. Translated by Flora R. Levin. Grand Rapids: Phanes, 1994.

Nietzsche, Friedrich. *The Birth of Tragedy and Other Writings*. Translated by Ronald Speirs. Edited by Raymond Geuss and Ronald Speirs. Cambridge Texts in the History of Philosophy. Cambridge: Cambridge University Press, 2000.

O'Daly, Gerard. *The Poetry of Boethius*. London: Duckworth, 1991.

O'Hear, Anthony. *German Philosophy Since Kant*. Cambridge: Cambridge University Press, 1999.

Osborne, Peter. *From an Aesthetic Point of View: Philosophy, Art and the Senses*. London: Serpent's Tail, 2000.

Page, Christopher. "Musicus and Cantor." In *Companion to Medieval and Renaissance Music*, edited by Tess Knighton and David Fallows, 74–78. Oxford: Oxford University Press, 1997.

Pappas, Nickolas. "Aristotle." In *The Routledge Companion to Aesthetics*, edited by Berys Gaut and Dominic McIver Lopes, 15–26. London: Routledge, 2001.

Pillow, Kirk. "Form and Content in Kant's Aesthetics: Locating Beauty and the Sublime in the Work of Art." *Journal of the History of Philosophy* 32 (1994) 443–59.

Pippin, Robert B. "The Significance of Taste: Kant, Aesthetic and Reflective Judgement." *Journal of the History of Philosophy* 34 (1996) 549–69.

Plantinga, Alvin. "Methodological Naturalism? Part One." *Philosophical Analysis* 18:1 (1997). Online: http://www.arn.org/docs/odesign/od181/methnat181.html.

———. "Methodological Naturalism? Part Two." *Philosophical Analysis* 18:2 (1997). Online: http://www.arn.org/docs/odesign/od181/methnat181.html.

Plato. "Laws." In *Plato: Complete Works*, translated by Trevor J. Saunders, edited by John M. Cooper, 1318–616. Indianapolis: Hackett, 1997.

———. "Phaedrus." In *Plato: Complete Works*, translated by Alexander Nehamas and Paul Woodruff, edited by John M. Cooper, 506–56. Indianapolis: Hackett, 1997.

———. "Republic." In *Plato: Complete Works*, translated by G. M. A. Grube and rev. C. D. C. Reeve, edited by John M. Cooper, 971–1223. Indianapolis: Hackett, 1997.

———. "Theaetetus." In *Plato: Complete Works*, translated by M. J. Levett and rev. Myles Burnyeat, edited by John M. Cooper, 157–234. Indianapolis: Hackett, 1997.

———. "Timaeus." In *Plato: Complete Works*, translated by Donald J. Zeyl, edited by John M. Cooper, 1224–91. Indianapolis: Hackett, 1997.

Pliny. *Naturalis historia (Natural History)*. Translated by D. E. Eichholz. Cambridge: Harvard University Press, 1962.

Plotinus. *Enneads*. Translated by Stephen MacKenna. London: Penguin, 1991.

Plutarch. *De Musica*. Translated by J. H. Bromby. Chiswick, UK: Whittingham, 1822.

Potter, "The Communicative Rest." In *Silence, Music, Silent Music*, edited by Nicky Losseff and Jenny Doctor, 155–68. Aldershot, UK: Ashgate, 2007.

Privette, Jeffrey S. "Must Theology Re-Kant?" *Heythrop Journal* 40 (1999) 166–83.

Pseudo-Plato. *First Alcibiades*. In *Plato: Complete Works*, translated by D. S. Hutchinson, edited by John M. Cooper, 557–95. Indianapolis: Hackett, 1997.

Ptolemy. *Harmonics*. Translated by Jon Solomon. Mnemosyne Supplements 203. Leiden: Brill, 2000.

Quantz, J. J. *On Playing the Flute*. Translated by Edward J. Reilly. London: Faber, 1985.

Rameau, Jean-Philippe. *Treatise on Harmony*. Translated by Philip Gossett. New York: Dover, 1971.

Rasch, Rudolf. "Tuning and Temperament." In *The Cambridge History of Western Music Theory*, edited by Thomas Christensen, 193–222. Cambridge: Cambridge University Press, 2002.

Rée, Jonathan. *I See a Voice: A Philosophical History of Language, Deafness and the Senses*. London: Harper Collins, 1999.

Reich, Steve. "Music as a Gradual Process" (1968). In *Source Readings in Music History*, edited by Oliver Strunk, 1385–87. New York: Norton, 1998.

Riley, Matthew. *Musical Listening in the German Enlightenment: Attention, Wonder and Astonishment*. Aldershot, UK: Ashgate, 2004.

Rist, John M. *Plotinus: The Road to Reality*. Cambridge: Cambridge University Press, 1967.

Rousseau, Jean-Jacques. "Essay on the Origin of Languages, which Treats of Melody and Musical Imitation" (c. 1760). In *Source Readings in Music History*, edited by Oliver Strunk, 951–53. New York: Norton, 1998.

Rowland-Jones, Anthony. "The Baroque Recorder Sonata." In *The Cambridge Companion to the Recorder*, edited by John Mansfield Thomson, 51–73. Cambridge: Cambridge University Press, 1995.

Rubenstein, Mary-Jane. "A Certain Disavowal: The Pathos and Politics of Wonder." *Princeton Theological Review* 12:2 (2006) 11–17.

Russell, Bertrand. *The Problems of Philosophy*. Oxford: Oxford University Press, 2001.

Sacks, Oliver. *Musicophilia: Tales of Music and the Brain*. London: Picador, 2007.

Salem-Wiseman, Jonathan. "Modernity and Historicity in Kant's Theory of Fine Art." *Philosophy Today* 42 (1998) 16–25.

Schmidt, Kenneth L. *The Recovery of Wonder*. Montreal: McGill-Queen's University Press, 2005.

Schoenberg, Arnold. "Criteria for the Evaluation of Music." In *Style and Idea: Selected Writings of Arnold Schoenberg*, translated by Leo Black, edited by Leonard Stein, 124–36. London: Faber, 1975.

———. *Fundamentals of Musical Composition*. Edited by Gerald Strang and Leonard Stein. London: Faber, 1967.

———. "New Music, Outmoded Music, Style and Idea" (1946). In *Style and Idea: Selected Writings of Arnold Schoenberg*, translated by Leo Black, edited by Leonard Stein, 113–24. London: Faber, 1975.

———. *Style and Idea: Selected Writings of Arnold Schoenberg*. Edited by Leonard Stein. Translated by Leo Black. London: Faber, 1975.

Schopenhauer, Arthur. *The World as Will and Representation*. Translated by E. F. J. Payne. New York: Dover, 1969.

Schrade, Leo. "Music in the Philosophy of Boethius." *Musical Quarterly* 33 (1947) 188–200.

Schwarz, K. Robert. *Minimalists*. London: Phaidon, 1996.

Scruton, Roger. *The Aesthetics of Music*. Oxford: Clarendon, 1998.

———. *Kant: A Very Short Introduction*. Oxford: Oxford University Press, 2001.